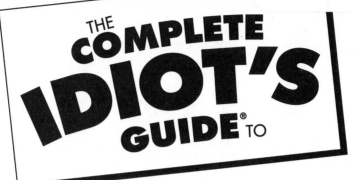

THE
COMPLETE
IDIOT'S
GUIDE® TO

Dream Jobs

by Brian O'Connell

ALPHA

A member of Penguin Group (USA) Inc.

ALPHA BOOKS

Published by the Penguin Group

Penguin Group (USA) Inc., 375 Hudson Street, New York, New York 10014, U.S.A.

Penguin Group (Canada), 10 Alcorn Avenue, Toronto, Ontario, Canada M4V 3B2 (a division of Pearson Penguin Canada Inc.)

Penguin Books Ltd, 80 Strand, London WC2R 0RL, England

Penguin Ireland, 25 St Stephen's Green, Dublin 2, Ireland (a division of Penguin Books Ltd)

Penguin Group (Australia), 250 Camberwell Road, Camberwell, Victoria 3124, Australia (a division of Pearson Australia Group Pty Ltd)

Penguin Books India Pvt Ltd, 11 Community Centre, Panchsheel Park, New Delhi—110 017, India

Penguin Group (NZ), cnr Airborne and Rosedale Roads, Albany, Auckland 1310, New Zealand (a division of Pearson New Zealand Ltd)

Penguin Books (South Africa) (Pty) Ltd, 24 Sturdee Avenue, Rosebank, Johannesburg 2196, South Africa

Penguin Books Ltd, Registered Offices: 80 Strand, London WC2R 0RL, England

Copyright © 2005 by Brian O'Connell

International Standard Book Number: 1-59257-382-7
Library of Congress Catalog Card Number: 2005928077

07 06 05   8 7 6 5 4 3 2 1

Interpretation of the printing code: The rightmost number of the first series of numbers is the year of the book's printing; the rightmost number of the second series of numbers is the number of the book's printing. For example, a printing code of 05-1 shows that the first printing occurred in 2005.

Printed in the United States of America

Note: This publication contains the opinions and ideas of its author. It is intended to provide helpful and informative material on the subject matter covered. It is sold with the understanding that the author and publisher are not engaged in rendering professional services in the book. If the reader requires personal assistance or advice, a competent professional should be consulted.

The author and publisher specifically disclaim any responsibility for any liability, loss, or risk, personal or otherwise, which is incurred as a consequence, directly or indirectly, of the use and application of any of the contents of this book.

Most Alpha books are available at special quantity discounts for bulk purchases for sales promotions, premiums, fund-raising, or educational use. Special books, or book excerpts, can also be created to fit specific needs.

For details, write: Special Markets, Alpha Books, 375 Hudson Street, New York, NY 10014.

Publisher: *Marie Butler-Knight*
Senior Managing Editor: *Jennifer Bowles*
Editorial Director and Acquisitions Editor: *Mike Sanders*
Development Editor: *Michael Thomas*
Production Editor: *Megan Douglass*
Copy Editor: *Molly Schaller*
Cartoonist: *Jody Schaeffer*
Cover/Book Designer: *Trina Wurst*
Indexer: *Tonya Heard*
Layout: *Ayanna Lacey*
Proofreading: *Mary Hunt*

Contents at a Glance

Contents

Foreword

A few years ago, even though I was riding a wave of success, I still felt lost at my job. I was only 37 years old but I felt frustrated with the day-to-day routine of being a senior vice president with a leading staffing firm. So I made a drastic move to save both my career and my state of mind—I took a leave of absence.

The top priority on my agenda for those next three months was simply to "recharge" and figure out my next course of action. I played with my one-year-old daughter. I exercised rigorously. And, most of all, I tried to figure out what to do with the rest of my time on this planet.

As a result I found my dream job and learned, once again, that you will always be most successful when you focus on what you are most passionate about and don't allow your daily life to distract you.

Now, thanks to the book that you hold in your hands, you can do the same. Whatever kind of job you've dreamed about, this book is for you. Brian O'Connell lays out 100 dream jobs—everything from the glamorous to the outdoorsy, the entrepreneurial to the altruistic. Step by practical step, in simple, easy terms, he spells out how you can make your career fantasies come true. In other words, if you can conceive it, you can achieve it.

Everyone has that "dream job" in mind—if only buried in their subconscious. This is the kind of job that meets *all* of your specs—it's more of a calling, really. What you know you were meant to do. Maybe your weekend hobby holds a clue, or something you loved in high school. Maybe it's that one aspect of your job that just puts a huge grin on your face or perks you up for the coming week. The key is to work hard to simply identify that dream and then to pursue it with vigor.

My own dream job took some time in coming. I tried my hand at accounting with a top firm for a while, but even with my head for numbers, I felt uninspired. It would have been a great, safe career, but it wasn't built around my passions. I considered going into advertising, but didn't. Then I entered executive recruiting and, playing to my strengths in salesmanship, communications, and personality, everything started to click. My job was to help other people find jobs. I was making a lot of money and had control over my own destiny. Later, 15 years out of college, I found myself fed up and burned out. I realized something was missing. I had achieved my goals in the organization and bought that nice house and those Armani suits, but I wasn't tapping into my passion. I also realized what I always knew—that money won't make you happy. Your passion makes you happy. And your passion leads you to money!

When I came back from my three-month sabbatical, I was recharged and focused on either taking my job to the next level (and restructuring it to do what I love most) or moving on to a more senior position elsewhere. What I didn't know was that the opportunity of a lifetime loomed right in front of me. Through a quirk of fate—not to mention some brash initiative on my part—I was promoted to Chief Operations Officer of my existing company and then to its President shortly afterward. I saw an opportunity and I took it. My energy and passion for what I wanted to accomplish was evident to the "powers that be."

Now how that happened—that sudden shift in career fortunes—is much less important than why. The simple truth is, from early on, I was meant to be a boss. Not just any boss, but one who liked to do things from a different perspective. I reveled in the world of creative change. At 14, I was elected mayor of the summer camp I attended. I became the youngest Division Head in my camp in later years. In college, I led my fraternity to victories over rivals. Later on, within 18 months of taking a job, I rose above the former supervisor who had hired me. I discovered that I thrived on being in charge, on empowering people, on having the authority to influence an organization and to make the big decisions. Now I am, and do. I realized that I could never allow the fact that I decided to major in Accounting at 18 years old (I felt it was a safe move then) affect the entire direction of my life. I recognized what I was good at, what inspired me, and where I should take risks. I knew that passion leads to success, and not the other way around.

Your day in the sun can come, too. To start, all you really need to know is yourself and your dreams … and this terrific book.

—Neil Lebovits

Neil Lebovits is President and COO of Ajilon Professional staffing, one of the world's leading specialty staffing firms and a division of the world giant Adecco. A graduate of The Pennsylvania State University with a BS in Accounting, he started his career as a CPA with Ernst & Young in New York City. He lives in New Jersey with his wife, Christine, and daughter and son, Jenna and Jamie.

Introduction

This book was personal for me.

I've written 10 books—some on career management and entrepreneurship, some on making money on Wall Street, and some on getting into college and managing your life. I felt a kinship with each one. (I've always thought that when you finish writing a book and ship it off to the publisher, it takes a little bit of you with it.)

But none of those books have been like writing about finding your dream job. That really hit home for me.

Why? Because I am lucky enough to have found *my* dream job—writing books for good people like you. It's not just books, actually. In fact, I'll write anything: magazine articles, newspaper columns, web blogs, speeches, my laundry list. You name it. The truth is I can't believe I actually get paid to write. It's something I love so much that I'd do it for free. (Um, don't tell my editor that.)

But I didn't start out so fortunate. After graduating from college in the 1980s, I abandoned my journalism degree in favor of the easy money and adrenaline rush of Wall Street. I spent five years in the financial markets, first as a trading clerk on the Philadelphia Stock Exchange and ultimately as a bond trader at a major mutual fund house.

Sounds like a cushy deal, right? Not for me—I hated it. No disrespect to the savvy and street-smart people who spend their days investing our money, but I wasn't cut out for the financial world. Yes, I made money. Yes, I made friends. And yes, I contracted an ulcer over being stuck in a job that *just wasn't for me.*

So at age 28 I walked away from the Philadelphia Stock Exchange to a job as a magazine writer for a high tech publisher in my hometown of Boston: low pay, low perks, low man on the totem pole.

But I loved every minute of it. When I first saw my byline in the magazine I felt like somebody had just walked up to me and handed me the keys to getting my life back. I kept writing and kept seeing my bylines in print and knew I was hooked for life. I also knew I'd never return to Wall Street (not that there was a clamor for that, anyway).

I'd love this to happen to you. And I'm sure it can.

But you have to have a plan first, the cornerstone of which should include the ability to identify your passion and create a road map for making a career out of it. This book is part of that plan.

In it you'll find more than a hundred dream jobs, along with a job description, facts and figures about the job, salary range, and key tips and resources on how to land that job and succeed at it. These dream jobs already exist in a wide variety of industries—entertainment, publishing, politics, fashion and style, nature and the environment, and many, many more. Some jobs are fairly traditional, like fashion magazine editor or Alaskan fisherman. Some are offbeat and unusual, such as professional hand model or paparazzo. Some are more spiritual in nature, like Peace Corps volunteer or Feng Shui consultant. And some are only for the stout of heart, like forest fire smoke-jumper or NASCAR pit crew specialist. The one thing they have in common is that the people who do these jobs love them and never want to leave them. These are the people who have found their dream jobs and don't want to consider doing anything else. These are the people who never want to retire—they want to do their dream jobs for the rest of their lives. These are the lucky ones.

You can be lucky, too. Start by reading this book, getting some ideas (and some confidence), and then crafting a watertight plan for getting yourself into your dream job. It might not happen overnight, and you'll surely face some obstacles along the way, but don't let that stop you. The important thing is to get the ball rolling. After you get some momentum you'll be surprised how exhilarating it is to change your life on the fly, and for the better. You only have to plant the seeds first and take it from there.

Let me end with a story about Solomon Rothschild, founder of the Austrian branch of the famous House of Rothschild. One day he was walking with a friend along the streets of Vienna. A pickpocket followed them and tried to lift a red silk handkerchief from the banker's breast pocket. The friend noticed and alerted Rothschild: "My dear Count, this fellow is trying to steal your handkerchief!"

"So what? Let him be," answered Rothschild. "We all had to start somewhere."

How to Use This Book

The book you hold in your hands is carefully organized to maximize the information on the dream jobs presented inside.

The format is easy to understand. Each job is broken down as follows:

- ◆ **Facts and Figures.** Statistics and trends about the job and the industry associated with it.

- ◆ **Job Description.** What you can expect to be doing on the job.

- ◆ **Pay and Perks.** The salary range for each job, along with commentary on nonsalary-related issues.

- ◆ **Key Attributes.** Talents, abilities, and characteristics that you need to bring to the job.

- ◆ **Key Tip.** Advice on getting the inside track to landing that dream job.

- ◆ **Key Resource.** A "go to" place for more information on your dream job.

See, I told you it would be easy. Now, here's what you'll find in the upcoming pages.

In **Part 1, "An Introduction to Finding Your Dream Job,"** I discuss the keys to merging your passion in life with your career. Unfortunately, it's not enough to yearn for a job in a vocation that fairly screams your name. Nope, you have to understand what you need to bring to the table to get a job in your dream industry.

After reading this section, you'll know how to do just that. You'll not only begin to understand how people get away with having jobs where they love what they do, you'll begin to understand how easy—and how important—it is for you to do the same thing.

In **Part 2, "Footlights, Fame, and Fortune: Glamour Jobs,"** we'll cover the kinds of jobs that place you square in the limelight, either in front of an audience as a radio DJ, or behind one as a film screenwriter or paparazzo. It's all about creativity and promoting your talent—after all, nobody can sell you to the public like you can.

Part 3, "The Rugged Type: 'Physical' Jobs," is for you if you like more physical work. We'll look at occupations that not only are physically demanding but also fulfilling, rewarding, and virtually loaded with adrenaline. Think forest fire smoke-jumper or alligator trapper and you begin to get the idea.

So you want to be your own boss? In **Part 4, "The American Dream: Being Your Own Boss,"** I discuss careers that emphasize individuality and entrepreurism—cast-iron American traits where you call the shots, you take the risks, and you are responsible for the outcome. Whether you want to open your own bed and breakfast or see yourself fulfilling every amateur golfer's dream as a backyard putting green designer, this section will provide a blueprint for finding the perfect business for you to run … and master.

Part 5, "Mind, Body, and Soul," focuses on the Zen that lives inside each and every one of us. If you believe that your destiny is tied to the, well, tides, and the moon and the stars for that matter, here's the section for you. In it you'll harness the inner you to find gigs that speak to the spiritual you. That could mean communing with Mother Nature as a professional orchid grower or opening people's abodes to serene spirituality as a Feng Shui consultant.

And finally, **Part 6, "Finding Coolness Where You Work,"** is about harnessing your favorite pastimes and passions in life to your professional career. After all, there's no rule that says you can't have fun—loads of fun—in your job. Imagine parlaying your love of barley and hops to a full-time job as a pub owner; or leveraging your mastery of online retailing into a lucrative post as a professional eBay seller. You can also make a difference with a political or civil service position, the subject of Chapter 17. I conclude this section with a look at the hottest jobs in the future.

In addition, you'll find the following informative sidebars throughout:

On the Job

Here you'll find tips that will give you an edge on the competition.

Balancing Act

These boxes encourage you to keep an eye on the big picture as you seek your dream job.

The Water Cooler

These sidebars provide general or little-known information about the job being discussed.

Acknowledgments

Researching, writing, and editing a book with over 100 dream jobs isn't a solo effort. Even though my name is on the cover, I had plenty of help getting this book into prime time. I'd especially like to thank my friend and fellow writer Micki Gorman, who acted as my sounding board during the manuscript process and provided just the right comment or tip to make the book look its best. I'd like to thank my crack staff of researchers, Scott O'Connell, Elisabeth Flynn, Raquel Pidal, Kate Chapman, and Keith Bandelin. To each and every one of you I say "thank you." You're all young, talented, and going far in life.

I'd like to thank my editor, Mike Sanders at Alpha Books, who exhibited the patience of a saint as I touted a "can't miss" career one day only to change my mind and tear it down the next. He made the final call on the jobs in this book and invariably, each one was right on the money. Thanks also go out to my development editor, Mike Thomas, whose creative stamp is firmly imprinted on the book you hold in your hand.

A special tip of the hat goes out to my agent, Marilyn Allen, who steered the book in my direction and convinced me I'd be perfect for an *Idiot's* book. As usual, she was right.

Lucky for me—and for the readers of this book—you guys make it all look so easy.

Trademarks

All terms mentioned in this book that are known to be or are suspected of being trademarks or service marks have been appropriately capitalized. Alpha Books and Penguin Group (USA) Inc. cannot attest to the accuracy of this information. Use of a term in this book should not be regarded as affecting the validity of any trademark or service mark.

Part 1

An Introduction to Finding Your Dream Job

You, Inc. is the term some career consultants are using to drive home the point that you alone are responsible for your career growth and for the paths you take to get the job you've always coveted.

I like the term *You, Inc.* I also like the sound of *CEO of Your Life*. Anything to convince people that the best way to get the dream job they want is to take matters into their own hands to make such a momentous life shift happen.

That's what I talk about in Part 1—finding the change-ready warrior inside each and every one of us who can shake up the status quo and create new avenues for growth in the career and job that matters.

So welcome to *You, Inc.* To find your dream job, you've got to realize that, by and large, it's all up to you.

Changing Workplace, Changing Workers

In This Chapter

◆ The importance of finding your passion

◆ Keys to finding your dream job

◆ Using the Internet

◆ Becoming an in-demand, gold collar worker

Academic types like to use the term "tipping point" to determine at what juncture an issue changes—inevitably and, sometimes, dramatically.

Such was the case on September 11, 2001, when New York City and Washington, D.C. came under attack by terrorist bombers. The pain and anguish Americans felt after the attacks—pain and anguish that continue to this day—demonstrated the heartfelt feelings Americans have for their country and their fellow citizens.

But after the smoke cleared, and things calmed down, many Americans also took an impromptu inventory of their souls, asking themselves, "Am I really happy doing what I am doing?" With no guarantees in life, did they want to stay at the jobs they had? Or did they want to try to grab the brass ring, follow their passion, and spend the rest of their working lives in a career they loved?

My take on that subject is that people have also questioned whether they could do better in their chosen career. They want to spend the time they have here on Earth in vocations that offer fulfillment, spiritually and financially. They also want careers that will enable them to spend more time with their families.

In short, they wanted a dream job. This book you hold in your hands could very well be the key to finding *your* dream job.

A Changing Culture

Times have changed, and so have Americans' work lives. It's the rule now rather than the exception that most people average five or six careers during their working years. Instead of holding down something steady for several decades as their parents did, Americans are now switching from job to job, acquiring new sets of skills.

Technology plays a big role in why Americans have changed their work habits. Thanks to the Internet, e-mail, voicemail, and cell phones, more people are able to work from home—and from train, plane, or automobile.

Corporate culture has changed, too, and unfortunately, words like *outsourcing* and *downsizing* have become part of our vocabulary. Many people have struggled with the anxiety caused by office politics and have turned to options outside the traditional 9-to-5 cubicle-farm office. By examining personal passions, talents, and goals, more professionals are creating their own careers and finding them very satisfying.

The sad reality is that many people don't think they will ever have the job of their dreams. They fear leaving the stability of their current jobs; and with today's shaky economy, who wouldn't? Major airlines are declaring bankruptcy, telecoms are going bust, and scandals like Enron are becoming more commonplace. It's a scary work world out there, whether you're fresh out of college or have been working for 20 years. CareerBuilder.com recently conducted a survey in which almost three-fourths of participants claimed to be searching for their dream jobs. That's a big number.

People become unhappy with their jobs for numerous reasons, including feelings of boredom and stagnation, a sense of the meaninglessness of the job, and the approach of retirement. Yes, retirement has its advantages. But if you reach your golden years and realize, in the pit of your belly, that you spent all those years in a job you tolerated, at best, and hated, at worst, then some of retirement's luster is regrettably lost. After all, those are years you can never get back.

Does this sound like you? Do you feel like your dream job will never come true? Think again. It's not as hard as it seems.

Stop thinking of yourself as just another cog in the corporate machine, and instead envision yourself as the boss of the most important company you'll ever be apart of—you.

Learning from the Entrepreneur

This book will guide you through the essentials of turning your blah job into a dream job, and shows you how to develop winning entrepreneurial skills. Every job in this book requires a bit of the entrepreneurial spirit. You might be thinking, "There's not an entrepreneurial bone in my body." It's true for many people. Few people are actually born leaders; instead, they become leaders through their personality and life decisions. If you're just starting on the journey for your dream job, or if you're a seasoned veteran, you'll quickly learn that there are certain characteristics entrepreneurs possess. Keep an open mind and develop the characteristics that best suit your goals and personality.

> **Balancing Act**
>
> Some people go through their whole life never loving their job. In fact, people who do love their work don't even call it a "job." They call it their passion.

Seven Characteristics of the Entrepreneur

Take a page from the successful entrepreneur's handbook and merge the following valuable attributes into your dream job career search.

Believe in Yourself

If you want to be a successful entrepreneur (after all, what else would you call yourself when you strike on your own to find the job you love?), you must learn to trust your instincts and ideas. You must be willing to be persistent, determined, self-confident, and disciplined, from start to finish. As you become wiser and more confident, you'll find that your belief in yourself grows stronger as well. You need desire and passion to start the journey toward your dream job. Think of believing in yourself and your ideas as the vehicle for getting to your destination.

Think Creatively

Don't be afraid to think creatively. Many people get frustrated because their thinking involves business ideas that already exist. That shouldn't stop you. Instead, you should think of ways to improve, expand, and enhance existing ideas. "Thinking outside the box" is a well-worn cliché, but entrepreneurs know it's true, and adopt it as a motto. They put their imagination to work to try new things and work toward a vision. To be a successful creative thinker, pay close attention to how well your strategies are working, and be willing to change your approach if you find that something isn't working well.

Explore and Use Your Skills

Successful entrepreneurs know they aren't good at everything, so they focus on the things they can do exceptionally well. By evaluating your own skills, you can determine those that will help you work toward your goals. Entrepreneurs are also willing to let other experts help with things they aren't as good at. Staying open to change is important so that an entrepreneur can move forward and continue to be successful.

Create and Follow a Plan

To achieve success as an entrepreneur, you must follow a plan. You wouldn't take a road trip without a map, and you shouldn't expect to reach your professional destinations without a guide to follow. Along the way, you might find that another road seems more appealing and effective, but you wouldn't have reached that point without an initial plan. By all means, take detours if you must—but always make sure you have a plan for reaching your goal. Start out by writing a basic business plan that will guide you and your accomplishments. Don't worry about making it elaborate or long, but make sure you include goals, ideas, ways you'll be better than the competition, and ideas for marketing. You should make sure to update your plan according to your new ideas.

Envision Your Success

Remember how they told you not to daydream in school? Ignore that advice. Take time to envision your final business goals. You'll find that visualization is a powerful motivator. Athletes routinely envision how they want each performance to play out, and it helps them achieve their sporting goals. Imagine how you want things to turn out and how good you'll feel as a successful entrepreneur; it will help make your dreams seem like a more tangible reality.

Respect Your Peers

The old saying, "To have a friend, be a friend" rings true in the business world, too. Recognize everyone you meet as a peer deserving your respect, and you'll find that people return the favor. You'll never know if someone you meet could become part of your business strategy. Good entrepreneurs let others work with them to the best of their abilities, giving everyone the chance to reach personal goals. The success of your team relies on each person's contributions. By putting others on an equal level, you'll find that they respect you and give you their best performance.

Don't Give Up

To be a successful entrepreneur, don't give up on your dreams. This doesn't mean successful entrepreneurs don't have discouraging moments, bad days, and disappointments; they just see these as part of the journey, not as the end. Successful entrepreneurs must have the determination to overcome these difficulties, and this determination is the result of self-trust and self-confidence. Entrepreneurs know that when the chips are down, they should turn to people who know them and their ability to succeed, because these people offer encouragement and put the entrepreneur enthusiastically back on track. To be successful, you must accept the ebb and flow of good and bad periods. This will keep you going long after others have given up in frustration.

On the Job

Keep a journal of your job-finding process. Make notes of things you did, right or wrong. For instance, if you found a website that offers loads of education on becoming a disc jockey—your passion—make note of it either in a ledger or online. That way you'll have it whenever you need it.

Get Plugged In

If you're searching for your dream job, the Internet is probably the most important tool you'll ever use. Not only is it useful for helping you find exactly what you want to do with your life, it's also helpful in establishing yourself as a freelancer. Globalization has been a blessing for self-starters, because now companies can't afford to have a full-time staff at their disposal. Enter the freelancers. Businesses now rely on people to step in part time, and they contract out a great deal of work to freelancers.

Some people might feel squeamish about not having a regular paycheck or inexpensive health benefits, but it hasn't deterred the millions of Americans who are currently working as independent contractors. Desktop publishing, designing website content, running public relations and marketing firms—the list of freelance businesses is growing by the day. Freelancers find themselves in demand and in control of their careers.

Be In Demand

The twenty-first century has no shortage of material for the history books. An increase in terrorism, divided politics, a global marketplace, and the widespread use of the Internet will surely fill the pages of books reflecting on our times.

These books are sure to include sections devoted to our changing workplace, too, discussing how corporate workers have morphed into their own bosses, creating their own careers. These dream job gurus deserve their own special section in the history books for taking their jobs into their own hands.

These modern professionals—or gold collar workers—are driven to use their strengths to map out and create their own success. These are the people who know that there are options other than simply stepping into a job for life, receiving raises on schedule, and getting a pension at a pre-determined retirement age.

Gold collar workers are determined and flexible, willing to learn new skills, and re-innovate what they do again and again. Their approach is all encompassing: they understand how their individual job fits into a whole company, instead of isolating themselves. These people know that companies are faced with tough economic decisions, meaning that only the best will survive. This leads them to make themselves extremely marketable and indispensable. They are relentless networkers, valuing each connection they make as a potential professional avenue. And these workers have an ongoing curiosity about their field, which keeps them ahead of industry trends. It also enables them to learn which jobs are most in demand, letting them acquire appropriate skills and making them in-demand employees.

Learn these skills, and you, too, will be an in-demand gold collar worker.

The Least You Need to Know

- First and foremost, to find your dream job, you must believe in yourself.

- Outsourcing, downsizing, and technology have created an ideal atmosphere for the modern dream job seeker.

- The key: find your passion.

- Take the attributes that comprise good business owners—confidence, goal-setting, good research—and plug them into your dream job search.

- Conduct some real self-assessment. It's not always pretty, but you need to know where you are right now so you have a jumping-off point into your dream job career search.

- Be a gold collar worker—that is, someone who is determined, flexible, and willing to learn new skills. Those are the characteristics that employers look for when they hire good people.

Chapter 2

Keys to Finding Your Career Passion

In This Chapter

- Getting on the right track
- Being your best advocate
- Negative thinking can sink you
- Learn career strategy from "The Hot Dog Man"

It is said that all that is necessary to break the spell of inertia and frustration is this: act as if it were impossible to fail.

That's a great mantra for people searching for their dream jobs: failure is not an option.

After all, people have many attitudes about work. The most important one you can have, however, is a can-do attitude. Other people might think your ideas have no practical value, but the world's greatest human contributions have come from those who ignored this negativity and instead focused on following their dreams, saying, "I can do it."

Think of various historical figures and how they believed in the power of their own ideas, even when others discouraged them. Michelangelo sculpted his masterpiece, *David*, from a block of marble that other sculptors found useless. Christopher Columbus persisted in finding a shorter route to the West Indies, making an "impossible" voyage and discovering the Americas. And Henry Ford stubbornly held on to the idea of making a motorized car, even when Thomas Edison told him to give up and come work for him instead. Take a lesson from these and countless other individuals—hold on to your great ideas, and be prepared to start on the path to success alone.

In this chapter, you'll learn how to figure out your own career passion—and what to do when you find it. Some of it is physical—getting out and networking or writing a great resumé—and some of it is, for a lack of a better word, spiritual—like believing in yourself. That's okay. You'll find that a good balance between the physical you and the spiritual you is helpful in centering yourself and finding your dream job.

Making Your Career Search Manageable

It's happened to most Americans at some point: the unhappiness of being stuck in a dead-end job. Many people imagine their dream jobs, but feel too overwhelmed by the job search process to even begin making a change. And who can blame them? Job hunting is time consuming and frustrating. There are plenty of things that might hold you back: fear of leaving your current job stability in a shaky economy, under-valuing your skills, or assuming there isn't anything better available. It's almost too overwhelming even to begin, so many people give up before they've started. But viewing your search as a series of steps makes it manageable and helps alleviate your apprehension.

Balancing Act

From a career passion point of view, 9/11 changed everything. Tens of millions of Americans watched in horror as the World Trade Center, and then the Pentagon, were attacked. After mourning the loss of their fellow Americans, many people began reflecting upon their own lives. Staring into the walls of their cubicle, they asked themselves, "Do I really want to be doing this the rest of my life? Especially knowing it could all end so fast?" Upon further reflection, many Americans determined they didn't—and resolved to spend the rest of their lives working in jobs they love.

Explore Your Dream Job Options

Start by evaluating your options. Do some research. Investigate job listings in the paper and online. Talk to your friends about their positions, and learn about other positions within your own company. View everything as an opportunity. Try compiling ads for positions that seem interesting to you. If you do this for a while, you'll discover the types of jobs that most appeal to you—and some of your choices might surprise you.

Take the time to go someplace quiet and brainstorm. Make sure you have a notebook and all your want ad clippings. Use the time to record your feelings about the kind of career you want. Also reflect on the kinds of ads you cut out. Were they the types of ads you expected to cut out? Did you make any choices that surprised you? Free write and record your aspirations, apprehensions, and any other thoughts that come to mind. Challenge yourself to write at least two pages. After you finish, review what you wrote and find any recurrent thoughts. What you wrote should reveal the types of jobs you're most interested in. Look through the ads you have with you and find the jobs that match your reflections on your ideal career. Completing this exercise will start you on a career search path.

Be Your Own Cheerleader

Writing daily self-affirmations might seem alien to you at first, but it will ultimately become comfortable and will be quite valuable. Use your notebook to write positive messages about yourself and your dream career. Focus on creating messages that relate to your ideal job. For instance, if you want to be a record producer, your messages might read something like this:

"I am the best record producer at my company."

"My skills make me a great record producer."

"Producing records is my greatest strength."

After you fill a page with these messages, imagine yourself at your ideal career. Visualize your work space, the clothing you'll wear, what a typical day will be like. Do these exercises for at least a week, and watch your confidence in your abilities and potential grow. By visualizing yourself working your dream job, you'll feel your imaginings becoming a reality. You'll find that your professional image will change according to how you want to be viewed by future employers and colleagues.

Create a Stellar Resumé

Now comes the hard part: your resumé. Because so much of your job search depends on the strength of your resumé, it's no wonder most people find it stressful. Don't let the process bog you down. Set aside enough time for yourself to work on your resumé. Do it in increments throughout the week; perhaps set aside an hour or so every day before or after work to develop it.

Get yourself a resumé writing guidebook or do some research on the Internet for resumé guidelines. Use existing resources, like past resumés and job descriptions, diplomas, certificates, awards, and other relevant information to start crafting a new resumé. Record all your employment accomplishments, even those that don't seem relevant to the job you want to apply for. Fill pages—it's better to have too much information that you can edit later.

On the Job

Limit your resumé to one page. Human resources managers and hiring executives prefer a quick read, even if it's an online version. Any more than one page and people might get the idea that you can't think quickly and cleanly—key attributes that decision makers look for in an employee.

Create the first draft of your resumé and have someone you trust look it over. Ask him or her to be honest. Remember that it's best not to take your resumé to co-workers at the office you plan to leave. Make corrections to your resumé, put it away for a week, then look at it again with fresh eyes. You'll be able to pick up on and correct any grammatical errors. Your resumé must be perfect when you send it out. And don't forget to tailor your resumé to the specific jobs you're applying to, listing the most relevant experience first for each.

Follow a Timeline

You've explored your job options, built up your self-confidence, and created your resumé. Now you need to create a timeline for yourself. Create a timeline that works for you. Choose a day for starting your new job. Write down your target career start date in your notebook with your affirmations. Writing it down will make it more real. Take into consideration personal, professional, and family obligations when making your timeline, so that you won't create any additional stress for yourself.

When you're making your timeline, schedule in "send" dates for your resumés. Send out multiple resumés at the same time. Don't be afraid to apply for jobs that you don't feel you're qualified for. Employers will see that you're ambitious, and might be willing to offer you training.

Stay Confident and Don't Accept Failure

Keep writing your affirmations every day. This will keep you motivated and confident, and will also be useful when re-evaluating your goals. Continue your path to your dream job one step at a time. Your confidence will be important in helping you keep a positive attitude. You should never accept failure when it comes to your career.

Keep in mind the attributes of successful dream job candidates: ambition, enthusiasm, determination, discipline, integrity, attitude, and a good work ethic. These attributes make Dream Jobbers more versatile and in-demand by employers.

Most people have some or all the attributes of Dream Jobbers. But how exactly do you go about getting the opportunity to put these skills to use in your dream job? Here's how.

Know Your Turf

Want to get promoted? Your chances will be infinitely improved if you know exactly how your company operates. Learn whether promotions are given to people based on experience, creativity, communication skills, or other factors. Work toward promotions in areas where your skills are strong, or seek to improve your skills in areas where you're weaker.

While you're at it, get to know your industry as a whole. Stay up to the minute on what's going on in your field—whether you work for a small bistro or a Fortune 500 Company. It's a lot easier and less time-consuming than it sounds. Read industry newsletters or trade publications that your company subscribes to—it's almost a given that you'll find a few issues lying around the break room or reception area. Use the Internet to get information from sites like Lexis-Nexis (www.lexisnexis.com), PR Newswire (www.prnewswire.com), Hoovers Online (www.hoovers.com), or Business Wire (www.businesswire.com). Of course, there's always good old Google (www.google.com). And you should also try to develop some industry contacts that you can check in with periodically for a chat. Warm bodies can be the source of inspiration, breaking news, and invaluable leads.

On the Job

One great way to get better known both in your industry and your community is by joining your local Chamber of Commerce. You'll meet plenty of people who are in a position to help you find a dream job, either through recommendations, mentoring, or hiring you themselves. Most meetings are early—think breakfast—so you won't miss too much, if any, of your work day.

Be an Expert

While we're on the subject of knowing something inside and out, I'll mention expertise. It's crucial that you actively gain expertise by observing others and learning from their successes and mistakes. Proactively increase your levels of expertise instead of just waiting around for someone to wave the expertise wand and proclaim you an "expert" in something. When you've learned a lot in a certain field, let everyone know it. This doesn't mean handing out flyers or screaming, "I'm the best!" through a megaphone. It does mean you should get your name out there. Write articles for newsletters or industry magazines, offer to give lectures or workshops, and share what you know with others. It will take some hard work, but it will definitely pay off.

Network, Network, Network

Remember all those business cards you've collected and thrown in your desk drawers? Take them out and treat them like gold, because those names will probably come in handy someday. Other professionals, in any industry, are one of your best resources for getting ahead. Connect with people who can help you, and also remember to be generous and help others, too. Swap cards as often as you can, and fill up that Rolodex or address book.

Find Someone to Look Up To

While on the subject of making connections, it's good to mention the importance of mentors. If you truly want to learn and advance in your field, find someone with more expertise than you and look up to him or her. It could be someone you know personally at your company, such as your supervisor, or someone in the industry that you meet at a conference and communicate with over e-mail. Model your mentor's behavior and learn from his or her experience, and you'll have a winning advantage over other job hunters who are going it alone.

Create Opportunities for Advancement

You can't move forward if you stay still. Makes sense, right? That means you have to constantly look for opportunities to move ahead in your career—and they start right in your own office. If you're not particularly busy, ask your supervisor if there's anything you can work on to help. Or if you hear about a new project launching in your office, get involved. Your higher-ups will take notice of your contributions to the company, and they won't forget that you're a motivated self-starter. If you're passive, you'll watch the rest of the world go by—and won't get what you want. Take initiative!

Be the Boss of You, Inc.

When you take control of your career, you're basically becoming your own boss. A boss's job is to oversee the company and make sure all operations are running on all cylinders. When you become your own boss, you take steps to correct any deficiencies in your professional life and ensure the success and longevity of *You, Inc.*, the most important company you'll ever be a part of.

Value Yourself

I know I touched upon this in Chapter 1, but if you want to land your dream job, you'll need to become a valuable commodity. But here's a secret: when you work to the best of your ability, you already *are* valuable! Value should be compensated accordingly. Don't undersell yourself. Stay aware of competitive salaries in your industry by reading the classifieds, talking to employment recruiters, or checking other annual reports on salary information. Your talents plus your time equals dollar signs, so educate yourself to make sure you're earning what you know you're worth.

Finding Your Dream Job: The Hot Dog Man

Although a positive attitude is the foundation of a Dream Jobber's success, a negative one will just as surely reduce one's chances of finding that job.

There's a great story, called "The Man Who Sold Hot Dogs," about how a negative attitude can derail the greatest career prospects. A 1930s-era man lived by the side of the road and sold hot dogs. He was hard of hearing, so he had no radio. He had no formal education, so he couldn't read. But he sold great hot dogs.

He spent his days standing at the side of the road hollering "Buy a hot dog, mister?" And people did. So many did, in fact, that he doubled and then tripled his bun and hot dog orders. He built a nice roof for his stand so people could eat his hot dogs in the rain or snow. He grew so busy that he called on his son, recently home from college, to help out.

But his son didn't want any part of selling hot dogs. He told his father, "Dad, don't you read the papers or listen to the radio? There's a war brewing in Europe and we're in a recession at home. Things are terrible all over." Thinking the son, being a college graduate, must know what he was talking about, the man reduced his hot dog orders and pulled back on his bun deliveries. He took down his roof and sold the spare parts. Soon he stopped selling hot dogs by the side of the road altogether. Naturally his bank account dwindled and debts piled up in his mailbox.

The father said to his son, "You know son, you were right. We *are* in the middle of a great depression."

So don't let other people's negative attitudes poison your own. Keep your own course and stay positive. Believe me, it will get you noticed.

And it'll get you that dream job you've always wanted.

The Least You Need to Know

- ◆ Think of yourself as a small business. Target your favorite employers and treat them like valued customers. That means marketing and selling yourself, establishing value in what you offer, and closing the sale.

- ◆ Get help via networking and mentoring. You may be able to find your dream job alone, but why take the chance? Find a seasoned veteran you know in the business you want to be in and ask for some tips. You'll be surprised how eager people are to help.

- ◆ The dream job game is a people game. Meeting people in your industry, developing mentorship contacts, and leveraging the contacts your friends and family have in the industry you love are all about selling yourself to other people.

- ◆ Learn from the Hot Dog Man and trust your instincts. Even though you'll have help in your dream job research, you, and you alone, have to make the key decisions.

Part  2

Footlights, Fame, and Fortune: Glamour Jobs

Humorist Fred Allen once said that a celebrity is someone who works hard all of his life to become well-known, and then wears dark glasses to avoid being recognized.

He's got a point. But if your goal is to someday see your face on a 50-foot billboard in Times Square or on Hollywood Boulevard, a career in the "glamour" world of film, fashion, publishing, or television and radio is a great way to get started.

To paraphrase Allen, get the fame first and the sunglasses will follow.

Chapter 3

Lights, Camera, Action: The Entertainment Industry

In This Chapter

- ◆ Cool jobs under the hot lights
- ◆ Dream jobs on radio and screen
- ◆ On the road: stand-up comics and roadies
- ◆ Being a celebrity assistant
- ◆ Makeup and wardrobe arts

The entertainment industry can be a tough racket.

Commenting on the film *The Tycoon*, critic James Agee wrote that several tons of dynamite are set off in the movie. Unfortunately, none of it is under the right people.

Tough business, indeed.

But if you have a thick skin, a steely confidence in yourself, and the ability to make people stop coughing while you're acting up there on stage or screen, or working with the people who are, then the entertainment industry might be for you. There are interesting ways to break into the business in posts like animator, screenwriter, or even voice-over specialist—and make a good living in the process.

Animator

Animation is defined as "the state of living or being alive," but cartoon and movie lovers often think of another interpretation. From *Bugs Bunny* to *The Lord of the Rings*, film animation has been entertaining generations of audiences for more than 70 years. You can see the connection, because animators literally use their artistic—and increasingly, their technological—skills to bring ideas to life.

> **The Water Cooler**
>
> Producing animated sequences is like producing any complicated art-and-technology product: you have to know where you're going, what you're doing, and how you're going to get there. Animators who master these themes often leave the profession to go on to software development and design. Some continue on to work on mainstream movies, cartoons, commercials, illustration, or whatever area emphasizes their strongest skills.

These days, animation has become both highly sophisticated and much more popular—as films like *Monsters, Inc.*, *Finding Nemo*, *The Incredibles*, and many more can attest.

These films and others rely extensively on 3-D computer animation—which can produce incredibly realistic characters and seamless sequences. The video-gaming and Internet industries are booming, and proliferation of cable TV channels is also providing a wider outlet for animated entertainment—and proving that it's not all kids' stuff anymore.

If you're a visual artist or computer "geek" who can't get enough of all this flash and flair, then perhaps *you* ought to be in pictures.

Facts and Figures

In 2002, the U.S. Department of Labor/Bureau of Labor Statistics reports there were 74,826 people employed as "multimedia artists and animators"—with a projected growth of 15.6 percent in the field over the next decade. The Disney/Pixar explosion is only one piece of the industry—in addition to feature films, animation is used in commercials (of which 20 percent use animation these days), pop videos, computer games and interactive videos, newspapers and magazines, and a host of other commercial projects, from automotive design to medical research.

If you're dead set on film or television animation, you'll be looking at the bright lights and big cities of L.A. and New York. But in the broader field of computer graphic design, jobs are popping up all over the country—anywhere software programs and web and advertising projects are produced. Video game designers require a team of animators to bring their vision to life—from character animation to texture mapping, lighting, and other special effects. In addition to full-time gigs, freelance opportunities abound in this project-oriented industry.

Job Description

Simply put, an animator creates a sequence of images that are then put in motion to tell a story or communicate an idea. Animation can be 2-D images drawn on to clear film or "cells" and then photographed; it can also be "modeled," using 3-D objects or puppets that are manipulated and filmed, then replayed in sequence to create the illusion of motion. Hand-drawn or modeled work can be scanned and manipulated via computer. These days, more and more images are originated by sophisticated computer software.

Although formal education is not a requirement, to achieve the level of professionalism demanded in most animation jobs today you'll need to know your stuff, technologically speaking—and prove it. A Bachelor's or graduate degree in graphic design with a focus on the necessary computer skills can help land interviews or portfolio reviews.

For an aspiring animator, the single most important factor is the quality of your work. To perfect your craft, you might want to sign on as an intern or apprentice (albeit a low-paid one) to an established animator, designer, or programmer.

> ### The Water Cooler
>
> Short of a full degree program, many colleges and universities offer short-term courses in specific animation programs. Among the key ones to know are Alias PowerAnimator/Maya, Kinetix 3D Studio Max, SoftImage, and Lightwave.

Pay and Perks

Salaries in the animation field range from $40,000–$60,000. In 2002 the Bureau of Labor Statistics reported that animators and multimedia artists earned an average of $43,980. Median salary in the video and film industry was higher, at $58,840. As with every career, the salaries animators earned varied greatly by employer and geographic region.

As with most creative fine arts fields, the supply of wannabe animators still outstrips the demand, so positions are highly coveted. Some animators begin their own production companies, and recruit funds to develop their own animated products, usually for foreign markets, sample shorts, or animation festivals. The odds of big-time success are relatively low, but most animators truly enjoy what they do.

Key Attributes

From a personality standpoint, creativity and originality are both key. You must be positive, confident, and a team player and have a strong work ethic and the ability to meet deadlines. A good animator must also be flexible—as with all artistic industries, you'll not only be drawing characters, you'll most likely be working with some "characters," too.

Key Tip

You'll want to produce a short demo reel that shows off your best work—this is your all-important, 3-D resumé. Take some time to figure out what your strengths are (modeling, scene composition, lighting, and so on). Naturally, the clips should be carefully selected to highlight your very best work. Many art schools now offer classes on how to prepare and produce a "killer" demo reel.

Key Resource

www.adigitaldreamer.com contains information on being a graphic designer and a section called Graphic Design Career Answers, featuring a school finder, articles, forums, and more.

For industry news and updates, also check out Animation World News at www.awn.com.

Radio DJ

Getting paid to play your favorite records, chat with rock stars, and give away concert tickets sounds about as good as it gets. It's also, increasingly, too good to be true. There's much more to being a successful DJ. The job requires skill, charisma, and an ability to think on your feet.

The days of a renegade DJ planning his or her own set, or "discovering" new bands—even taking live requests—are for the most part long gone. The dramatic concentration of station ownership in the last decade or so, and the ensuing corporate atmosphere of most broadcasting has drastically altered the field. These days, most stations' playlists are programmed by computer, and dictated by market research.

Today's on-air talent is at the whim of ratings, mergers, and format changes, which can mean receiving a pink slip practically overnight. But for all the closed doors in the industry, others seem to be opening someplace else—so experienced and talented DJs generally do land on their feet. And there are pockets of independent broadcasting around the country that refuse to be silenced. So far neither video nor big business have quite killed the radio star.

Facts and Figures

According to the U.S. Bureau of Labor Statistics, announcers held 76,000 jobs in 2002; about one-third of these were employed part time. More than half worked for broadcasters, but some were freelancers working on a per-project basis for various stations, advertisers, or independent producers.

Competition for DJ positions is stiff, because the field attracts so many people. Small stations in minor media markets (for example, small cities and college towns) are more inclined to hire newcomers, but the pay there is low.

Employment for on-air announcers is expected to decline slightly, by 1 percent or more, through 2012 due to the lack of growth of new radio and television stations.

> **The Water Cooler**
>
> Internships (most of them, unfortunately, are unpaid) have become par for the course to gain entry in radio. Students might rack up valuable experience at campus radio or TV stations and by interning at commercial stations during school. Internships give students hands-on training and the chance to establish working contacts.

Job Description

A good DJ is primarily a good communicator, a familiar and friendly voice to his or her listening audience, keeping them entertained or informed, helping them pass the time in the car, at work, at play, or at home. In the increasingly competitive world of radio, your job is to keep people tuned in—prevent them for getting restless and changing the dial.

Landing a job in radio broadcasting can be extremely competitive. Despite the proliferation of academic programs, holding a communications or broadcast degree is no guarantee of future employment in the industry. Most station managers look and listen for audition tapes that showcase your polished delivery and style. Experience at college stations and professional internships will also help. DJs typically start at a smaller, local station, build up some time on the air, and gradually make the move to larger, more lucrative spots.

You might advance by hosting a regular program as a disc jockey, sportscaster, or news announcer. At the bigger city networks, competition is especially fierce, and employers look for college graduates with several years of successful on-air experience.

> **The Water Cooler**
>
> In addition to smooth and skillful announcing, a DJ also acts as producer and should learn expert technical skills that help in creating first-class promotions, commercials, contests, and public service announcements—making sure they all fit the overall "sound" of the station.

Announcers at smaller stations might cover all of these areas and have more off-air duties as well—from operating the control board, to selling commercial time to advertisers, to keeping a daily programming log.

A good DJ also manages to "take the pulse" of his or her local audience, finding out what they want and need, talking to them on the phone, and making personal appearances at promotional events, nightclubs, and wherever they might be gathered.

Pay and Perks

The BLS reports the average annual salary for the on-air radio personality is $43,800, but pay varies greatly from place to place. There are few Howard Sterns out there, and the fact is most DJs don't earn much money. Average salary in the smallest cities is $13,000, while some prime-time, big-city jocks earn superstar-level salaries in the six figures or even more. The prime spots are working "drive time" slots at leading stations in major cities. Commercial broadcasting pays more than public broadcasting, though turnover there is more frequent due to the market's shifting whims.

Most radio talents are in it for the love, not the money. For many, the intangible rewards include creative work, making personal contacts, having a "voice" on the air, and gaining the satisfaction of becoming known in the community. These can outweigh the drain of irregular and often unpredictable hours, work pressures, and disrupted personal lives.

Key Attributes

Multitasking ability is important. You must switch from music to news, weather, and traffic reports; take phone calls; respond to feedback and tight schedules; and manage all this in an allotted time slot. Vocal talent, spontaneity, and quick-thinking skills are critical to radio work.

Key Tip

Search the Internet for area voice talent agents and scouts, who represent professional narrators and voices who do commercial work, comic voices, cartoons, and so on. You'll want to produce a "demo" or audition recording (CD or tape) that can be sent to potential stations or commercial employers.

Key Resource

www.nab.org (National Association of Broadcasters) contains links to conventions, seminars, career development programs, and more.

Screenwriter

Hey, satisfying Hollywood moguls with great screenplays isn't easy. Fabled film producer Samuel Goldwyn once exasperatedly told a screenwriter about the nuances of writing for one of his movies: "What we want is a story that starts with an earthquake and builds to a climax!"

If you can handle that request, then you'll get a lot of work in Hollywood.

Facts and Figures

In 2001 M. Night Shyamalan was Hollywood's highest paid writer, commanding more than $10 million per film. The entertainment world is famously fickle, though, and what's hot can change like the weather.

Television responds very quickly to ratings and pop culture trends, whereas the theatrical film world involves longer lead times and far bigger budgets, and is therefore slower to adapt. The Writer's Guild of America West (WGAw) reported 3,169 writers employed in television in the year 2000, not including those who worked in pay or cable TV. The number of writers employed in theatrical films was 1,819 that year.

Los Angeles and New York are still the capitals of the film world in the United States, and the best places to make connections, but the American Screenwriters Association boasts members in 939 cities and 32 countries worldwide. Unlike acting or directing, the writing can be done anywhere.

> ### The Water Cooler
>
> In recent years, numerous competitions and contests have emerged with the aim of uncovering fresh talent, such as HBO's "Project Greenlight." These schemes have enjoyed mixed commercial results, but have certainly garnered attention and inspired a small army of wannabe scribes.
>
> In addition, a number of screenwriting seminars are offered around the country these days, ranging from colleges and community centers to online classes.

Job Description

Screenwriters write the scripts for all types of filmed entertainment, from sitcoms to feature films, soap operas, workout tapes, late night infomercials, and even corporate videos. Because it's considered a "glam" industry, and paychecks are often substantial, screenwriting is extremely tough to break into. Most who attempt it never see a script actually produced. Success in this field requires luck, good contacts, persistence, and most of all, talent.

Depending on your background and the particulars of the assignment, writing a screenplay might involve considerable research and plotting out before you get started. After it's turned in, your work will typically go through a series of edits and revisions from the original treatment. Screenwriters spend considerable time negotiating and modifying their draft until it's a working shooting script, and at the request of a script developer, editor, producer, or director, they might be asked to perform several rewrites. (What's more common is for somebody else to get hired to revise your work.)

Like Rodney Dangerfield, writers in Hollywood like to lament their notorious lack of respect. That's because few people go to a movie based on its author, so writers are considered all-too expendable in the world of film and TV execs. The script you were hired to write might go through six or seven revisions, each one by a different hand, before it appears on screen—as a story you no longer recognize.

This is why screenwriters have to learn to "let go." Unless you're exceptionally well known and can negotiate otherwise, your work stops belonging to you when it leaves your hands. The paycheck is expected to compensate!

Pay and Perks

Writers' fees in Hollywood are often governed by the Writers Guild of America (whose rates are listed at www.wga.org). Nonunion productions pay less, although they might be a foot in the door. A few big-name writers (Nora Ephron, David Mamet, M. Night Shyamalan) might earn headline-grabbing script sales—but most would-be script writers are working "on spec" (i.e., for nothing, still hoping for their big break) and working day jobs to make ends meet.

> ### The Water Cooler
>
> According to the Writers Guild of America West, the highest paid 25 percent of employed writers earned more than $575,000 each in 2000, with the lowest 25 percent earning less than $30,000.

Freelance writers negotiate and agree to a set fee for each piece of work. The writer of a script for a one-hour television drama could receive at least $10,000 and might earn considerably more.

Usually the pay per project is great, but income is highly unreliable unless and until you become a big name.

Although some writers complain of being low on the Hollywood totem, there are undeniable perks to working in the industry. You might have the chance to work with talented, creative, or just plain famous people. Feature film writing can be an isolated endeavor, but TV writing is much more collaborative, involving a team of writers as well as interaction with a cast.

Key Attributes

To be a successful screenwriter, you must have creativity, patience, and persistence, and be able to meet deadlines. As with all writing, there's a strong likelihood of rejection, again and again, before you find success.

Key Tip

If you're serious about starting a script, invest in one of the many available screenwriting software packages. There are several good ones out there, any of which will help make sense of the complex formatting requirements a script needs in order to be considered.

Key Resource

Get your hands on the book *Screenplay* (Dell Publishing, 1994) by Syd Field. There are legions of screenwriting guidebooks, but this is considered one of the very best. Field has his own website at www.sydfield.com.

Voice-Over Professional

Some of the most familiar voices in our lives belong to people we've never met—and wouldn't recognize on the street. Think of all the television broadcasts, commercials, cartoons, radio spots, and other recorded information that fills up our airspace. Somebody somewhere gets paid to do that.

A few of the highest paid commercial voice-overs are recorded by big-name actors such as James Earl Jones, Alec Baldwin, and Gene Hackman. But there is also a legion of professionals who make their living strictly off-camera and out of sight. For these pros, cultivating vocal techniques, neutralizing or developing accents, and caring for and training the vocal instrument is just as critical as for any singer or actor. Their voices are their instrument—and they're often highly paid to play.

Facts and Figures

The majority of voice-over professionals have had little or no acting experience. What gets them going is when a friend or colleague tells them they have a great voice, and that they could profit from it. Fair enough.

If you do go for a voice-over role, the pay is worth it. Although there's more info below under "Pay and Perks," the scale (minimum) rate for a local radio spot is $220 per session. A local TV spot is even better—paying around $375 to $500 (off- and on-camera, respectively). And national spots can pay thousands of dollars more. Even gigs such as animation, books-on-tape, industrial narration, and audio tours pay at least $100 an hour.

Job Description

A voice-over announcer provides scripted narration and other on-air services for live and/or prerecorded television programming, films, books on tape, advertising, and other types of recordings, as needed. Voice-over professionals might participate in the development and writing of their material.

Most of us can read the words on a page. But it's the ability to express a whole range of emotions—joy, anger, enthusiasm, pity, wonder, sarcasm, sadness—by adjusting the pitch and pace of his or her voice that is the mark of a true voice-over artist.

Mastering a range of accents is a highly marketable skill, as more and more recorded books, advertisements, television programs, and films make use of them.

Like all acting gigs, voice-over work is cyclical, with its good and its lean periods. Having a range of skills or accents helps keep you employed, so it's worth investing in voice classes to develop your skills. Ask around among agents, teachers, and fellow actors, casting directions, and so on for well-regarded classes or instructional tapes to give you a boost.

Pay and Perks

For union gigs, rates are generally predetermined, and are based on variables such as how often the TV or radio spot will air and in how many markets. It's common for top-level professionals to earn more than the base union rate. Newcomers may be paid what's called a "buy-out," which offers one set fee for the job, with no additional payments. (A contract known as a "talent release" will spell out the conditions.)

> **The Water Cooler**
>
> AFTRA, the American Federation of Television and Radio Artists, is the main union representing voice-over artists. They define a voice-over performer as someone who reads copy and is not seen on-camera. Radio and television commercial performances up to three minutes in length are considered voice-overs; anything over three minutes is considered voice-over narration.

> **The Water Cooler**
>
> Author James Alburger author of the book *The Art of Voice Acting: The Craft and Business of Performing for Voice-Over*, identifies pacing, volume, and range (or "PVR") as the keys to a captivating vocal performance. Pacing refers to the speed of your delivery, which usually reflects the rhythm and timing of the script. Volume is obviously how loud or soft you speak in places, and range is the ability to vary the pitch of your voice to capture attention or express an emotion.

Rates for nonunion jobs are negotiated between the voice-over artist and a particular client. Again, rates vary with the size of the advertiser, how long the spot will air, and whether it airs in one market or many. A local cable ad, for example, might pay $50, but a corporate spot on network TV might net you fifteen times that. Narration jobs often pay by the hour, based upon the project budget, length of work, audience (in-house or general public), and ultimate purpose (training tape or soundtrack for a major documentary).

At the stratospheric end of the spectrum, the cast of Fox's long running animated series *The Simpsons* settled a highly publicized contract dispute in 2004. Though final amounts were undisclosed, Daily Variety reported they had been seeking a raise from $125,000 to $360,000 per episode, or $8 million for the season.

Key Attributes

A voice-over artist should have superb articulation, a flexible voice, and acting talent. Hard work, persistence, and the ability to market yourself is a must for getting steady work.

Key Tip

Having a great voice alone isn't enough; you need to learn how to utilize it and show-case the kind of skills and talents casting agents really need. You'll want to get a first quality demo tape produced (you can make your own, but get feedback from others before sending it out). If you know a voice instructor, have him or her give a listen and share any advice.

Key Resource

You should definitely check out *The Art of Voice Acting* by James Alburger.

Celebrity Personal Assistant

We've all seen it: the frazzled or spoiled movie star, dictating rapid-fire orders to a sharp-witted lackey (usually with a headset attached) who makes the calls, pays the bills, and confirms the appointments.

Although high-powered people have always enjoyed help, these days the celebrity personal assistant (or CPA) is a genuine and growing cultural phenomenon. Qualified

CPAs can earn up to $100,000 per year—and enjoy the lifestyles of the rich and famous up close. A good assistant functions as secretary, accountant, and whatever else is required to provide his or her client peace of mind and some privacy.

And it's not just actors and rock stars who are looking for CPAs—busy professionals from CEOs and politicians to authors and athletes will pay for this kind of assistance.

On the Job

Referrals from trusted sources are the most common way to get hired in this field, which makes networking essential. Make use of any connections you have in the field of your interest (sports, entertainment, etc.). Seek out work as a production assistant on a movie set or volunteer opportunities at charity events celebrities will attend. You might start by assisting a corporate or noncelebrity type to gain experience and a sense of the skills that will be required of you.

Facts and Figures

Fabjob.com, a Canada-based company that publishes information on nontraditional careers, reports that the celebrity personal assistant field is growing at a rate of about 15 percent per year.

The celebrity personal assistant field is one of the hottest and fastest growing careers today.

Job Description

There's plenty of errand running involved, but many personal assistants are educated professionals performing high-level tasks for their employers. Some act as personal shoppers, manage the household staff, and pick up dry cleaning. Others read scripts, handle media queries, and act as liaison between the client and his or her agent, manager, or the rest of the world.

Celebrities—and plenty of other busy professionals—look for highly organized, tech-savvy types who'll help them transfer their schedule from a handheld device to a computer, keep track of finances, and find the perfect birthday gift for Mom. Also helpful are etiquette knowledge and party or event planning experience. On your

On the Job

There is currently no formal long-term education program to become a personal assistant, but you can develop many of the necessary skills in related programs, such as computer courses, household management courses (for butlers and household managers), and event-planning courses offered by community colleges.

resumé, highlight any skills and work experience that point to successfully managing people's lives.

In addition to being polished, professional, and organized, it takes a little something extra to succeed as a celebrity personal assistant. You really check your ego at the door. Personality match here is critical—as is flexibility, patience, and an ability to anticipate an employer's needs. You'll have to deal with difficult and demanding people in a skillful and diplomatic manner. Perhaps most important of all is discretion, because you'll be privy to sensitive personal information. A good CPA will observe a "code of honor" when it comes to keeping secrets.

Pay and Perks

On average, pay ranges anywhere from $20–30 per hour, but the most experienced celebrity assistants working for well established celebrities can earn upward of $100,000. Needless to say, the perks of this job can be priceless: jetting off to exotic locales, attending VIP social events, picking up hand-me-down clothing or jewelry. You might go behind the scenes at a film shoot, or score VIP seats to a concert, premiere, or ball game when your celeb can't attend.

With all the glitz and glamour comes a downside. The fast-paced nature of the job can be stressful and can consume much of your personal time. You might have to travel at a moment's notice, or take a 3 A.M. "emergency" phone call. The unusual nature of the job—and the fickle temperaments of some celebrities—can make it hard to maintain a personal life. But for the resilient and resourceful there can be a reward, as more and more assistants make the transition to other careers in the entertainment industry.

Key Attributes

Discretion, multitasking, and resourcefulness are invaluable to the CPA—you might be called on to answer any number of crises, from dry cleaning to dinner reservations to last-minute travel arrangements. You can't be an expert in everything, but you will need to know where to go for the answers.

Key Tip

You can't reach most celebrities directly, but you can usually contact their publicist, agent, or even their current personal assistant. If they're not hiring, they might keep you in mind for the future or recommend you to somebody else. Don't gush or sound over-eager; be highly professional and diplomatic, focusing on what you have to offer.

Key Resource

www.fabjob.com/celebrity.asp lists more than a dozen CPA agencies that can help you get an inroad into the industry. Their advice is to sign up with as many as possible; send a brief query e-mail asking whom you should contact and what your next step should be.

Stand-Up Comic

Thanks to the success of sitcoms, cable television outlets, and talk shows, stand-up comedy has come a long way from the world of seedy, smalltime nightclubs to the well publicized, multimillion-dollar contracts that Jerry Seinfeld, Jamie Foxx, Rosanne Barr, Ray Romano, Ellen Degeneres, and others have landed.

But anyone can tell you that it's still a long, hard slog through the "minors" for a shot at comedy's big league. Few professions require you to put yourself out there in such a public and potentially humiliating position. Everybody bombs—it's the ones who can learn from the experience, adjust their material, and get back out there night after night who stand a chance. If comedy truly is in your blood, you might be hooked after getting one or two good laughs on stage.

Just know there are still plenty of seedy joints to endure.

Facts and Figures

It's estimated that more than half of those starting out don't last more than two years in the profession, simply because failure, disappointment, and rejection are so prevalent. It takes tremendous self-confidence to get on stage night after night. In terms of visibility, New York and Los Angeles are the best cities to start your career in— though the competition in both are intense. With comedy clubs and venues all over the country these days, relocating is far from essential. Many comics get their start by logging hundreds, even thousands, of miles on the road. It's not unusual for an aspiring stand-up to log over 200 days a year away from home.

Job Description

A stand-up comedian performs in comedy clubs, relating a well-paced succession of scripted and sometimes ad-libbed jokes, from one-liners to humorous stories, making up what's known as a monologue. Some immerse themselves in characters, or build a more elaborate form of story-telling into their act. The end goal is the same—getting laughs from a crowd of total strangers.

On the Job

Any comic will tell you that his or her life source is coming up with fresh, funny material on a consistent basis. Carry a notebook wherever you go to jot down observations or ideas. In addition, set aside scheduled writing time every day. Strive to be as descriptive as possible—use words that will paint a picture and put the audience into the scene you describe.

Stand-up comedy is in one sense the easiest of the entertainment fields for beginners to enter, with "open mic nights" at venues across the country for anyone brave enough to take a shot at performing. More and more venues, from cruise ships and college campuses to corporate events, offer a chance for stand-ups to strut their comic stuff and be seen.

It's also probably the most difficult field to endure, because a stand-up comic is always at the mercy of a live audience. On a given night you might face aggressive heckling or simple indifference; a truly great comic feeds off the mood and responses of a particular crowd, and can adjust his or her act accordingly. As a solo performer your mission is to win them over—with humor as your only weapon.

The Water Cooler

Comedy troupes develop, perform, and publicize their own material. Most of the members maintain freelance or day jobs that allow them to pursue this career. They usually schedule a weekly show, bracketed around rehearsal and workshops where they critique each other's sketches and performances. Because attendees will not return to see the same material, it is a highly pressured large-output environment. A troupe comedian must adapt to peers' comments and take criticism well. The ability to work with others is critical to success in comedy groups. Troupes are often formed in major urban centers where actors and comedians congregate due to the larger opportunity for work.

Pay and Perks

Comedians work long hours for little and sometimes no pay, and suffer near constant uncertainty about their next gig. Average pay runs about $50 for two twenty-minute sets at a comedy club—which might sound good for the time, but consider that a new comic might perform four sets a week, while writing new material, watching other comics, and working a "real" job on the side. Not surprisingly, corporate gigs are more generous, offering up to $100 for a 10–15 minute spot.

Realistically, those without trust funds should consider stand-up a hobby when they're starting out. Keep your day job, but focus on getting stage time wherever and whenever you can.

Key Attributes

Persistence, persistence, persistence. Flexibility, confidence, and thinking on your feet help, too. Successful stand-up comics are thick-skinned in the face of hecklers, low pay, and long nights and have the ability to take criticism and learn from failure. Sense of humor should go without saying!

Key Tip

Comedy is based on truth—so being "yourself" is essential, even when you're doing imitations or other characters. Without some emotional connection to your material, it will surely ring flat. Your comic voice or point of view—be it aggressive, soft spoken, observational, opinionated, or self-effacing—should always come through.

Key Resource

Your key resource is *The Comedy Bible: From Stand-up to Sitcom—The Comedy Writer's Ultimate "How To" Guide* (Fireside, 2001) by Judy Carter.

Rock and Roll Roadie

Nothing says glam like the lifestyle of a rock 'n' roll star. But let's face it—outside of daydreams, few of us will ever be on stage in tight pants, performing for adoring throngs. So what about the guys (and they're still nearly all guys) who work behind the scenes? Whether it's the bar band circuit or a big-budget stadium spectacle, it takes a whole crew of hard-working people to put on a rock show.

If you've got a thirst for loud noise, late nights, and life on the road—along with a lot of heavy lifting—then the roadie's life might be for you.

Facts and Figures

Live music is very big business around the world. According to *Billboard* magazine, Madonna's "Re-Invention" Tour earned the star $125 million in 2004, when she sold out over 50 shows. In the same year, the artist-known-again-as Prince raked in $90.2 million on his tour. All told, the top ten pop music acts earned well over $500 million through touring in 2004—and that's just a small sampling of the shows that go on in every city, every night.

On the Job

Theatrical work is one way to break into road work. The International Alliance of Theatrical Stage Employees (I.A.T.S.E) has hundreds of local chapters you can look up on their website: www.iatse-intl.org.

Meet local bands through school, college, bars, casinos, and festivals. Work in your school or college's theater for the experience. Work for a sound and/or light company.

Job Description

Although the term *roadie* conjures up about as loose and informal a job as you can imagine, the members of a rock 'n' roll band's road crew are in fact highly trained, specialized technicians, who provide essential services for the band while they tour and perform live shows. It's kind of an umbrella term that encompasses many different roles—and might describe anyone from the lighting technician, to the stage designer, to the security detail. You might be a one-man show for a local band that's just starting out—maybe even your own—but for the really big tours there are drivers, make-up artists, caterers, even day-care providers.

Roadies get the late nights *and* the early mornings—carting truckloads of heavy equipment on and off the bus, making early connections, turning that empty hockey arena into a multi-million-dollar, multimedia rock 'n' roll spectacle in 12 hours or less.

Unlike the band members, these guys show up early. Each will have a task—guitar tuners, mixers and sound boards, lighting equipment. They should work like a well-oiled machine, so teamwork is highly important. Essentially, roadies work hard so the band can play hard—and make it look effortless.

On the Job

If you want to work with the instruments, get to know your gear. Musicians are a finicky and brand-loyal bunch, so you'll want to know if your drummer lives and dies by a Yamaha drum key, for example. Is there a reputable music shop in your area? Their staff are the experts, and can help school you on the particulars. It's also a great place to scour want ads for musicians and crews in your area.

Pay and Perks

A roadie's "salary" truly runs the gamut, from free beer and minimum wage to six figures, depending on your skills and experience—and sometimes the success of "your" band. In the beginning, you can expect little, if any, money. Mostly local bands can't afford to pay out, so they tend to be self-supporting or use a volunteer crew. When you move up to "regional" work (i.e., touring the Northeast, Midwest, and so on), pay for a lightman may be $50–100 per gig, while a soundman might earn slightly more at $300–500 a week. Reaching "the Big Time" means working national or international tours—reserved for crew with significant experience and excellent technical and people skills. The pay here, not to mention the perks, can be remarkably good—up to $50–$60,000 a year for a top-flight rock and roll gig.

The truth is, few if any roadies do it for the pay. Most are friends of the band and/or musicians themselves, eager to be part of the rock 'n' roll lifestyle and happy to add their own skills and muscle to the mix. It can take hours of backbreaking labor to put a big show together, but when the lights go down and the band takes the stage, you realize you've helped make it happen.

Oh, and those magic words: "I'm with the band."

Key Attributes

To be a good roadie, you must be a team player, be able to keep a cool head amidst a million distractions (screaming groupies, travel delays, equipment failure), and most important, *love* the music: it's what you'll be eating, sleeping, and breathing, night and day.

Key Tip

Even better than brawn, having quick hand-eye skills, a good tuning ear, and timing are incredibly useful—especially when the band is on stage. Anything can happen during a live performance, and a truly expert roadie might need to replace a drum head or re-string or tune a guitar on the fly.

Key Resource

www.crewpro.com is a subscription-based website for touring personnel, musicians, and employees who advertise their skills or staffing needs. The cost is $30 per year for "rookies" with one year or less in the business, $60 for one year, and $95 for a lifetime membership.

Stuntman

In the 1980s ABC action series *The Fall Guy*, Lee Majors played Colt Sievers, a stuntman cum bounty hunter whose daily routine included chasing cars off of bridges, jumping bad guys, and rescuing beautiful women—only to hand them off to the "real" stars. As the show's country-style theme song lamented, Sievers had been the "unknown" who made Eastwood and many others look unbeatable onscreen.

Unknown is still by and large the stunt person's fate; but exceptional is the job they do. They can tumble down stairs, dive off of high buildings, survive a hair-raising car chase, explosion, or sword fight, and bounce right back for the next take. Stuntmen and women are a truly rare breed.

The common perception of them is as daredevils or simply madmen, but stunt people are an extremely careful and detail-oriented bunch—planning, preparing, and training for years to produce stunts safely, and only after a thorough consideration of risks.

Facts and Figures

As opposed to the legions of (mostly unemployed) "regular" actors, there are only about 2,000 working stunt people in Hollywood. About half the stunts in film or television are fight scenes—the rest involve car stunts, falls, fire, crashing through windows, and so on. The vast majority are men, because that's still what most scripts call for, but the growing number of heroines in action pictures has provided an opportunity for stuntwomen.

As with most film and TV work, the places to be are Los Angeles. and New York—though you might find jobs here and there on location shoots in places like Vancouver, Toronto, and other cities. Contact the union and/or local casting agencies to learn more.

Job Description

As you might expect, there's no such thing as a "typical" stunt person. He or she might be an expert at archery, horse riding, climbing, jet skiing, snow skiing, boxing, fencing, motorbike riding—the list is endless.

The essentials are gymnastics and stage combat training—but the more you can do, the better. It's good to get as many licenses and qualifications as possible—which might include a motorcycle license, first-aid certificate, martial arts belts, diving qualification, or whatever else, depending on your interests and strengths.

Stunt people have their own training schools (such as the Academy of Theatrical Combat in Hollywood) and a union that ensures they are well compensated for the tough work they do. They tend to be young and athletic, and have usually mastered a variety of different physical skills, with one or two specialties.

Needless to say, stunt work can be dangerous, and nearly every stunt person suffers broken bones or serious injuries at some point in his or her career.

Pay and Perks

Stunt people can pull in anywhere from $500 to $1,500 per day on a typical shoot. The perks of this career are numerous—from being sent to glamorous, exotic locations to working with actors, directors, and other creative professionals to create an

The Water Cooler

The Stuntmen's Association of Motion Pictures (www.stuntmen.com) was founded in 1961 with the goal of professionalizing the world of stunt work, establishing highest standards of safety, integrity, and preparation. As they like to say, there is no "dare-devilry" in the profession, but rather a highly talented, exceptionally well-trained and prepared breed of professionals.

On the Job

All Hollywood stunt workers are members of the Screen Actors Guild (SAG)—but the more specialized stunt associations (International Stunt Association, Stuntmen's Association, and Stunts Unlimited, for example) are tough to crack. Because networking is essential to getting work in the industry, one tip is to find a gym where stunt people train and start working out there.

exciting and believable sequence on film. For most, the satisfaction of a job well done more than compensates for the frequent bruises.

Key Attributes

Though some would say you have to be crazy to do what stunt people do, in fact it's knowledge, experience, physical discipline, and a can-do attitude that are the keys to success.

Key Tip

You should know at least two martial arts (which might include boxing)—not necessarily at the black belt level but well enough to be convincing and not injure your partner onscreen. Judo's great for learning how to break falls.

Key Resource

The United Stuntman's Association, a licensed and registered school based in Mukilteo, Washington, offers an intensive, professional-oriented training course each year. Over three weeks you'll get 150 hours of immersion in everything from fire work and horseback riding to stage combat. Find them online at www.stuntschool.com.

Hollywood Makeup Artist

If it's your passion in life to get famous actors ready for their close-up, then why not a career as a Hollywood makeup artist?

You get to flex your creative muscles, rub elbows with celebrities, and when you're done, you can write a "tell-all" book about the experience.

Facts and Figures

The fact is that if you want to be a Hollywood makeup artist, you have to live near Hollywood. But Broadway actors need makeup, too, so New York is always an option. Canada is a big venue for filmmakers (the cost to film a movie is cheaper than in the United States), so Toronto and Vancouver are good bets, too.

Job Description

Your task is to make the beautiful even more beautiful … and bring them back to Earth again at the end of the day, when you'll also be peeling makeup off of touchy and tired actors.

Of course, there is much more to the job than that. You want to help actors immerse themselves into characters, as well. Think Boris Karloff in *Frankenstein* or Cicely Tyson in *The Autobiography of Miss Jane Pittman* (where the character gradually ages from pre-teen years to old age) and you get the idea.

Being a makeup artist is a challenge. Yes, you'll be applying blush or mascara to doe-eyed actresses, but you'll also be asked to create black eyes or bloody wounds for characters, too. One of the most interesting corners of the makeup world is in horror films, where makeup artists really get to make their chops turning Willem Defoe into the Green Goblin (in *Spider-Man*) or Gary Oldman into Dracula. For those jobs, extensive research is required to get to the heart of the character. In the modern movie era, makeup artists also produce prostheses using rubber, plastic, fiberglass, or even latex paint. They also create or purchase hairpieces, wigs, and beards. Makeup artists sketch final designs for hairstyles and makeup.

Pay and Perks

Good Hollywood makeup artists can earn up to $3,000 per week for your average Hollywood film. For big-budget blockbusters, top-of-the-line artists can earn $3,000 per day. Starting out can be tough, though. To apprentice for a working Hollywood makeup artist—a good idea—you may make little or no money. Usually, makeup art students do so to gain experience and build a much-needed portfolio and develop some contacts in the industry.

Key Attributes

Some formal makeup schooling is usually required to land a makeup job. Course-work in television, film, or theater will add luster to your resume. The ability to get along with often prickly celebrity types helps. An academic background in film, television, modeling, or marketing can boost your chances. You'll need some money, too. A good makeup school may charge up to $4,000 for its classwork. You can also expect to pay up to $500 or so to put together a decent "book," as it's called in the trades. To the rest of us, it's a portfolio of your best work, comprised mostly of photos and testimonials.

Tool-wise, you'll need camera-ready pressed powder; velour powder puffs to apply the powder; a collection of lipstick colors; and hairspray, brushes, combs, scissors, tweezers, and disposable razors.

Key Tip

Get an agent. Aside from completing an apprenticeship with a good LA-based makeup artist, the fastest way into the film makeup industry is through a reputable agent. Expect to pay your agent 15 percent of whatever you make in the field—but only from the gigs he/she gets you.

Key Resources

Take a look at the Worldwide Alliance of Makeup Artists website at groups.msn. com/WorldwideAllianceofMakeupArtists/schools.msnw.

Wardrobe Artist

If you have the cojones to walk up to George Clooney or Val Kilmer and say "Sorry, dude, but brown corduroy is so last year," then you have the brass needed for a career as an entertainment industry wardrobe artist.

Facts and Figures

About 400 films are produced in Hollywood each year (India leads the world with 800). About 700 TV shows are produced in the United States, as well. Film and TV are also sliding in different directions. Film production is down about 10 percent annually while television, with added advantage of cable, satellite, and a growing number of networks, is growing at about 3 percent annually.

So there is work out there for dedicated wardrobe artists, particularly in TV land.

Job Description

With clothing as your calling card, your job is to dress actors and prepare them for performances on film or on stage. Musicians are also big on using wardrobe artists for their performances. If you can't stand the west coast, where most of the wardrobe work is, the modeling industry (can you say "Venice?") is a good place to start a career, as well.

Not only do you have to know and understand fashion, you need to be nimble enough to change gears from gig to gig. A Hollywood civil war movie will have you immersed in haversacks and basic running stitches. Four weeks later you could be measuring cummerbunds for a 1930s-period romp. A good working knowledge of clothing patterns, fabrics, and styles is therefore highly important.

Most of the work is indoors, which is only worth noting if you are a sun worshipper or are particularly susceptible to allergies from old clothes and dusty film or theater stages. You work when the cast works—often at night and on weekends.

Pay and Perks

For wardrobe artists in Hollywood, a good, steady gig on a television show should bring in at least $250 per day—and up to $1,000 per day based on experience, reputation, and the success of the show involved. Wardrobe experts on film sets, who work for the movie studios, can do even better—up to $2,000 per day in some cases. As you gain experience, expect to slide up the income scale even more.

The perks include a chance to work closely with talented (in some cases testy) celebrities. Plus, there are plenty of clothes to choose from, which is a good deal if you're working on a modern-day film with New York or Paris fashions. It's not such a good idea if you're working on a Fellini-esque film where the wardrobe is pretty much limited to black-hooded robes.

Key Attributes

Besides a sense of style and a good historical knowledge of clothes and fashion, a good artist's eye for drawing sketches is a necessary trait for a wardrobe artist. After you research the clothing needed for your latest film or play, you'll likely be asked to whip up some sketches to give the director and actors a sense of what the cast will be wearing—and how they will look—once shooting starts.

It helps to be a real people person. You might also be asked to sit in and read through scripts with the cast (to understand the details that affect the character's appearance), consult with the director or producer on new ideas or changes, and shop for bargains at wholesale clothing stores or fashion boutiques.

Key Tip

The best move for a wardrobe artist is to spread his or her wings and diversify. That means that if there is a lull in the television end of the market, you should have the resources and contacts to slide over to the music or modeling sector until the thin market blows over.

Key Resources

Wardrobe artists are big on unions. Two of the biggest and best are:

Costume Designers Guild (IA Local 892)
13949 Ventura Blvd., Ste. 309
Sherman Oaks, CA 91423
818-905-1557
818-905-1560 (Fax)

Theatrical Wardrobe Union (IA Local 768)
13949 Ventura Blvd., Ste. 307
Sherman Oaks, CA 91423
818-789-8735
818-914-6532 (Fax)

The Least You Need to Know

- ◆ Breaking into the entertainment field takes confidence. A stand-up comedian, for example, has the tough task of ensuring that his audience hangs on his every word—and laughs, too.

- ◆ Find people who can help you get hired. I know, the networking thing again. But a would-be stuntman or rock and roll roadie stands a much better chance of getting hired if they know someone in the same business.

- ◆ Find a talent, hone it, and then exploit it. Celebrity assistants, for example, likely have a talent for listening well and being very detail oriented. Prove that to a celebrity and you stand a much better chance of getting hired than if you didn't.

- ◆ Be a joiner. By that I mean join organizations that cater to and accommodate the professionals in your chosen career. Stunt-people, professional comedians, wardrobe artists—all have unions and join them. After all, there is power in numbers.

Chapter 4

It Speaks to Me: The Fine Arts

In This Chapter

- Opportunities for creative types
- The many hats of the documentary filmmaker
- Get rewarded for your perfect "part"
- The self-employed jewelry designer
- On stage: playwriting and stage managing

Oscar Wilde wrote that life imitates art far more than art imitates life.

If so, then there should be plenty of opportunities available for creative types looking to break into the field of arts and leisure.

But like a master sculptor, there's a great deal of prep work involved before you can actually get your fingers in the clay.

Documentary Filmmaker

Documentary or nonfiction films can range from hour-long cable or public television specials to full-length features in commercial release. They can be highly personal or sweeping in scale, covering topics from biography and history to science, politics, and the arts. (The recent and highly successful film *Supersize Me* even chronicled one man's steady diet of McDonald's products and how it affected his health.)

The common thread is that all documentaries have a story to tell. But it takes much more than a story to make a successful documentary—producing a film means countless hours of behind-the-scenes work, lining up investors, scheduling interviews, and putting in hours of research, writing, shooting, and editing, usually for little acclaim or attention. The Ken Burnses and Michael Moores of the world are very few—but their success has generated fresh attention to this medium. It's a long, hard road to the final cut, but if you have a passion for documenting real-life events, people, or ideas on film, you've got the first essential ingredient.

On the Job

Capable editors are always in high demand in the film and television industry, where an experienced editor can earn about $60,000–$80,000 in a major market. You'll need experience with nonlinear editing systems (mainly the Avid Media Composer), or if you're a newbie, an editing class at a community college or university. If you're just starting out you'll probably have to take work as an assistant editor or on corporate industrial marketing projects, for a lot less money, until you've cut your teeth.

Facts and Figures

Like all films, documentaries are a risky business financially—which makes getting your great idea off the ground a hard sell. If you have solid entrepreneurial or fund-raising skills, you might be able to interest private investors (or apply for grant money, if the film has serious educational or cultural potential), then hire a professional producer to develop the idea into something ready for pre-sale to a network, which would then raise the rest of the budget.

Most cable documentaries are made with co-production financing from the network. The Discovery Channel, for example, might put up 60 percent of a film's budget, with the production company or its investors providing the balance in anticipation of making it back (along with a profit, of course) in ancillary sales such as foreign markets and home video.

Although documentaries can be made anywhere, beginners in the industry will find the best prospects for employment in Los Angeles, New York, or Washington, D.C.

Job Description

Most documentarians wear many hats. You might be writing or researching one day, then directing or filming an interview the next, then supervising the editing process. An assistant or associate producer might pitch in as production coordinator, production assistant, receptionist, and secretary (among other things).

Most commercial documentaries today are researched by the writer and/or associate producer. Staff positions are few and freelance work is the norm, especially for those new to the business. You might get your start as a cameraperson, editor, or a producer of news or some other type of programming. Some documentarians emerge from the ranks of film schools or the numerous film festivals.

If you're hoping to get your own film or program produced, you need to start by writing up a brief (1–5 page) proposal or "pitch," explaining what the show is about. You'd send your idea to all the TV networks that might possibly be interested—and nine times out of ten, they shoot you down. But once in a while, the network will take the bait and actually pay you to make your film or show.

Although a cheap-and-quick one-hour program can be completed in just a few weeks, a good quality documentary usually takes 4–6 months, or often longer. Public television documentaries can take years to produce, either because a high budget allows for it, or a very low budget forces the work to be done on a part-time, piecemeal basis.

Pay and Perks

The size of your paycheck depends on whether you work in the commercial or noncommercial (for example, public television) arena. An entry-level salary for an assistant producer might be $30,000 or less. Experienced commercial documentary makers can average anywhere from $50,000 to $85,000 a year—but because it's mostly a freelance business, that figure can change dramatically from year to year. Noncommercial documentarians generally earn less than their commercial counterparts.

Short of fame, fortune, and prestigious awards, the main perk of the job is a stimulating environment with lots of variety. You'll get to learn about all kinds of different subjects and turn your raw material into a coherent and compelling story. Although the process is engaging, seeing the end result is generally the greatest perk for filmmakers.

Key Attributes

Though it's often not very glamorous work, documentary filmmaking is still a form of show business; and making it requires a thick skin and huge amounts of patience and persistence.

Key Tip

If you're in the exploratory phase, try applying for work as a researcher or production assistant with a documentary production company in your area. Check the credits at the end of a documentary to find out which company made it, then give them a call.

Key Resource

Check out the job listings at mandy.com and maslowmedia.com, as well as any local resources, schools, or production companies.

Body Part Model

Less celebrated than high fashion modeling, body part modeling is a specialized category of fashion and commercial modeling that can be a lucrative and enjoyable line of work. Many so-called supermodels who might look great in full length shots are much less impressive up close—especially around the hands and feet. That's where a body part model comes in.

Think of all the products, from lip gloss to diamond earrings to a luxury wristwatch, that require close-up photography. In every instance, the aim is to create the illusion of perfection around whatever they're selling—and finding the "perfect" body part is harder than you might think. So if you've got what it takes, you'll be rewarded accordingly.

Facts and Figures

Modeling remains a fairly elite occupation, with approximately 4,600 people employed in the field nationwide. Most jobs are concentrated in New York, Los Angeles, and Miami, where the fashion industry lives and breathes. Most models work through modeling agencies.

Nearly half of all models are self-employed, which means looking after your own health insurance and retirement needs.

Job Description

The most common areas featured in print and TV ads are the hands, feet, legs, torso, and facial features. Most body part models specialize in just one of these. Parts models follow similar career paths as regular models: finding modeling agencies, building portfolios, and making connections. With hand modeling, employers tend to look for long, slender, graceful hands and fingers. They want to see smooth, clear skin (no wrinkles, hair, or large pores; no blemishes or irregular color) and very good nails. Being able to pose the hand in a relaxed, graceful fashion—i.e., avoiding the "claw"—is important.

> **The Water Cooler**
>
> Selection of an agency is an important factor in getting jobs. An agency with a good reputation is more likely to find jobs for their models. Most agencies review photos or have open calls, where models are seen in person. Some agencies sponsor modeling contests or searches.

Much the same goes for other body parts. With facial features, the requirements of shape, color, and so on will vary, but symmetry is nearly always a factor.

You might be hired as a hand "double" if the model they're using has less-than-perfect hands. Or you might be hired for a solo gig to emphasize a particular product.

You'll want to create a portfolio or package to market your priceless part. Have a professional photographer do the job, to ensure proper lighting and clarity, and be ready to submit at least three different pictures of said body part (preferably from different angles).

Your photos can be color or black and white, preferably in 4×6, 5×7, or 8×10s—definitely no larger. Be sure to include the following personal info: name, contact information, height, weight, clothing sizes, hair color, eye color, and age. You might also need to submit your glove or shoe size, if appropriate.

Pay and Perks

Wages vary greatly for different types of modeling; they also depend on the experience and reputation of the model. As a body part model you can expect to earn about

$100 an hour, but keep in mind that these shoots generally don't last more than three hours. A reputable agency will help land you gigs, but the work is still hit or miss unless and until you're established. (And your agent will collect 15 to 20 percent of your earnings in return for their services.)

Perks include working in the fashion/model industry, which is excitement enough for some. Models might also receive additional benefits besides wages, such as job-related travel expenses, clothing, jewelry, or discounts on the merchandise being promoted.

Key Attributes

A good body part model must be well-groomed and flexible and have a professional attitude. In the highly competitive world of modeling, personality plays an important role in landing a job—and landing future recommendations. All models should be professional, polite, and on time for auditions or bookings.

If you are self-employed, you need to be organized to manage your finances and schedule. Patience and persistence are also a must, as the work might build slowly.

Key Tip

A working hand model needs to keep his or her assets protected, which means wearing sunscreen every day on the hands. Keep nails filed and strong by applying a strengthening product two or three times a week. Always wear gloves when washing the dishes (or take advantage of a dishwasher, if possible). Even fairly routine cleaning and household chores can take a toll on your hands, so give them a rest whenever possible. When a job or audition approaches, schedule a professional manicure.

Key Resource

www.mymodelingagency.com links to a vast number of agencies nationwide, in every niche category.

Jewelry Designer

You've heard that diamonds are a girl's best friend—and we all know how Audrey Hepburn felt about Tiffany's. For many men and women alike, the fascination with jewelry goes beyond merely consumption, and into the art and science of creating something beautiful for others to enjoy.

These days, both men and women can be seen sporting jewelry of all kinds—from the classic and formal to the cutting edge, punk, artistic, or exotic—in every imaginable style and price range. This popularity has opened doors for artisans of all ages and backgrounds to get creative and, with some luck, get paid.

If you've got a flair for visual arts or design, are skilled with your hands, and have the patience and vision to work with very small materials, you might be able to turn an enjoyable hobby into a genuinely rewarding venture.

Facts and Figures

In 2000 the consumer market for fine and costume jewelry in the United States reached close to $40 billion. Contributing to the growth in the jewelry market is the expanding availability of jewelry at the retail level, at places such as Wal-Mart, Sears, QVC, Zales, J.C. Penney, and many others. Some jewelry designers work for large-scale manufacturers—and might specialize in an area like gemology or horology (the science of time-keeping, for building and repairing wrist watches).

If you're among the majority of self-employed designers, your costs and considerations will depend a great deal on your materials. If you work at the high end with diamonds or precious metals, fluctuating prices of these items in the world market will affect your production costs.

On the Job

Museum stores and art galleries often feature the work of local artisans and crafts-people. Visit as many as you can in your area and get a feel for what kind of jewelry they carry—price range, materials, and overall style. After you've got a strong portfolio of sample pieces to show off, set up an appointment with the shop buyer to consider carrying your stuff (usually on a consignment basis at first, until they see if it sells).

Job Description

Jewelers design, make, repair, adjust, or sell jewelry, such as rings, pins, bracelets, necklaces, earrings, lockets, and watches. They work with gold, silver, platinum, or other metals, gemstones, beads, and plastic, and these days all manner of other materials. They use a variety of tools to saw, cut, solder, weld, polish, and clean pieces of jewelry.

The work itself isn't as delicate as you might imagine. You might create your initial design by shaping metal or carving wax to make a model for casting metal. Other times you'll be tying or twisting gold or silver wires together and bending them to form rings. You'll want to be adept at welding, to smooth soldered joints and rough spots.

Many art schools and community colleges offer introductory classes in jewelry design. Some colleges and art schools offer programs that lead to a Bachelor's or even a Master's degree of fine arts in jewelry design. There are also technical school courses in areas such as sample making, wax carving, computer-aided design and manufacturing (CAD/CAM), and gemology.

Some learn the skills by apprenticing with a master jeweler, but these days most people start with a keen interest in jewelry. You might start with something relatively simple, like beading, then work up to fabricating a few pieces of your own, and find yourself hooked on the combination of mental creativity and highly skilled handiwork.

Pay and Perks

Pay in this field varies widely, as many people start out with jewelry design as a hobby in the hopes it will eventually become a full-time career. Yearly earnings can range from the high teens to $50,000 or more. There are a select few who become recognized jewelry artists and can command big dollars for their designs, but for the vast majority it's a labor of love.

Key Attributes

You should be creative, dexterous, and energetic at self-promotion. Precision and attention to detail are very important.

Key Tip

Visit craft fairs, jewelry expos, and trade shows in your area and talk with designers and vendors to get their take on the field. It's a competitive field, but with a polite and friendly approach you might gather helpful information on working with different materials and techniques, as well as pricing your own stuff to sell.

Key Resource

Contact the Jewelry Design Professionals' Network at:

Jewelry Design Professionals' Network
12 East 41st Street, Suite 701
New York, NY 10017
www.jdpn.org

Also take a look at *Jewelry Design: The Artisan's Reference* by Elizabeth Olver (North Light Books, 2000).

Playwright

For thousands of years, audiences have flocked to see stories performed on the stage. The authors of such works, from Aeschylus to Shakespeare, have been celebrated through the ages, and the best of their plays continue to captivate audiences today.

The modern era has produced its share of stage giants—from Tennessee Williams and Arthur Miller to Tony Kushner, Eve Ensler, and more. These days producing a play is a costly business, and competition from television and the movies has chipped away at the audience. Few if any contemporary playwrights become household names—but that doesn't stop legions of theater buffs from pursuing their passion. If you're a gifted wordsmith with a strong sense of story and a genuine love of live performance, then perhaps the play's the thing for you.

Facts and Figures

U.S. News and World Report provides annual rankings for the top 70 creative writing programs in the country, most of which offer the aspiring writer an M.A. or M.F.A. (Master of Fine Arts) degree. Prerequisite for this is usually a Bachelor of Arts degree. But as with other writing careers, holding a degree is no guarantee of employment—only a sign that you've spent time honing your craft. Still, a degree can help land you a teaching or related position.

In addition to these degree-granting programs, there are literally hundreds of writing workshops, seminars, and competitions offered year-round that allow you to practice your craft in the presence of instructors and fellow scribes. These range from a one-day or evening workshop to several weeks in the country.

> **On the Job** _____
>
> A quick Internet search will turn up a vast number of playwriting contests; most charge an entry fee, but some will allow you to enter for free. Obviously, the more prestigious and well known the contest, the longer your odds—but there's no harm in trying. Aside from prize money, winning a contest can lead to prestige and further opportunities, including publication or the chance at a full-fledged production. Be sure to follow contest guidelines to the T, so your hard work gets at least a fair chance to be read.

Job Description

A playwright will spend months or years developing his or her ideas into a well-crafted play—drafting, revising, proofreading, editing, and formatting. Unlike novelists and other kinds of writers, the playwright's work doesn't simply end on the page. Playwrights rely on actors, directors, set designers, and most important of all, a live audience, to see their dream through to the end.

Whether it's a staged reading or a full-scale production, playwrights are always looking for ways to get their works seen and heard. There are various paths toward the goal of getting your work out to the public: contests, theatres, publishers, and residencies.

Across the country, there are theaters in cities and towns on the lookout for new material for upcoming productions, although the competition is stiff. It's always best to inquire before submitting a script. Check play writers' market listings for details on how best to query a particular theater (i.e., sending a synopsis versus a complete manuscript; whether the theatre accepts unsolicited submissions or only those from agents). Theater magazines or individual websites might give you more detailed information on rights, compensation (i.e., royalties), and the theater's response time if they're interested. Working with a theatre allows playwrights a chance to form contacts in the field, which could lead to further productions.

Because landing a major theater remains a long shot, some first-time playwrights choose to produce and stage their own plays—a tough haul, but one that does ensure maximum creative control. To do this, you should be prepared to provide and/or raise the finances, assemble the cast and crew, and publicize the play.

Just like new writers in other genres, playwrights generally seek an agent to represent their work, pave the way to larger, more prestigious markets, deal with contract negotiations, and recommend scripts to contacts they might not have on their own.

Beginners will find it a challenge to land an agent without some track record of success in the field. (Agents, after all, earn their money based on a writer's returns.) A good agent will certainly help open doors, but even playwrights with agents need to continually market themselves.

Pay and Perks

Unfortunately, the odds of making a full-time living from playwriting are tragically slim. Most playwrights supplement their income through additional writing (screenplays, TV writing, magazine stories, essays, and so on) or teaching courses in playwriting and drama. Some are hired to direct the works of other playwrights, or find alternate work in the theater.

Established playwrights might apply for a variety of "playwright in residence" positions at a growing number of colleges and universities. Potential perks here include receiving a regular salary or stipend, the chance to lecture on your craft, enjoying a schedule and atmosphere conducive to writing, and maybe even overseeing a school's production of your work.

A working playwright's income derives mainly from performance royalties, script sales, and contest prize money. If their work has been published they will receive royalties each time a drama department or theater group orders a copy or pays for the right to stage a particular play.

Still, the odds of success remain long, and most playwrights will tell you that it isn't the monetary rewards that keep them writing. The real prize is seeing their words come to life on the stage.

Key Attributes

You should be creative, patient, and persistent.

Key Tip

Writing is essentially a solitary pursuit—and sometimes it can feel downright lonely. That's why joining a playwright's organization can offer benefits for the beginner as well as the veteran playwright. These groups (whether in person or online, if there are none in your area) can offer a great way to meet and connect with other playwrights through informative newsletters and magazines, business contacts, and upcoming workshops and retreats.

Key Resource

Budding playwrights should check out these two key resources: the Dramatists Guild at www.dramaguild.com and the Playwright's Noticeboard: www.stageplays.com/markets.htm.

Stage Manager

The great film star Spencer Tracy once said of acting: "It's not hard—just remember your lines and try not to bump into the furniture."

If you want a career in film or stage and it's not the lines that interest you, but the furniture, a stage management gig might be right up your alley.

Facts and Figures

About 6,000 stage managers operate today in the United States and Canada, primarily in entertainment hubs like Hollywood, New York City, Las Vegas, Orlando, Toronto, and Vancouver (both big filming locations for Hollywood producers). Most belong to unions like the Stage Managers Association (www.stagemanagers.org) or Actors Equity (www.actorsequity.org). It's hard to find work as a stage manager without being a member of a union, although you can certainly try.

Job Description

Essentially, the stage manager is the eyes and ears of the production (usually film or stage, although musical acts, Las Vegas performers, TV news, and other entertainment venues need stage managers).

It's a demanding job that begins in pre-production, when the stage manager meets with the producers and director to discuss what stage equipment, props, costumes, furniture, and razzle-dazzle special effects the production is going to need. Then the stage manager assumes responsibility for making sure everything is purchased, set up, and looks superb by opening night. The stage manager will also schedule rehearsals, make sure everyone who should be on the set is on the set, lay out "marks" for performers, and provide actors with hand signals noting when they should enter or exit the stage. When the production ends, it's the stage manager's job to supervise the dismantling of the set.

The stage manager is also involved in keeping a tight schedule through production and rehearsals, working closely with the director and basically supervising the nuts-and-bolts tasks that the director does not have time to do. The best stage managers are a strong link between the director and the cast and crew.

Pay and Perks

Stage managers usually earn anywhere from $30,000 to $60,000 annually. The better, more-connected managers can earn up to $1,000 per day. Stage managers who can manage to find long-term work, such as at regional theaters, seem to do better financially over the long run. Most stage managers, however, hop from gig to gig.

Key Attributes

People-management skills are a big plus in the stage management market. You'll be asked to act as a "go-between"—between the director and the performing talent—time and again to work out problems.

You should also take theater classes to learn all you can about stage sets, lighting, props, and costumes. Classwork in directing can help, too. As a working stage manager you'll be undertaking many directorial tasks, such as rehearsing understudies and communicating directly with actors.

Key Tip

Be alert and in good physical shape. Stage managers work long hours, up to 80 hours per week in rehearsals and production. You'll be on your feet most of the time, troubleshooting and herding cast and crew to meet rigorous scheduling deadlines. Stage management is a control freak's dream job, but it's a demanding one.

Key Resource

The Stage Managers Association (www.stagemanagers.org) is a good resource for would-be stage managers. The site has a great job bank to give you a head start on good gigs in theater and film. The site's "Ask Us" section allows members to communicate directly with working stage managers.

The Least You Need to Know

♦ The fine arts industry is looking for talented people with a flair for the dramatic and the creative.

♦ Hiring emphasis is on well-groomed, positive people. After all, you'll be selling yourself—this is as far away from the corporate world and its insular culture as you're going to get.

♦ Pay, across the board, is erratic. But the creative rewards are numerous and your chance to leave a mark even better.

♦ Be prepared to work alone. Artists, playwrights, and the like spend solitary hours honing their craft.

Chapter 5

Stop the Presses: Media and Publishing

In This Chapter

- ◆ The great communicator's guide to the media spotlight
- ◆ Becoming a traffic reporter
- ◆ Don't take "no" for an answer: talk show booker
- ◆ The literary scene: romance writer, book doctor, literary agent
- ◆ Crossword puzzle craftsman

Welcome to the world's biggest megaphone—the media and publishing market. If you have an itch to say what you think and want to influence public opinion, the media spotlight is a great place to be.

So keep your eyes open and your ear to the ground. The next big scoop just might be yours.

Traffic Reporter

There's nothing quite like the thrill of breaking a news story at 1,000 feet in the air from the all-seeing eye of a helicopter.

But that's exactly what can happen when you become an air traffic reporter.

It's a great field for those risk-takers and news-breakers who deal in the flow of information, and who like a little risk thrown into the equation for good measure.

A good traffic reporter knows that consumers are more sensitive to change today because of the speed and the style in which we receive information. In 1805, it took six weeks for word of British Admiral Nelson's victory at Trafalgar to reach Montreal. But with the merger of aviation and instantaneous digital broadcast technology, an air traffic reporter can get the news out on a highway traffic jam or a high-profile criminal on the lam across to viewers in a matter of seconds.

Facts and Figures

Studies show that U.S. drivers spend more than 40 hours a year tied up in traffic. And employers bemoan the fact that over 5.7 billion person hours and productivity are lost to traffic jams. Consequently, there's a big market for traffic reporters who can get drivers on the open road.

Job Description

The job of air traffic reporter is probably best filled by someone with print or broadcast journalism experience who has little fear of heights. Traffic reporters report on everything from breaking news to the weather to traffic snarl-ups.

Typically, your day starts early, often at three or four in the morning. The morning drive in most broadcast areas starts at 5:30 A.M. or so. That's when most local news broadcasts kick off. A typical helicopter news reporter will be in the air until around 9 A.M., when rush-hour traffic peters out. Although many news outlets go back on the air at 11:30 or 12 noon, eye-in-the-sky traffic reporters have to be ready to fly at a moment's notice. A high-speed police chase, news of a major fire, or a hostage situation are all part of the job for helicopter reporters.

Some traffic reporters don't get involved with general news coverage—they stick to riding high in the sky reporting on weather and traffic conditions. But with tight station budgets, some reporters will and do wear both hats.

Pay and Perks

Compensation varies, depending on the market you work in. A traffic reporter in New York or Chicago will obviously earn more than a reporter in Dayton or Baton Rouge. A small radio station, for example, might only offer traffic reporters a salary of $15,000 per year. TV stations pay better. Starting salaries for helicopter reporters can be as much as $60,000. Normal starting salaries for broadcast reporters, according to Salary.com, is about $30,000.

Key Attributes

The best path to a helicopter reporter's job is through your high school math and science books. Local television stations will hire a helicopter reporter well versed in weather and climate patterns and put him right to work. For general news, the station editor might just send up an on-staff news reporter who only rides in a chopper to cover major stories. For traffic and weather reporters, riding high in the sky is more of a regular occurrence, especially for a traffic reporter. A degree in meteorology is especially helpful. Knowledge of aviation will get you to the front of the resumé line, too.

Finding a mentor is a good idea. Someone who has experience on the air in a chopper can level with you and provide a good idea of the risks and rewards of helicopter reporting.

Also, get the basics down. Learn how to operate an onboard camera system. And practice your reports in front of your bathroom mirror. TV producers will overlook some lack of technical knowledge, but a lack of on-camera presence is a real career killer.

On the Job

To get your foot in the door of a television news studio, it's best to have a high school and a college degree in broadcast journalism or communication. Even better is a minimum three years of television reporting experience with prior helicopter reporting experience.

Key Tip

If you can manage it financially, take some flying lessons. It's a much easier sell for broadcast station managers to hire a reporter who knows a thing or two about wing drafts and blade grips.

Key Resource

Try out www.tvjobs.com. It's a paid site, but it's a must read if you're serious about a career in broadcast journalism. Another worthwhile site is www. theweatherprediction.com/jobs. It has a good list of pros and cons to weather-related broadcasting jobs.

Talk Show Booker

Can you flip through a Rolodex in no time flat? Can you spot a trend before it happens—and find a book author or industry specialist to appear on the air to talk about it before the competition does? Do you know what's hot and what's not?

If so, then a career in talk show talent booking might be in the cards for you.

Facts and Figures

The United States has over 2,000 talk shows on air today. And all of them need people to book interesting guests.

Job Description

Talent bookers on talk shows work closely with the show producer to identify qualified experts who can appear on the broadcast and add some heft, cachet, and education on whatever issue the show is shining its spotlight on that day. You'll be dealing with people—often celebrities—with big egos, and with agents and talent agency representatives who'll promise you the moon. But it's up to you to make sure they deliver.

Pay and Perks

As with the traffic reporter job, a talent booker's pay varies from broadcast market to broadcast market. A recent ad for a talk show booker for court TV advertised an $80,000 salary. But that assumes a bloated Rolodex, years of experience, and a demonstrated track record getting celebrities and experts on your show. More likely you'll start at the station doing other tasks first and then work your way up to the booker post.

Key Attributes

As a talk show booker, your primary job is to never take the word "no" for an answer. You must be relentless—but diplomatic. You also have to be creative enough to know how to make your pitch stand out from the rest of the pile. If a major breakthrough on the war on AIDS hits the front page of *The New York Times* that morning, why should the director of a leading HIV research laboratory appear on *your* show? Such are the challenges of succeeding as a talent booker.

The willingness to volunteer your services to learn the trade can go a long way, too.

Contact your local TV or radio station—a college station will do just fine—and ask to help out around the studio. Before long you'll get a chance to screen callers and talk to show hosts to see what makes a talk show tick. You'll also get a good grip on how potential guests (or their handlers) call, mail, or in some cases actually come to the station to book interviews. Discovering how the talk show books its guests and responds to would-be guests—as well as how actual interviews are carried out—is a big advantage in your fledgling talk show talent booker career.

Key Tip

Have a good sense of humor. You're going to face some difficult personalities as a talent booker. So the ability to laugh at yourself (and the often chaotic situation around you) is a critical component to any good talk show booker. Plus, when you laugh, others laugh with you—and agree to appear on your show.

And leave your beeper on. Talk show bookers are expected to be on call nights and weekends. No telling when Tom Clancy will call back; when he does, you have to be ready.

Key Resource

Your best resource is your local television or radio station. But it's also a good idea to subscribe to the major talk show periodicals. *Talkers* magazine is a good place to start (www.talkers.com).

Romance Novelist

If you grew up reading Harlequin romance novels and think you can do better, then writing about love and romance might be your ticket to fame and fortune.

Getting into the romance racket is a bit of a catch-22. Often you can't get an agent or a publisher to return your phone calls unless you've written a book. And you can't write a book unless you get an agent or a publisher to return your phone calls.

But there are ways to crack the code of the romance writing racket, if you try hard enough.

Facts and Figures

Over 50 percent of all mass market paperback books bought in the United States are romance novels. The romance novel industry generates more than $1 billion in sales each year.

Job Description

Writing bodice-rippers takes a great deal of creativity and discipline.

A good romance writer can churn out one or two novels each year. That means writing every day for at least a few hours. If you are fortunate enough to travel, you can take notes while in Paris or Venice and inject some interesting backdrops for your novels. Otherwise, you're left conducting background research on the Internet and through books and magazines. So you have to take research time into account, as well.

Writing is hard work, but those who do it for a living love it. And romance writers are no different. You do get to make your own hours, answer to nobody but your publisher and your readers, and find yourself the center of attention at parties and book readings. Be prepared to do some newspaper, magazine, radio, and television interviews, as well. Publishers love romance authors who can toot their own horn and sell books through media appearances.

Pay and Perks

Romance writers are usually paid in the low-to-mid four figures for book advances. Somewhere between $2,000 and $10,000 is realistic. If the book takes off and sells well, you can expect to be paid royalties of between four to ten percent of total book sales. Advances are paid against royalties earned by the sales of your book, so your book sales have to exceed the amount of your advance before you'll receive any royalty payments.

Usually, first run printing of your book by a respectable publisher will be between 10,000 and 20,000 books.

The perks are good, too. One great benefit of being a romance writer is being able to work at home, churning out best-sellers in your jammies or sweatpants.

Key Attributes

Obviously, the ability to write is paramount. And the ability to tell a good story is mandatory.

Time is another valuable commodity for a romance writer. Many authors can't subsist on writing wages for a full-time gig. So they do it part time and find themselves in a quandary about squeezing their book work into their daily calendar. Consequently, discipline enters into the mix. When you get a book deadline from a publisher, you have to meet it. Failure is not an option in the publishing world.

A keen eye for how men and women relate to one another and interact, as well as how their word play unfolds and what fuels their passion for one another is very helpful. As a romance writer you are part psychologist and part anthropologist. Understanding the human dynamic between the sexes might be the most important ingredient in writing a romance novel.

To beat that catch-22 issue I mentioned previously, start out by writing short stories and magazine articles and place them in women's magazines and websites. Don't expect a lot of pay, but the bylines will prove invaluable when you try to sell your book to an agent or publisher.

Key Tip

Join a writing group where participants critique each other's manuscripts. You'll need a thick skin, but a group of savvy readers can help you sharpen up your dialogue and your delivery.

On the Job

To better your chances of becoming a romance novelist, make sure you know how to prepare a good book proposal. That's the mini version of your book. Agents and editors swear by them. A proposal consists of the first three chapters, a synopsis of the plot and a cover letter. Sending them a SASE is old hat; e-mail it instead.

Also, if you can't sell your book through a publisher, explore self-publishing. Companies like XlIbris (www.xlibris.com) will help you print your book for as little as $100.

Key Resources

Check out—and join—the Romance Writers of America (at www.rwanational.org). It's an organization of 9,000 romance writers that holds seminars and conferences on romance writing and offers fledgling writers tips on how to get started in the romance writing market.

Paparazzo

Got the nerve of a cat burglar? Do you have the patience of a saint? Can you stand in the hot sun or the freezing rain for hours on end, waiting for Nicole Kidman to emerge from a hotel?

Can you operate a camera with a security guard's hand in your face?

If so, then you're well on your way to a career as a celebrity photographer—otherwise known as a "paparazzo."

A paparazzo's life is certainly not dull. Although the notion of standing on a sidewalk, sometimes for days on end, to get that shot of Al Pacino that *People* magazine desperately wants might not appeal to a lot of folks, the adrenaline rush from the thrill of the hunt is like a tonic to professional celebrity photographers.

Facts and Figures

The word *paparazzo* derives from a character's name in the classic 1959 Fellini film *La Dolce Vita*. Fellini thought the name, suggesting an insect, was fitting to describe the shadowy types who hounded his actors.

Italy's pesky shutterbugs were noted for scooting through Italy's largest cities on Vespa motorcycles and snapping away at celebrities such as Sophia Loren and Claudia Cardinale. Soon the trend caught on in (where else?) Hollywood—where photographers found there was a lucrative market for celebrity snapshots.

Job Description

Most of a paparazzo's day is spent standing around waiting for a movie star to show up. Professional celebrity photographers say they can wait for weeks on end for the right celebrity supernova to appear. There is no law against taking someone's picture, so interference from the police usually is not a problem. Security guards are another story. They go to great lengths to keep their charges away from harassing shutter-bugs.

To gain an edge, many paparazzi will have a network of paid "informers" who can tell them when a celebrity is set to leave a gym or has a dinner reservation at the Ritz. For a paparazzo, bribing an employee of a celebrity to find out when the starlet is having her hair done is a common occurrence. Anything to get that shot.

Having the technological know-how of manipulating a camera is not a major requirement of paparazzi. With today's sophisticated digital technology, taking pictures is easier than ever. Small, easy-to-hide cameras make it easy to surprise unsuspecting celebrities. Picture quality is no big issue, either. Magazines and newspapers just want a reasonably good shot of Will Smith as long as he is recognizable.

Hiding in trees, or popping up from bushes and hedges, is a regular task for paparazzi looking to take their quarry by surprise. Some will even rent helicopters to catch hard-to-get celebrities.

When you capture the picture you want, go ahead and e-mail it to the magazine or newspaper you have targeted. Multiple submissions to different publications are fine. Some paparazzi make good money selling the same photo to different magazines. E-mailing the photo to the editor in question is best. After you have sold the picture, go ahead and mail the hard copy to the editor—along with an invoice.

When negotiating a price, consider the following issues:

- Who is the celebrity?
- Is the photo verifiable?
- What is the celebrity doing?
- How high is the quality of the photo?
- What is the availability of similar photographs from other paparazzi?

Pay and Perks

Although no solid numbers exists that tell us how many people make a living as paparazzi, a glance at any tabloid magazine shows that there is a huge marketplace for celebrity photographers. With an insatiable appetite for candid celebrity snapshots, paparazzi can make up to $1 million a year for those hard-to-get photos of movie stars cheating on their spouses or presidential candidates kicking their dogs. Garden-variety shots are much less profitable, going for a few hundred dollars apiece.

Key Attributes

Patience and nerve seem to be the twin keys to success in the paparazzo field. The reason that magazines and television shows pay so much for celebrity snapshots is that celebrities, by and large, don't like to have their privacy invaded or their pictures taken while in a state of less-than-glamorous fashion.

Key Tip

Use wireless cameras or video cameras to capture your quarry unaware. Paparazzi often plant tiny wireless cameras in their clothing or even attach them to telephone poles or car windshields. Transmitters inside the camera record the celebrity and broadcast video footage to receivers carried by the paparazzi.

Key Resource

Get a subscription to a media database like Bacon's Directory (www.bacons.com). There you'll find the names, phone numbers, and e-mail addresses of all the major magazine and newspaper editors, and the editors of TV news and celebrity-oriented TV shows.

Literary Agent

"Dahling, I'm going to put you on the best-seller list."

That's a promise made by many literary agents to their favorite authors. But the best-seller list has only so much room, so only the hungriest and most well connected agents can actually deliver on that promise.

If you're that kind of agent, you'll go far in the publishing world.

The book publishing industry is huge—almost $24 billion worth of books were sold in 2004 alone.

Job Description

If you abhor cell phones, avoid long lunches with publishing house editors at fancy restaurants, and can't stand the prospect of attending book parties with smart, funny people, then literary agent is not the job for you.

What does a literary agent do? Besides the parties and lunches, a literary agent negotiates between authors and book publishers. If the author's book is a success, then an agent might also handle negotiations with Hollywood film producers.

Responsibilities include …

- Reading manuscripts to decide which authors to represent.
- Offering editorial advice to authors.
- Advising authors on career strategy.
- Negotiating deals with producers on the author's behalf.
- Sending out scripts.
- Building up contacts throughout the producing industry.
- Updating producers about author's work.

Pay and Perks

The good news for authors is that literary agents only get paid when they sell an author's book. Normally, agents get anywhere from 10 to 20 percent of the author's advance and royalties. A good agent might sell three or four books per month. If the combined total cash amount for those books is, say, $150,000, then an agent can make up to $25,000 in fees.

Key Attributes

There's no hard-and-fast collegiate major for literary agents. Most come from a publishing industry or marketing background. But any experience negotiating contracts is a plus, as is a fat Rolodex full of contacts in the publishing industry. For a literary agent, access is everything.

A good eye for editing and the written word is essential for a literary agent. You'll be an extra set of eyes for your author clients, and reviewing book proposals and manuscript chapters is a regular part of your job. Reading unsolicited manuscripts is another facet of a literary agent's job. Many higher-end agents hire college students and young graduates to read manuscripts and book proposals for them. That, by the way, is a great way to break into the literary agent game.

Because you'll be negotiating contracts for clients, it also helps to have a sharp legal mind. The best agents might be tenacious in their hunt for the best deal, but they are also savvy and comfortable in the world of contracts management.

It also helps to have good people skills. You'll spend hours on the phone with editors and writers, and you'll spend hours schmoozing both at lunches, dinners, and cocktail parties. A clean, well-groomed look is essential. No nose rings or Hell's Angels tattoos allowed.

On the Job

There is no shortage of competition over good authors in the literary agent world. So be prepared to hone your negotiating and people skills. Knowing when to back off and move in aggressively is as important for a good literary agent as it is for a good poker player.

Key Tip

Move to New York City. That's where all the action is in the publishing field. Although the Internet and cell phone have made business communications a mobile and global game, there is nothing like seeing editors and writers in the flesh to build those long-lasting relationships that literary agents must have to succeed.

Key Resource

To get a better grip on what you can make as an agent, review the Regional Wage Comparison Chart(s) for "Agents and Business Managers of Artists, Performers, and Athletes" produced by the Occupational Employment Statistics (OES) survey at www.iseek.org/sv/13000.jsp?id=100228.

Crossword Puzzle Creator

Who's the lead singer of the band The Go-Go's?

Here's a clue. Fifteen letters with the second letter being "e."

If you guessed Belinda Carlisle, and you have a thing for Number Two pencils and horizontal and vertical grids, then a career creating crossword puzzles could be on the horizon.

People who can create clever, complex crossword puzzles for newspapers, books, and magazines (hey, even the Internet has crossword puzzles) are in high demand these days.

All it takes is creativity, an uncanny ability to merge popular culture into random word patterns, and some connections with editors at your local newspaper (or any newspaper).

Facts and Figures

About 100 to 200 crossword puzzle mavens craft more than 5 puzzles per year in the United States. Another 100 to 200 more do variety puzzles, such as cryptograms, metacrostics, and word search puzzles, in addition to—or instead of—crosswords.

Job Description

Creativity is job one for a crossword puzzle craftsman. Puzzle editors usually insist that all crossword puzzles be original. Clues that have been used before are frowned upon by editors.

You can create crosswords two ways—randomly or as theme puzzles. *The New York Times* recently offered a theme puzzle on snakes. Three of the answers were "Dodge Viper," "Monty Python," and "feather boa."

The best puzzle creators are the ones who know the individual tastes and quirks of the newspaper editors who they have to please. Some editors don't approve of abbreviations, but others don't mind them at all. So make sure to do your homework and get to know the editor's tastes in crossword puzzles.

Puzzle experts say it's best to start your puzzle with longer words. It gives you more options as you continue constructing your puzzle. Most crossword creators use basically the same kind of grid to craft their puzzles. In this techno age, puzzle gurus often opt to use software compilers to create their grids.

Pay and Perks

Besides being the hit of the cocktail party circuit for constructing the latest *New York Times Sunday* crossword puzzle, you can earn money as a puzzle creator. The major papers pay about $75 or so for an original puzzle. Local papers and websites pay less, about $40 to $50 per puzzle. Sunday crosswords command more financial respect. They can bring in $350 per puzzle. Unfortunately, as one puzzle creator points out, there is only one Sunday each week. Most puzzle professionals are freelancers who work under "work for hire" arrangements. So don't expect health benefits.

You can create your puzzles from the comfort of your own home, and your hours are your own to manage. Although larger newspapers prefer fresh material, the regular premium markets aren't as picky—so you can easily resell and recycle your puzzles.

Key Attributes

Clever phrasing, an encyclopedic mind, and an affinity for providing good clues are the prime ingredients for a successful crossword puzzle creator. A background in English and engineering—engineers are notoriously good problem solvers—is a big eye-opener for puzzle editors looking for fresh talent.

Key Tip

Make sure you can document your clues in case there is a problem or a question about their veracity. Also make sure you invest in some good crossword puzzle compiling software.

Key Resource

Learn how to make a crossword puzzle at www.crossdown.com/howtomake.htm.

Book Doctor

Is there a book doctor in the house? Thousands of would-be book authors sure hope so.

Many book projects would never see the inside of a Barnes & Noble without the services of a book doctor. The pay is good, the work is rewarding, and by hopping from interesting project to interesting project, you'll rarely get bored with the workload.

Facts and Figures

There is no real hard-and-fast number of book doctors operating in the United States today. Best estimates place several thousand ghostwriters working on books. But because the publishing industry publishes 20,000 books a year (not counting self-published projects, the biggest growth area for ghostwriters), there is plenty of work to go around.

Job Description

Let's face facts. Most people can't write. But that doesn't stop them from writing books. Celebrities, business titans, and industry experts such as doctors, stockbrokers, and lawyers all clamor to pen a manuscript that will wind up on the best-seller list.

When they begin slogging away on the book, it soon becomes apparent that they can't do it alone. A call is placed to an agent or a publishing house editor, who in turn places a call to a book doctor or "ghostwriter" to jump in and save the day.

Usually that means taking the manuscript and rewriting it. Sometimes book doctors have to start from scratch and produce new copy. Whatever the situation, book doctors must be able to write clear, concise, compelling copy on very short deadlines.

Book doctors are free agents, who must negotiate their own deals with book authors, agents, and editors.

Pay and Perks

A good book doctor can make anywhere from $5,000 and up for polishing up a manuscript. Complete rewrites can net you more—even up to $100,000 in some cases. Salary.com pegs the average annual salary for book doctors at about $35,000.

You also get to rub elbows with famous people looking to publish their own books. This can be a good or a bad thing, depending on the "author" in question.

Key Attributes

A solid background in English, grammar, punctuation, and spelling is critical for the career advancement of a ghostwriter. The ability to manipulate words and turn a clever phrase doesn't hurt either. Good copyediting skills are also a must. Fiction writers have it tougher than nonfiction book doctors do. They have to understand plot, pacing, character development, dialogue, and structure.

Consequently, book doctors attend a lot of writing workshops and seminars to hone their skills. They write all the time and can demonstrate to clients that they have completed book projects to supreme client satisfaction. A background in newspaper or magazine editing is okay, if you don't have actual book publishing experience.

One great idea is to specialize in one specific area. A writer who knows Wall Street cold or understands the ins and outs of the information technology industry can likely count on a steady flow of work, given the high amount of books that come out of that industry. Fiction writing is murkier. If you excel in historical novels, for example, then you can probably build a good career from working with history book writers. Note that fiction book authors are finicky and probably won't like too much hands-on work on their manuscripts. Nonfiction book authors might wind up asking you to overhaul everything. Thus the money on that side of the aisle is better and the work is more plentiful.

> **The Water Cooler**
>
> To be a good book doctor means being a good reader. Reading other books, magazine articles, or newspapers can give you ideas to make the book you are working on that much better. Reading is time consuming, true. But to a good ghostwriter, being a good reader is no luxury—it's a necessity.

Key Tip

Create a website and put the first chapters of the books you've handled on the site. Also, get testimonials from clients and put those on your website. Word of mouth is manna from heaven in the ghostwriting business.

Key Resource

Two good places to go to learn more about ghostwriting are The Dabbling Mum and Vault.com. Visit them at www.thedabblingmum.com/writing/want_freelancebookdr.htm and www.vault.com/nr/main_article_detail.jsp?article_id=21807902&cat_id=0&ht_type=1.

The Least You Need to Know

- If you have a passion for the written word, there's a good chance you can turn it into a career in media and publishing.

- Being curious about the world is a big plus in the media market. Wanting to know what makes people tick is the hallmark of a good reporter or writer.

◆ The book publishing world is a cutthroat business. Only a few people make it big. But you can make a career out of it if you find a niche and keep on writing about it.

◆ Media firms are really into "specialization" these days. If you're an expert on a given subject, you can leverage that expertise into a good job with a newspaper, magazine, or broadcast media outlet.

Chapter 6

"Say Cheese": Fashion and Style

In This Chapter

◆ Breaking into the fashion and style industry

◆ Sketching and photographing

◆ Setting the tone: fashion magazine editor

◆ The high demand for model scouts

◆ Psssst: Being a gossip columnist

Everyone pays attention to fashion, but not everyone admits it.

Bono, lead singer of U2, once said, "I've no regrets other than a really awful haircut in the 1980s—a haircut that launched a thousand third-division soccer players."

It's only natural to want to be a leader rather than a follower. And the fashion and style industry loves leaders. Preferably creative, ground-breaking, prone-to-the-outrageous leaders who can see a trend before it happens and turn it into a fashion statement and a profit.

Fashion Photographer

"Smile, darling. Act like the star you are!"

So it goes in the land of the flashbulb glitterati.

It's a vibrant, competitive business where talent is important, but so is knowing the right concierges, nightclub owners, and public relations agents. It's the ultimate access game, where you party down with divas and cover girls at night and shoot them first thing in the morning. (With a camera, that is.)

As one world-weary fashion photographer puts it, "This business is so much about who you know. You can walk in with the best portfolio, but if you aren't hanging out with the right people, you don't get the job. It's a subjective business and it's all based on a taste level. Do you aspire to *Harper's Bazaar* or *New Jersey* magazine?"

Facts and Figures

The good news is that with the soaring popularity of fashion magazines and television style and makeover shows, the continued growth of the industry looks good. Most photographers work for large commercial studios or big fashion and style magazines. Many, however, freelance, opening their own studios and hiring themselves out. The idea there is to snag some reputable, high-profile clients.

If you live in rural or even suburban areas, you're really hurting your chances of making it in the fashion world. Move to New York City or Los Angeles, or even Milan, Paris, or London. That's where the action is.

Job Description

The average day for a photographer is spent taking photographs of models on location and in studios, developing tight bonds with models, and putting out fires in the form of pouting starlets and egomaniacal bosses. Shoot in sunny, well-lit studios for best effect (not many photographers work nights). You'll have to learn a great deal about skin tones and how they look with specific fabrics. At night, enhance your career by nurturing relationships with stylists, art directors, agencies, and fashion editors. Above all, be unique and make your own statement. You'll get noticed faster that way.

You'll also need a solid, ready-to-show portfolio for clients. Use basic imaging of 4″ × 5″ transparencies or tear-sheets (pages ripped from a magazine). Aim for about 15 or 20 pictures in your portfolio.

Pay and Perks

Fashion photographers can expect to see a wide salary range, the amount of which depends on experience, education, talent, and—oh, yes—connections. Entry-level pay starts at around $15,000 to $25,000. The best photographers easily earn six-figures and more—and all the free shrimp they can eat.

Key Attributes

As always, patience is a virtue. You won't break in as an Annie Leibovitz right away. Get in the door as an assistant and show confidence and resiliency. Master photographers love assistants who can tackle tough tasks. The key is to earn their trust. That will come in handy because later on, you'll use that knowledge to gain the trust of fashion models, style magazine editors, and other industry heavyweights (if you'll excuse the expression). Be aggressive, too. If you have industry contacts, use them. The style editor at *Allure* won't even look at a portfolio without a direct recommendation.

Key Tip

It's a competitive industry, so the best way to break in and move up is to serve as an apprentice or assistant to a talented fashion photographer. Keep your ears open and be resilient. You'll face long hours, but the wait will be worth it.

Also, to develop a brand new portfolio, offer to shoot younger, newer models for free. You get the portfolio and they get pictures for free—so they can market themselves, too.

Key Resource

Your cell phone. You'll spend as much time on the phone as you will taking pictures—booking gigs, talking to casting directors, begging models to get out of bed to show up at shoots, getting directions to on-location shoots, things like that. You'll always be on the move, so make sure your lines of communication are open. Also check out

Toppest.com. The site (www.toppest.com/fashion.htm) has loads of information and news on the fashion industry.

Fashion House Sketcher

Anyone who ever whipped out a notepad and drew pictures of their brothers, sisters, families, and friends as a youngster knows what it's like to create inner beauty out of thin air.

That's what fashion sketchers try to do. Sure, they draw gorgeous models and beautiful celebrities much of the time, but the idea is to bring out the human side of their targets.

It's all about capturing images out of ideas, be it a *Sports Illustrated* bikini model or a pair of glasses for a high-end retailer.

Facts and Figures

With the acceleration of digital imaging and photography technology, the numbers of fashion sketch artists who work strictly by hand are dwindling. Still, even good digital photos can't express an original idea like a good sketch can, so there is work available if you know where to find it. Start with advertising agencies and design firms, but also consider companies that develop fashion patterns or firms that forecast future design fashions. They just love good, creative illustrators.

Job Description

Like most high-profile, high-cachet careers in the fashion industry, the fashion sketcher market is ultra-competitive. You'll spend your time working on drawings, paintings, and even website illustrations for a variety of clients, including advertising agencies, design firms, public relations specialists, and retail and fashion outlets.

You'll meet with designers and editors to create a vision of the images and ideas they want to capture. Your work might show up in a newspaper or magazine advertisement, direct mail catalogs, television commercials, and other media outlets. Most illustrators work for ad agencies or design firms, but a growing number strike out on their own as freelancers, hopping from gig to gig.

Pay and Perks

A fashion illustrator, working steadily, can earn up to $60,000 annually. Much of the work can be done in your home studio or on-site, if you like. Getting to see your work in print or on television is extremely fulfilling, and you really get to flex your creative muscles. If you like to draw, and inking *The Simpsons* or *The Family Guy* isn't for you, then fashion illustration is a great option.

Key Attributes

A high priority is given to illustrators who know how to interpret high-end fashion concepts. Technical know-how is key, too. Many fashion sketchers work on powerful computers, using sophisticated computer-aided design (CAD) software, the same software that carmakers in Detroit, Tokyo, and Milan use.

Educationally, two or four years at an arts-oriented higher education program is advisable. Unlike fashion photographers, who gain as much work through their social networking as they do their talents, fashion sketchers ply their craft in a fairly lonely trade: it's just you, your sketchpad or computer, and a vision.

Key Tip

One often overlooked market for fashion illustrators is children's book publishing. Book authors are talented writers, but most can't draw worth a lick. That's where you come in. So send your portfolio to the major publishing houses—most have children's book divisions. And see if you don't get noticed—and hired.

Also, if you're asked to submit what's called a "pencil"—a preliminary sketch—do more and provide three or four sketches. Show people you want the job. Make them hire you to get rid of you (a good tip for any career).

Key Resource

A fashion illustrator's best resource is his or her own website. Even if you live in Topeka or Tacoma, you can get hired by a New York magazine or newspaper if your work stands out. Your own website—with plenty of clips available—can get people's attention.

The Water Cooler
The global fashion industry is huge—it's a $300 billion market.

Fashion Magazine Editor

Anyone who read *The Devil Wears Prada*, by Lauren Weisberger, a thinly veiled view of life at a major fashionista magazine with an editor-in-chief who makes the Wicked Witch of the West look like Mary Poppins, has a good idea what life is like at the *Vogue*s and *Allure*s of the world.

If you can stand the long hours, jet-set lifestyle, and layers of free designer clothing from some of the hottest houses on Fifth Avenue, then a fashion editor slot might be perfect for you.

Facts and Figures

There is no hard-and-fast number of fashion editor jobs in the United States today. Most are employed by magazines located in urban areas like New York or Miami, although many of the new style magazines have popped up in high-end suburban locales like suburban Philadelphia's *Bucks County* magazine.

Over 2,600 consumer magazines are up and running in the United States today. According to *Halls Magazine Report*, of the issues covered in that category, fashion and style magazines are among the top three on the list. That includes general fashion and style, bridal magazines, dressmaking magazines, wearing apparel, and beauty and grooming.

Job Description

A fashion editor sets the tone for a magazine's style and attitude.

That's the big picture.

A good fashion editor also must establish strong connections with design houses, retail and apparel stores, and publicity agents. Don't forget the business side. An editor also has to have a bit of the bean counter in him or her, and must work within a budget, often at the behest of a board of directors or senior management, and make sure the magazine comes out under budget and on time.

Much of the job is demanding, but it's a great deal of fun, too. You'll break bread with the hottest fashionistas, sip cocktails with industry movers and shakers, and fly to Europe and Rio de Janeiro to view fashion shows. You'll visit showrooms and help choose the clothing from designers that you'll want to profile in your magazine.

You'll pour over shoes styles, lipgloss, hairstyles, and even visit sidewalk boutiques on your way to and from work to find the next hot trend.

Pay and Perks

Top-notch magazine editors in the fashion sector can earn up to $1 million annually (at top magazines such as *Elle* or *Vogue)*.

Perhaps it's more realistic to discuss how to break in to fashion journalism and work your way to an editor's post. Entry-level fashion writers earn up to $40,000 annually, depending on the size and budget of the magazine. But many fashion magazine editors started out as administrative assistants or photography assistants, where the opening salary is even lower (as low as $15,000 annually).

The perks are tied up in your workday, which is hectic. Lunch is usually eaten in (the bigger magazines will pay for your lunch) and access to free, high-end clothing, make-up, and shoes is a good possibility. If you get to know the shoes editor, then she might throw a pair of Pradas your way from the many she gets every week or so from the manufacturer.

Access to fashion shows and high-cachet social events is also easy to get. Magazine editors and writers consider networking to be a key part of the magazine's success and will make sure to spend time schmoozing each other at parties and cultural events.

Key Attributes

Unfortunately for the less-than-well-connected, the path to a fashion editor perch is easier if you know the right people. If, for example, you attended the right Manhattan private school, and your best friend's mom is the editor of *Seventeen*, then you're in like Flynn.

But if you possess nerves of steel, a good fashion eye, and a flair for originality and getting along with people—and you can write—then you've got a chance. Like most industry jobs, the ability to be where the action is—New York City or London, for example—is almost a necessity.

Key Tip

Cultivate relationships with showroom specialists, especially those in the areas of fashion that interest you. Get a job at a fashion magazine and don't worry about starting at the bottom.

Another tip: get a job as a public relations intern at a top fashion house like Gucci's or Tod's. They're proving to be great breeding grounds of fashion magazine talent.

Key Resource

I hate to repeat myself, but the best move to make is a geographical one. If you want a job at a fashion or style magazine, move to New York City. One good web resource to study before you go is fashionnet.com. The site tells you how to dress for your interview and what to expect on the job.

Model Scout

Wanted. Ambitious go-getter to spend all day looking at beautiful men and women and sign them up for photo shoots for glamorous style magazines. Pay is great.

Gee, where do I sign up for *that?*

Model scouts are in high demand in this, the glamour age. The market for new modeling talent has never been larger. Consequently, the market for people who know how to find those models is on the rise, too.

Facts and Figures

There is no hard-and-fast association that caters to model scouts, but the numbers indicate that the demand for model scouts is high. The cosmetics industry alone is a $20 billion yearly cash cow. And the industry is always looking for models to market their wares. And that pales in comparison to the fashion and textiles industry, which clocks in with annual earnings of $300 billion.

Job Description

Model scouts are energetic, outgoing types who won't rest until they find the next Kathy Ireland or Christie Brinkley. Scouts spend most of their time attending concerts, ballgames, movies, theaters, CD release parties, modeling conventions, and professional photo shoots.

You'll spend a lot of time interacting with clients and potential clients. Responding to portfolios sent by prospective models can be tedious, but it's the backbone of the job. You'll also be reviewing fashion magazines and television shows that feature fashion and style issues, to keep up with the current trends. There are details to attend to, as well. You'll be negotiating with agents and arranging photo shoots with fashion magazines.

After you find and sign a new model, you'll help train him or her and accompany the new talent to photo shoots and fashion shows. It's the ultimate "people person" job.

On the downside, you'll also be the one responsible for telling model candidates that they didn't make the cut. So pack a lot of tissues.

Pay and Perks

A good model scout can earn $80,000 annually (starting salaries are about $40,000). You might also be paid by commission, for signing up new talent. Commissions start as low as $50 per model.

Key Attributes

An obvious eye for talent is required, as is the ability to network and get out to various social events and schmooze with clients. Personality counts for a great deal as a model scout—you spend a lot of face time with clients and agencies. The model scouts who fare the best are the ones with the best contacts. So a little smile goes a long way.

Key Tip

I know I'm starting to sound like a broken record, but it's imperative that you be where the action is. So a move to New York City, Milan, or London might be in your future.

Key Resource

For a deeper look at the modeling industry, check out www.careersurfers.com/Modeling.php. The book *Guide to Talent & Modeling Agents* by Rachel Vater (Writer's Digest Books, 2001) is a great resource. Writers Digest Books is very helpful to would-be model scouts.

Personal Stylist

Gianni Versace had it right.

The famed fashion stylist, gunned down before his prime outside his Miami Beach mansion, knew that to be a great stylist, you manipulate minds as much as you do bodies.

"I like to dress egos," Versace said. "If you haven't got an ego today, forget it."

A good personal stylist, also known in the trade as a wardrobe consultant or a personal shopper, must appeal to that singularly human characteristic known as ego. People want to look good and they expect their personal stylist to recognize that need and fill it—preferably with something nice from Gucci or Saks.

Facts and Figures

In most states, personal stylists must be fully licensed to ply their craft. Virginia, for example, has a Board of Barbers and Cosmetology. Applicants in that state must be at least 16 years old. Often, a personal stylist must have 1,500 hours of training—about one year—before they can be certified. You might have to also pass a written exam before you can obtain your license.

Job Description

A personal stylist primarily creates relationships with individual clients—some do work with groups of people in classrooms or corporate settings—to provide some fashion advice and drape them in the most complimentary attire possible. You'll work with clients to feed their egos and meet their desired image and fashion goals. That means recommending styles, shopping for clients, and picking out accoutrements like jewelry, makeup, and shoes.

Your nose will be buried in the latest fashion magazines and your eyes will be locked on what the stars are wearing to the various awards galas broadcast on television.

If you're fortunate, you'll be working in the entertainment industry, where such jobs are more plentiful. Game shows, soap operas, and movie studios all count on personal stylists to provide clothing and fashion gear for the "talent." Your job is to go out, find it, and spend other people's money to get it.

Pay and Perks

Personal stylists work—and get paid—by the hour or by salary. Chances are you'd start out making not much more than you did as a counter rep at Chico's or Laura Ashley. It's not uncommon for a new personal stylist to make $10–$20 an hour. As your client list grows, so will your hourly rate. Day rates for a good stylist range from $600 to $1,000 per day. Compare that to the average hair stylist who earns about $24,000 annually. Tips are also a big part of a stylist's income.

Key Attributes

Some experience working in high-end fashion boutiques is usually the clearest path to a career as an independent. A job as a merchandise buyer at a fashion retailer is also a great springboard into a career as a professional stylist. The ability to think like a small business owner is essential. You can always open up new revenue pipelines by teaching fashion and styling to small classes or at corporate seminars (where employees are encouraged to attend to learn how to look their best for clients). Connections are also made by moonlighting. You might wind up representing a famous athlete or TV personality from such connections. And when your name is attached to a celebrity, you've got it made.

A good personal stylist knows things nobody else knows. Where are the best pet clothiers? Can you find a sailor uniform on short notice? Which tailors can handle fast alterations? Clients pay handsomely for that kind of information.

Academically, a college major in fashion design can help you get your foot in the door in fashion design or fashion merchandising. Obviously, pitch perfect fashion sense is a plus, as are good self-promotion and business management skills.

Key Tip

Find a personal stylist in your neck of the woods and offer to act as his or her apprentice. Even if it just means carrying her shopping bags around, you'll learn a lot about the trade that way. And you'll have a good reference, too.

Key Resource

Your best resource is probably your favorite local fashion boutique. Hang out there—ideally, work there—and soak up all the information you can on identifying fashion trends.

Gossip Columnist

"Psssst … wanna hear a secret?"

That's the calling card of the wild, untamed gossip columnist. In the supply and demand game of celebrity knowledge, those who can discover the best secrets will soon find themselves at the top of the heap in one of the entertainment industry's most competitive occupations.

So sharpen those claws and let's get scratching.

Facts and Figures

There are really no figures on the number of gossip columnists operating in the United States today. In New York City alone, there are a dozen or two working at city and neighborhood newspapers. The Internet has created a new market for gossip, as many websites are turning to gossip columnists to attract more "hits."

Job Description

You'll go far in the gossip world as long as you recognize that the public is a hungry and demanding animal that constantly needs to be fed. So daily deadlines are a part of the trade, and those who aren't careful can find that they burn out quickly, leveled by a constant swirl of social activities that demand your presence if you want to get the juiciest quotes and tidbits.

Most gossip columnists have weekly—if not daily—deadlines, and the pressure is thick in getting enough good material to fill a column. One page of copy in a major newspaper or magazine can be 600–800 words. And editors hate it when any of those words are stale or boring.

The key to surviving in the celebrity gossip maelstrom is being able to separate your work life from your private life. In many cases the two are locked together tighter than a barnacle on the hull of a boat. You'll quickly find that your sources become your best friends and soon you can't tell if you're out relaxing or if you're working on getting a juicy piece of news for your next column.

If you focus on entertaining, rather than harming, people, you should be just fine.

Where your byline appears will have an impact on your fortunes as a gossip columnist. In gossip, power rules. A gossip columnist for a New York City daily gets her phone calls returned. A gossip columnist for a small, regional weekly doesn't hold that power and won't get as many phone calls returned.

Pay and Perks

To write shallow copy with sinister intent and get paid for it is a good day's work for a gossip maven.

How good? Well, the top New York City tabloid gossips earn low-to-mid six figures easily. Even a columnist at a smaller city daily can earn up to $100,000 annually.

Plus, you get invited to the best parties and meet some very successful, interesting people. People have to invite you to their parties. In the gossip world, the longer and sharper the claws, the larger the fear factor from potential victims. To stay on your good side, people will consider you strictly A-List, sweetheart.

Key Attributes

Access to celebrities—or people who know celebrities—is important for a gossip columnist. But perhaps even more important is a sense of humor. A gregarious, campy personality who can see the funny side of any situation is a real commodity on the gossip circuit—that and the ability to write zinging copy on tight deadlines. Always remember that being snarky sells on the gossip market.

A background in newspaper feature reporting—where you might have built up a nice Rolodex of celebrities, publicists, and agents—is a big advantage for a gossip columnist. That goes double if you have reporting experience at a supermarket tabloid, or a proven national weekly like *People* or *Us*. Also movie and theater reviewers have a leg up as gossip writers—they get to meet many celebrities. In gossip, a celebrity's phone number is high currency.

Key Tip

Get started as a gossip columnist by profiling celebrities as a freelance feature writer. Major magazines pay as much as $5,000 to $10,000 for good celebrity profiles.

Key Resource

Read *The New York Post's* infamous *Page Six*. It's the blueprint for the killer gossip column.

The Least You Need to Know

◆ A sense of style and a dedication to your craft are at the top of the list of things fashion employers look for in hiring good talent.

◆ Have thick skin. There is no shortage of prickly egos in the fashion business.

◆ Subscribe to magazines like *Vogue* or *In Style* to see what's hot and how fashionistas frame the latest trends. Check out the ads, too. They tend to reflect current fashion norms.

◆ Contacts are important for professionals in the fashion industry. Many jobs are handed out to people who employers are already familiar with, usually via the social scene. So be a player and be visible.

Part

The Rugged Type: "Physical" Jobs

"Drop and give me twenty, maggot!"

Okay, a job in the U.S. Marines might not be your idea of a dream job (although it is for some people), but having the physical conditioning and stamina to thrive in any one of the dream jobs in this section is an absolute must.

This section is for people cooped up in a cubicle all day, pining for a job in the great outdoors. It's chock full of jobs Mother Nature would surely approve of, in fields like sports, the environment, pets and animals, and travel and recreation.

So take a deep breath, pound your chest, and dive right in. After all, you don't want to keep Mother Nature waiting.

Less Popular Outdoor Jobs

Anchor Retriever

Turf Replacement

Bear Tickler

Chapter 7

The Great Outdoors

In This Chapter

- The career benefits of communing with Mother Nature
- Fishing and windsurfing work
- Keep the fun going: cruise ship activities director
- Smoke jumper: for adrenaline junkies only
- The pits: NASCAR pit crew member
- Training dolphins and other marine mammals

You've heard of Tarzan? King of the Jungle, Lord of the Vines, the legendary Ape-Man himself? Tarzan spent his days swinging from vines, running with the beasts, and frolicking in the cool rivers of the African savanna, with the bodacious, bikini-clad Jane at his side. Not a time clock in site, or a bitter, bumbling boss or cranky co-worker with an axe to grind. Just Tarzan, Jane, and the ample abundance of Mother Nature.

Now *there's* a guy who knows a dream job when he sees one.

After all, Tarzan got it. There's something about working outside, under cloudless skies with the sun shining on your back. All that liberating fresh air and expansive elbowroom.

If you yen for the great outdoors, you're in luck. These days there is no shortage of occupations that will have you communing with your inner jungle beast. From commercial fishing in Alaska to being a cruise ship activities director, making your mark in a career that keeps you away from those cold, heartless cubicles—with their soul-sapping artificial lighting and stale, recycled air—and gets you outdoors is easier and more attractive than ever. If this sounds appealing to you then, by all means, read on.

Alaska Fisherman

Professional contemplator Henry David Thoreau once said "Many go fishing all their lives without knowing that it is not fish they are after."

Not so for the great Alaskan fisherman—and woman.

Balancing Act

Working outdoors is great for your health. See for yourself. Just attach a pedometer to your shirt or belt for one week, and see how much you move every day. Some outdoors types walk between 10 and 15 miles per day.

To them, Alaska represents the last great frontier in an over-industrialized, crowded world. I'll put it this way: if you feel comfortable on the 7:50 subway into Manhattan, clutching to a metal pole so you won't bounce into the bored, hung-over-looking guy standing next to you, then Alaska fisherman is probably not your calling.

If you think you're up to the challenge, then you're really in for a treat. The Alaskan fishing industry is booming, with commercial fishing boats constantly on the look for strong, energetic types who like the outdoors, love working hard, and don't mind some risk and ruggedness in their job description.

Facts and Figures

With scenic vistas, vibrant cities like Anchorage, Fairbanks, and Juneau, and millions upon millions of beautiful, profitable salmon and other sea-faring delicacies inhabiting its waters, Alaska is a commercial fisherman's paradise. Over 65,000 people work in the Alaskan fishing industry. The fishing sector in our fiftieth state is broad and diverse, ranging from giant trawlers with 100 employees aboard to smaller, more agile gillnetting boats manned by one or two fishermen. The industry is also populated by pot boats (which target Alaska's famous king crabs) and trawlers that catch not only salmon, but bottomfish, halibut, and blackcod fish. Such boats have anywhere from one to twenty workers aboard. Job candidates can also target the state's 2,500 or so private charter boats looking for deckhands. Oh yes, Alaska has no state tax, meaning even more money in your pocket.

Job Description

Alaskan fisherman—called "harvesters" in the trade—are expected to have some experience working on boats. If not, a strong back and a willingness to show up and work hard could well land you a job in an industry that needs people, especially in the summer months when boat cargo holds groan under the weight of fresh salmon. The "busy season" gets going in May, with the major salmon runs petering out by the end of October. Consequently, seasonal work is a real option. Crab boats stay out later—often until November or December.

As a harvester on an Alaskan fishing boat, you might fill one of several roles—deckhand, skiff man, or captain. The size of the crew—and the number of job opportunities—depends on the size of the boat.

You'd handle every chore, from stocking ice, unloading fish, fixing lines, and cooking and cleaning the vessel. Expect a long day (15 to 16 hours) about three or four days a week. (Alaskan state law limits the days and even hours that boats can actually harvest fish.) Expect to be out to sea for up to 12 weeks. Best way to get the job? Hang out in the ports-side bars that fishing captains and crews frequent. That's where the networking and connections are made. Hustle enough and you'll make those connections.

Pay and Perks

Alaskan commercial fisherman can expect to earn up to $1,000 per week during peak season (most boats don't go out in the foul-weather months of January and February). Some fishermen have even earned $10,000 to $20,000 per month in abundant fishing seasons, but don't expect that kind of paycheck going in. Do expect to sign a contract giving you a percentage, or share, of the boat's take for a season. Deckhands on private charter boats can earn up to $200 per day on the water. Many companies pay health benefits, especially if you sign a contract before boarding any ship or vessel. Some companies will even pay your transportation to and from Alaska, providing you

On the Job

When applying for outdoors jobs with the federal government, think sooner rather than later. Most seasonal work is doled out early in the calendar year. Also, budgets are full early in the year, and federal employers have the money to hire. Aim for a completed application by January 15—or earlier, if possible.

have said contract and you can make a long-term commitment to your employer. Room and board is usually free, as chances are you'll be living on the boat.

Key Attributes

You should be a team player with a strong work ethic and no fear.

Key Tip

Don't show up without a signed contract. In fact, don't leave home without a signed contract. Your pay, living arrangements, and health insurance are at risk if you go without one.

Key Resource

Check out the *Alaska Fish Jobs Guide 2004*, published by Alaskafishingjobs.com. It can be ordered from their website www.alaskafishjobs.com.

Cruise Ship Activities Director

You might think that a show with the cringe factor of *The Love Boat* would have turned people off on a career in "cruising" as Captain Steubing would invariably say. But it didn't.

Instead, *The Love Boat* launched a veritable bull market in ocean-bound cruising, with companies like Disney, Royal Caribbean, Carnival, Cunard, and others rolling out their own mammoth cruise line operations.

Hence the need for onboard cruise directors to keep the fun going 24/7.

Facts and Figures

More than 60 million people have taken cruise trips in the past 20 years. That's big business, indeed. The U.S. cruising industry earned $17.9 billion in the year 2000. The news going forward looks even better. About 69 million Americans say they would like to take a cruise in the next five years, and more than 43 million will embark on a cruise during the same time frame. Such numbers add up to a potential $85 billion market for cruise liners, industry experts say. Your best shot at landing a cruise job? Start with Cunard Line (11 ships), Royal Caribbean (10 ships), Carnival Cruise Lines (9 ships), and Princess Cruises (9 ships).

Job Description

Cruise ships employ hundreds of people, and are especially on the prowl for upbeat, energetic "Julie your Cruise Director" types who know how to lead, organize, and manage large groups of presumably relaxed vacationers (including children).

To get the job, know the lay of the land—um, sea—first. Do your homework and find out a potential ship's size, its port of registration (for passport purposes), its schedule and regular itinerary, and the kind of passengers who frequent the ship. Disney, for example, attracts loads of families and young children. If you think that the little darlings should be seen and not heard, Disney might not be your best bet for a cruise line.

You likely won't start out as a cruise director on a major cruise line (but maybe a smaller one). Instead, target cruise jobs that put you in close contact with vacationers. Bartenders, fitness instructors, tour guides, and deck hands are great places to start. Expect to spend two to five years earning your cruise director wings.

> **On the Job**
>
> It seems obvious when you think about it, but it's worth pointing out that, volume-wise, most of the outdoor jobs are available in warm-weather states such as Florida. Head there after hurricane season (late September), when the need for strong backs and hard workers is critical, and well-paying outdoor jobs plentiful.

When you interview, know that cruise ship marketers (the marketing director will probably interview you) love team players who have experience coordinating events; can master (I'm serious) games such as bingo, masquerade, and—on certain ships—poker and other gambling games; can handle fickle tour groups; and have great customer service skills.

Pay and Perks

Cruise ship directors can easily earn up to $7,500 per month, industry sources say. Deck hands make out like Gilligan—they average about $1,200 per month (but you can save lots of money because your living expenses are covered while you're working). Living arrangements and meals, free of charge, should be part of any cruise ship contract.

Key Attributes

Only "people" persons need apply. Previous experience as a cruise director or experience in public relations is a plus. Great public speaking skills are a bonus, too.

Key Tip

Live close to warm water ports. Typically, cruise lines do not pay for airfare to ports for cruise departures. And leave your pets at home or in the care of a trusted friend. Ships don't allow Fido and Tabby out at sea. And if you're prone to seasickness, you should probably forget working as a cruise ship activities director.

Key Resource

The *2004 Cruise Line Employment Manual* (published by Cheryl Kerr, 2003) by Jim Ross is a great place to start. Find more information at www.cruiseross.com.

Forest Smokejumper

Want to run into burning forests when everyone else is running out? Well, adrenaline buffs, forest fire fighting might be for you.

The Water Cooler

Every fire season temporary smokejumper bases are set up in such places as Silver City, New Mexico; Grand Junction, Colorado; and LaGrande, Oregon. There are about 400 smokejumpers nationwide. There are also smokejumpers in Russia, and, off and on, in Canada.

Facts and Figures

The largest employer of forest firefighters is, no surprise, Uncle Sam. Why do I say "no surprise"? Because the federal government is the largest landowner in the country. To keep all that land from going up in smoke, various U.S. government agencies tend to our public lands, like the U.S. Forest Service, the National Park Service, the U.S. Fish and Wildlife Service, and the Bureau of Land Management. Chances are, your local state park service hires firefighters, too. Overall, national parks employ about 55,000 employees, according to government reports.

Even with all that land to cover, and all the danger that goes with the mantle of smokejumper, landing such a job isn't easy. Government estimates indicate that one job is handed out for every twenty-five applications. Of course, with this handy guide, your chances will increase by knowing what the various national park services look for in those applications.

Job Description

Uncle Sam looks for hardy souls who love the outdoors, can communicate clearly, have calm demeanors, and can make life-or-death decisions under pressure. From an experience point-of-view, smokejumpers should have a high-school education and be able to hike, climb trees, and lift heavyweight items such as rocks, boulders, and fire equipment.

Your best bet might be to start as a seasonal worker on a forest firefighting team as a member of a hand or engine crew and work your way up to smokejumper. Even a job as a clerk in a national forest office can increase the chances of working your way up to a firefighter post. Education-wise, a graduate degree in natural sciences is a big help, as is experience as a traditional firefighter or emergency technician. Expect to undergo a drug test and pass a work competency test (you must complete a 3-mile walk in 45 minutes or less while carrying a pack weighing 45 pounds).

If you land the job, expect to do a lot of heavy lifting. Although firefighting teams do have off-road fire trucks that might be able to get to trouble spots, it's more common for smokejumpers to clear brush and lift heavy rocks and trees. Get used to using chainsaws and hand tools—especially in hard-to-reach areas. Expect to spend up to five days fighting tougher hot spots. After fires are under control, smoke-jumpers do a great deal of environmental assessment, cutting down damaged trees, and removing burnt logs that, left unstable, can roll away and do more damage to the area. When there are no fires about, you might be required to search for lost hikers and conduct fire control tests.

Pay and Perks

Smokejumpers can make as little as $8 per hour. More seasoned firefighters can make up to $50,000 annually. In most cases with the federal government, free room and board are available and the health and retirement benefits are ample.

Key Attributes

A smokejumper must possess physical courage, a calm demeanor, and good decision-making abilities.

Key Tip

In the smoke-jumping world, timing is everything. If you want to go for a seasonal firefighter post, think about it by January. That's when most applications are due.

Key Resource

Check out the U.S. Department of Agriculture job website at www.fs.fed.us/ people/employ/asap/index_nw_centralized_temporary_hiring.htm.

Windsurfing Instructor

Windsurfers have a saying about "newbies" who can't seem to get the hang of the sport:

"Dude, 99 percent of success is failure—and you've got that down pat."

To those who have mastered the sport of windsurfing, who live their lives by the mantra "happiness is a handheld sail," teaching the craft for a living is an exciting possibility.

Facts and Figures

Windsurfing has been around for about 30 years, ever since the invention of the first sailboard by Californians Jim Drake (a sailor) and Hoyle Schweitzer (a surfer) in 1968. They called their design a Windsurfer. Early Windsurfer boards measured 12 feet long and weighed 60 pounds.

Although it's difficult to pinpoint exactly how many windsurfers are riding the world's waves, there is an abundance of interest in the sport by the people who count: tourists. Studies show that windsurfing is one of the most popular pastimes at tourist destinations.

With a professional windsurfer's tour that generates high-profile media coverage on ESPN and MTV, and with tourism hot spots like Maui, Aruba, and the Columbia

River Gorge touting windsurfing instruction as part of their tour packages, the wind is definitely at the back of the fledgling windsurfing industry.

Consequently, the need for good windsurfing instructors is growing, and fast.

Job Description

More than most vocations, training and equipment expertise are prerequisites for would-be windsurfer instructors. In fact, in most cases, teaching certification is required for instructors, through organizations such as the Windsurfing Instructors of America. On top of that, you must pass the same courses (advanced life saving certificate courses) that professional lifeguards must pass, meaning you must be a strong swimmer, knowledgeable about water rescue and safety instruction, and know first aid and CPR. You'll need experience and a license to drive a boat, too. Given the difficult nature of windsurfing, and the panicky nature of people who keep falling to the water, you probably should also possess the patience of a saint.

> **The Water Cooler**
>
> Windsurfing has caught a big gust in the past two decades, and meccas such as Maui, Aruba, and the Columbia River Gorge draw boarders and spectators from around the globe. Nowadays the sport gets coverage from television stations such as ESPN and MTV and draws big-name sponsors.

Oh, and it really, really helps to have a recommendation from a friend at the resort or beach windsurfing company you're targeting. Professional instructors maintain that's the shortest route to employment.

On the job you'll be, obviously, in the water a lot and working with some anxious, if not downright nervous, customers. Expect to be teaching beginning and advanced lessons daily. The good news is you won't be teaching at night, and probably not too early in the morning. Expect an 8 to 10 hour day, tops. Apart from teaching in the water, job responsibilities include rigging, maintaining, and repairing sailboats and motorboats, organizing weekly sailing/windsurfing regattas, and participating in demonstrations.

Pay and Perks

Windsurfing instructors can either be hired by a resort for an annual or seasonal salary, roughly averaging anywhere from $10 to $35 per hour, depending on the resort and the quality of the instructor. In most cases, accommodations are free—although you might be bunking with five or six other employees in less than plush housing. But, chances are, you'll be near the beach. Oh, and then there are the dating possibilities ...

Key Attribute

Impress employers with your passion for safety. Insurance-conscious resorts and windsurfing operations love instructors who love safety. They also like instructors to be enthusiastic, energetic, and patient, and able to perform repetitive tasks without getting burned out.

Key Tip

If you take a job on, say, a Caribbean island, you might get homesick fast. Either make plans to bring a friend or try to find a windsurfing teaching post closer to home.

Key Resource

Contact the U.S. Sailing Association for more information:

> PO Box 1260
> Portsmouth, RI 02871-6015
> Phone: 401-683-0800
> Fax: 401-683-0840
> Website: www.ussailing.org

NASCAR Pit Crew Member

So you feel the need for speed? And you don't mind spending your weekend afternoons surrounded by 100,000 screaming race car fanatics who would trade places with you in a heartbeat?

Then welcome to the land of the fast and the furious—the NASCAR Racing circuit.

It's not easy landing a slot on a NASCAR pit crew, but it's not impossible, either. That's especially true for someone with the right work ethic, experience, and connections in the competitive race car industry.

Facts and Figures

Did you know that 17 of the top 20 most-watched sporting events in 2002 were NASCAR races? On television, NASCAR ratings are second only to professional football in the United States, and NASCAR has inked big-time network deals with NBC and Fox in recent years. Sponsors love NASCAR, too. Studies show that NASCAR fans say they are three times more likely to try a sponsor's product or service than that of a nonsponsor.

Job Description

NASCAR race teams look for pit crew members who can keep a cool head on a blazing hot track with a cacophony of sound around them akin to sitting five rows back at a Metallica concert or being strapped to the bulkhead of an F-14 fighter jet. In other words, you need to be someone who is not cowed when it's loud.

The best way to sign on with a NASCAR pit crew is to warm up in the minor leagues on smaller tracks where you can learn the ropes, get used to making split-second decisions, and get a feel for the travel grind that comes part and parcel with life on the NASCAR circuit. With a NASCAR pit crew, the whole idea is to get your foot in the door. And the best way to get your foot in the door is to earn your way there.

The Water Cooler
New MBA students at Wake Forest University's Babcock Graduate School of Management are learning team-building skills on the fast track—literally. Incoming full-time MBA students at the Babcock School will participate in the Richard Petty Ultimate Racing Experience as part of their curriculum. This is the first time the university has used NASCAR pit crew techniques to instill the value of teamwork, and the Babcock School is the first MBA school to offer this experience as a team-building event.

Race car pit crew positions call for a wide range of skills, most prominent among them having good hand-to-eye coordination (for changing tires on the fly) and being small (it helps in moving quickly around tight spaces and enables other crew members to more easily move around you). Think baseball shortstop, basketball point guard, or flyweight boxer and you begin to get the idea. The best positions to break in are front-tire changers, rear-tire changers, gas catchers, and jack-men, who don't often have the experience or ability (at least not yet) to start tinkering with engine block problems or cranky manifolds with $750,000 on the line.

Physical fitness and stamina come into play in a NASCAR pit crew. Racing tires can weigh as much as 80 pounds and fully-loaded gas cans come close to that at 60 to 70 pounds. With most races on hot southern tracks, weather and fatigue have to be battled as well. The best pit crew workers, trackside gurus say, should have a combination of strength, speed, and coordination. Philosophers needn't apply. When changing a tire within a 7-second timeframe, race teams can't afford to have a pit crew member thinking about anything beyond "five lug nuts on and five lug nuts off."

Pay and Perks

If you can accept the organized mayhem of a NASCAR pit stop, you'll find the pay isn't bad, either. Salaries can often be as high as $75,000—plus bonuses. Crew teams are often paid on a scaleable basis. That means a pit crew that can get a car in and out of a pit stop in 12 seconds will be better compensated than a pit crew that averages a car turnaround time of 16 seconds.

Key Attributes

Be fast—especially at pit crew training school. Applicants who can prove they have the speed and agility to survive on the NASCAR circuit are the ones who are most recommended for jobs.

Key Tip

Take a pit crew course and practice, practice, practice. Even taking tenths of a second off a pit stop is enough to land you a job on a race tour.

Key Resources

Hone your craft at one of the growing number of NASCAR pit crew schools. Try Crewschool for starters. Find it at www.crewschool.com. Expect to pay up to $7,500 for a ten-week course.

Dolphin Instructor

The study and "mentoring" of dolphins is a relatively new, but now thriving, phenomenon. Thanks to new-age technology such as underwater cameras, sonar, and hydrophones that enable marine mammal specialists to get up close and study dolphins, marine scientists have learned a great deal more about the Princes of the Sea. Consequently, the market for people who love—and can work with—dolphins is wide open.

Facts and Figures

Over 50 species of dolphins survive and thrive in Earth's seas, rivers, and oceans. Classified in the small-tooth whale category, most dolphins are roughly six-feet long, with males being up to eight inches longer on average than females. Larger dolphin species, such as the killer whale (yes, "Willie" of *Free Willie* fame was actually a dolphin) can grow to 22 feet in length and weigh 10,000 pounds.

Numbers on employment as marine mammal trainers are hard to come by, but one of the most recent U.S. government studies shows that 75 percent of college graduates who earned degrees in marine sciences and wanted to work directly with marine mammals did find work in the field.

Job Description

Dolphin trainers answer to many names and titles. Topping that list are the terms *trainer*, *animal care specialist*, and *mammologist*.

One name you might also hear, but isn't as apt, is *marine biologist*. Although marine biologists do yeoman's work in the field of dolphin research, and some might even double up as dolphin trainers, they spend their careers studying the *environment* dolphins live in and the impact that habitat has on a dolphin's anatomy, behavior, and psychology.

Dolphin trainers are more hands on than their marine science compatriots. As a dolphin trainer, you'll spend your sun-burnt day caring for and feeding the mammals, giving them medicine, working in the water with them conducting cognitive training sessions, and in the case of marine parks and zoological tourist venues, spending time with the public educating them on the ways of the dolphin. Be prepared to do the latter up to five times a day.

Most marine mammal trainers are college-trained, and the majority go on to graduate schools that excel in the marine sciences field. After graduation, many go on to internships with aquariums and marine theme parks working directly with dolphins. Most are offered either part-time or full-time work at the same marine venues where they interned (or, in some cases, volunteered).

You might find that, given that there are only so many aquariums in the world, the dolphin trainer tides carry you toward the burgeoning career of marine mammal rehabilitation, i.e., working with sick, malnourished, or otherwise incapacitated dolphins. Such positions are most widely found at educational and marine laboratory institutions.

What do employers look for in the field? Primarily, people who love animals and the water (you'll be spending a lot of time with both), are creative, have solid manual dexterity, are persistent, and possess the social, visual interpretation (dolphins are experts in hiding illness and disease from their human handlers), and time management skills that can be found with the best dolphin trainers in the field. A background in veterinary care and medicine will also help open doors in a career of dolphin trainer.

Pay and Perks

Pay depends on whether you're pursuing a full-time career in marine mammal training (and have a relevant college degree) or whether you're working on a seasonal basis at a marine park or aquarium. The former can easily earn $40,000 annually; the latter might make an hourly rate of about $10 to $12. If you can handle that, perks include loads of time outside in the sun and surf, and the once-in-lifetime shot to swim with a dolphin pack.

Key Attributes

You must have a love of dolphins, obviously. By and large you can add knowledge of the animals, skill in operant conditioning training, especially bridge and target training, and public speaking and presentation expertise to the list of key attributes that employers seek.

On the Job

Looking for a conservation or environmental career? A great resource for your job hunt is the conservation jobs page at About.com. Find it at usparks. about.com/od/ environmentaljobs.

Key Tip

Take a scuba diving course and get certified. That will get you tapped for those ultra-cool ocean excursions where you visit dolphins in their natural environment.

Key Resource

Visit Dolphin Trainer at dolphintrainer.com or the International Marine Animal Trainers Association (IMATA) at https://www.membersolutions.net/organization/ IMATA/home.asp.

The Least You Need to Know

- ◆ Outdoor jobs are great, but conditions can be harsh.

- ◆ Consider seasonal work as a way to break into your dream outdoor job.

- ◆ For riskier jobs, like smokejumper or windsurfing instructor, you'll need to be certified.

- ◆ To land your outdoor dream job, be prepared to travel.

Chapter 8

Walk with the Animals

In This Chapter

- ◆ How to turn your love for animals into great career options
- ◆ Animal-related jobs you may have never considered: alligator trapper, dog walker, horse whisperer
- ◆ Ride 'em, cowboy
- ◆ Keep clowning around: rodeo clown

Woody Allen once said, "The lion and the calf shall lie down together, but the calf won't get much sleep."

However you view that line, it's a good (and humorous) take on the animal world—a place where both lion and calf may not be able to co-exist, but at least can share the same characteristics of the four-legged set: freedom, fresh air, and family.

If you love animals, then there just might be a place for you in that world. True, you must have the patience of a saint and the bedside manner of Florence Nightingale when dealing with animals, but the rewards are many and the career a fulfilling one.

Alligator Trapper

You might still think of alligators as an endangered species. They once were, but effective conservation efforts have resulted in a tremendous success story on the part of the old gator. In Florida alone, there are now more than a million wild alligators. Unfortunately, the gator population growth spurt coincided with tremendous human population growth, and development in the same areas. So now, instead of being endangered, gators are classified as nuisance animals.

But they can be much more than a nuisance. In fact, they occasionally pose serious threats to the human, livestock, and pet populations in the areas they inhabit. Gators eat dogs so commonly in Florida that the state refuses to keep records. And every once in a while, a gator grabs a human, causing serious injury or death.

Thus there is a need for the gator trapper. In locales where humans and gators collide, trappers work to keep the boundaries between the two populations clear, and in the process help keep both safe. So if you're comfortable hanging around in swamps, and you're not afraid of taking on a 14-foot gator in a wrestling match, you can carve out a career path in the world of gators.

Facts and Figures

Alligators occur from southeast Oklahoma and east Texas on the western side of their range to North Carolina and Florida in the east. They prefer fresh water lakes, slow-moving rivers, and wetlands, but they also can be found in brackish water habitats. You can find work as a trapper in any of these states, but the biggest demand for the job is in Florida, where increasing numbers of people and abundant alligator populations have led to a progressive rise in the number of alligator-related complaints.

Although the majority of the problems with alligators relate to their being in places where they aren't wanted, a small number tragically involve alligator attacks. More than 200 unprovoked alligator attacks on humans have been documented since 1948, with 13 resulting in fatalities.

The State of Florida contracts with anywhere from 35 to 80 licensed gator trappers every year. Trappers pay an annual license fee to the state and a small fee per hide as well.

Job Description

Gator trappers remove nuisance alligators found in swimming pools, wandering in bank parking lots, lounging on golf courses, or threatening children and pets along waterways. And there is certainly an ongoing demand for the job. In 2004 the commission received 16,749 alligator nuisance complaints, compared with 5,000 complaints in 1978. Much of the increase in complaints is related to gators being fed by people; the reptiles lose their fear of humans as a result.

In Florida, to qualify to be a nuisance-alligator trapper, you must ...

1. Reside in the region where the nuisance-alligator trapper is authorized to take, possess, or kill alligators.

2. Possess the experience and ability to handle wild alligators.

3. Be capable of supplying all equipment necessary to take alligators.

4. Have sufficient time to adequately and efficiently take designated alligators.

5. Not have been convicted of violating any law or rule relating to the illegal taking of crocodilians within five years of the date of application, or within ten years of the date of application if such conviction involved endangered crocodilians.

6. Assume personal liability for health, welfare, and safety while acting as a nuisance-alligator trapper.

Pay and Perks

The primary compensation for nuisance-alligator trappers is through the sale of alligator hides and meat from alligators harvested on the job. Trappers get a small expense reimbursement from the Wildlife Commission for each alligator harvested. In some cases, there is not enough "work" to make nuisance-alligator trapping a full-time job, and the income generated through the sale of alligator products might not be enough to support an individual or family. Most, if not all, nuisance-alligator trappers have other sources of income.

A study done by the wildlife department's Division of Law Enforcement found that trappers received a net income of about $100 per gator and an annual income ranging from $3,000 to $50,000, depending on the number of gators caught. Trappers can sell alligator meat to area restaurants for about $5 a pound.

One way to supplement your income if you have some skills with trapping alligators is to turn it into a tourism industry. Hunters visiting Florida will pay around $250 to go on gator-hunting expeditions led by professional trappers.

Key Attributes

Gator trappers act as ambassadors for the alligator. It takes patience to explain to a resident facing a large reptile that the resident is the invader who has bulldozed the natural wetland environment that hosts these magnificent creatures. And it can be emotionally difficult to have to kill a gator in the line of duty.

The Water Cooler
The word "alligator" is derived from the Spanish term "el lagarto," which means "the lizard."

Key Tip

Stay on top of your health insurance premiums. As a gator trapper, you can never drop your guard. Even a 6-foot alligator can easily drown you. Trappers sometimes find their health insurance companies become hesitant to insure them due to the risk associated with the job.

Key Resource

Look into the Florida Fish and Wildlife Conservation Commission. Contact them for more information at www.wildflorida.org/gators/nuisance.htm.

Dog Walker

Dog walking is a low-overhead way to merge your love of dogs with the seemingly never-ending stream of pet-related revenue. If you love the feel of warm puppy kisses, and like spending time outdoors, this might just be the perfect job for you.

Facts and Figures

The number of pet dogs in the United States has blossomed in the last 20 years. There are more than 60 million pet dogs in the United States alone, and their owners tend to spend lots of money on their care. The average dog-owning household spent 38 percent more on the care of their pet in 2001 than they did 1997. In fact, the pet-related industry is the second-fastest growing industry in the United States.

It might sound like an easy job—what can it take to leash up Fido and trot him outside for a brisk walk? But the job isn't nearly as easy as it looks. Most people start out working part time, as a pet sitter, a couple steps below the oft-desired position of dog walker.

Dog walkers have to be responsive to the demands of their clients, which can mean no vacations, no real weekends off, and crazy hours. It usually takes some time before most dog walkers realize their financial goals and create a schedule that works for them.

It is also a job that requires capital if you're going to strike out on your own with a dog-walking business. Commercial dog walkers are sometimes required to carry large insurance policies, and must be bonded and licensed. And it doesn't hurt to take classes and become certified in canine CPR and first aid.

Job Description

Dog walking is a pretty clear-cut job, although the needs of clients can vary dramatically. Some are regular customers, requiring care every day, and some only require dog walking services when they go away for weekend trips or vacations.

Dog walking is a great way to get exercise, make a little money, and play with pets. Sometimes, there's no actual walking involved. Clients with puppies or dogs with separation anxiety will hire dog walkers to spend time with their dogs to help with socialization or minimize destructive behavior.

For those who can look past the sometimes-inconvenient hours, the less-than-glamorous wages, and the waste removal, dog walking can be a very rewarding job. After all, there's nothing more rewarding to a dog lover than having those animals love you.

Pay and Perks

You probably won't get rich as a dog walker. It pays about as much as an entry-level office job, but of course you're not in an office, you're outside.

New York City dog walkers charge an average of $15 for one 30-minute walk. For dogs who require private walks (most walking services walk two to three dogs at a time) or who need and extra half-hour of exercise, prices rise to an average of $30. Owners who are gone longer than the average workday can expect to pay around $50 for their dog to be walked three times a day. A good professional walker with a solid client base can earn a solid annual income of over $40,000.

You might not be earning a Trump-like salary while walking the dogs residing in Trump Plaza, but on the plus side there's no one looking over your shoulder while you work. You won't hear complaints from your charges, as human language is not in their skill set. And while most people are stuck in office buildings all day looking out a window from their cubicle and hoping they can get outside before it gets dark, as a dog walker, you'll be spending 95 percent of your time outside with dogs.

Key Attributes

Dog walkers must be flexible, as schedule demands can change daily. And of course, you have to love dogs to enjoy the job.

Key Tip

Carry lots of plastic bags. Picking up poop is a key part of the job. If you're squeamish about scooping up after dogs large and small, this is not the job for you.

Key Resource

The folks at PetSit USA help dog owners locate qualified dog walkers and pet sitters throughout the United States, and they help people thinking about getting into this line of work find opportunities. Contact them at www.petsitusa.com.

Horse Whisperer

If the phrase *horse whisperer* conjures up images of Robert Redford, get them out of your head immediately. Although many people found the movie entertaining, most horse people were amused by the inaccuracy with which the job was portrayed.

That is not to say that horse whispering is not a fascinating and rewarding job. Indeed, for those with a love of horses and a desire to help people, "whispering" can provide a kind of therapy for both the whisperer and the whisperee. And in a country that in 2004 declared December 13 the National Day of the Horse, the demand for people who can simplify the training process is growing.

Facts and Figures

Americans have long had a deep relationship with the horse. The wild mustang is as much a part of American culture as apple pie and hot dogs. But, unfortunately, not every person bonds well with every horse. People looking to find just the right mount often spend a lot of time and money trying out different horses until they find one they can get along with well. This process can be costly and time consuming, not to mention heartbreaking for both the owner and the horse.

Tom Dorrance, born in the early twentieth century, recognized that traditional horse training methods were not terribly successful. He authored a book, *Natural Horsemanship*, that is now the bible of horse whisperers worldwide. Instead of using the horse like a vehicle or farm equipment, he developed a two-way communication system with his horse.

Dorrance realized that horses are a lot like people. After careful study, he found that the central nervous system of a horse is very similar to ours, which, he speculated, is why humans bond with horses so easily. For many people, this bond can be a life-changing one.

Trainers who follow Dorrance's methods are broadly referred to as "horse whisperers," partly because the methods they use require a kind of silent language, and partly because of the secrecy that has surrounded them as they work their magic in the equine world.

Job Description

Horse whispering is based on a simple premise: body language. A horse whisperer acts more as a psychologist for the animal than a trainer. Like dogs, horses are social animals that aim to please. However, because of the often strenuous and inhumane methods that some trainers use to get results, the animal's innate desire for companionship is often masked, causing the horse to turn into a problem horse. Whispering uses the horse's natural tendencies toward socialization to restore the animal's trust. Mimicking methods of discipline that horses use in the wild, the trainer uses his physical stance to either drive the horse away from him or allow it to come and connect with him. In physical terms, this usually takes place in a round pen, where the trainer uses his arm movements and sometimes a rope to get the horse moving around him in a circle. The method is called gentle, because little to no physical contact is used. Instead, eye contact is heavily relied upon.

Although horse whispering is based on a set of founding guidelines, training must be flexible to meet the needs of the individual horse. It's all about the psychology of horses, and understanding how their heads work to get the behavior you want out of them.

Pay and Perks

No one gets into horse whispering with the expectation of becoming a millionaire. But if you establish a successful practice, there is a good living to be made in horse whispering. You can also supplement your income by teaching others this technique through seminars and classes.

Key Attributes

Obviously, the best horse whisperers have a deep love of horses. Add to that a lot of patience, and empathy for sometimes brutal treatment that horses receive at the hands of their masters.

The Water Cooler

Horse trainer Buck Brannaman was the inspiration for the best-selling book *The Horse Whisperer* (later made into a movie starring Robert Redford).

Key Tip

Horse whispering requires a lot of physical exercise, so make sure you're in good condition before you head out to tackle your first equine.

Key Resource

The Man Who Listens to Horses (Ballantine Books, 1997) by Monty Roberts is a good place to start.

Rodeo Cowboy

What red-blooded American kid didn't grow up thinking about becoming a cowboy? It's the kind of job that has natural appeal—life on the range, days spent under the open sky on the back of a good horse, no care or worries from corporate life.

But how do you make a living as a cow-puncher, given that the wild west has been tamed? Well, you might be surprised at the options available to the job seeker still holding onto that childhood dream of living the life of a cowpoke—especially if you have a competitive spirit and like the idea of becoming a rodeo cowboy.

Facts and Figures

In the United States alone, there are about 750 rodeos held each year, attracting 22 million fans. The prize money for such contests is getting better—million dollar purses are growing more common.

Rodeo is a sport unique in the fact that it grew directly from an occupation. Early cowboys often did roping or riding tricks for entertainment during cattle roundups. Ranches, communities, and organizations began holding these cowboy competitions and exhibitions and the "rodeo" was born.

Professional rodeo has evolved into a major production, a show of theatrical proportions with professional rodeo cowboys taking home large purses and traveling to dozens of rodeos per year. Small-town and ranch rodeos still prosper with local and area cowboys, many of whom still work regularly with cattle and other livestock. Whether big-time professional show or small-town production, rodeos have two things in common: the skills involved are authentic and the "cowboy way" is a revered and honored tradition.

And although rodeo is traditionally a male dominated sport, cowgirls are an integral part of the rodeo scene. Belle Starr and her counterparts might seem like the stuff of Hollywood scriptwriters, but women have ridden, roped, and wrangled for years, and their future in rodeo is bright. More women are now participating in traditional "male" events, and with the growing purse for traditional "women's" events, cowboys and cowgirls are increasingly competing in the same events.

Job Description

Life is hard for the rodeo cowboy just as it was for the cowhand on the ranch a hundred years ago. In addition to being tough physically, the athletes have to pay their own expenses, including entry fees. This can be especially difficult considering that rodeo cowboys are not paid salary. They are awarded buckles and saddles, but the only money they make is the prize money that is awarded by the promoters of each rodeo.

Five-time PRCA world champ in bareback riding, Joe Alexander, put it well by stating, "There are a lot of cowboys that can rope and ride, but there is a much smaller percentage who can stand the pace and still win. That's one of the real tests of a cowboy. You will find out how tough he is real fast when he has to get out and go to rodeos. It's the original school of hard knocks!"

Here are the main events any rodeo cowboy will want to master.

◆ **Bull riding.** Stay on the bull for eight seconds to earn a score. The rider holds on to a rope (hopefully firmly tied around the bull) with one hand and uses the free hand for balance. The rider is never allowed to touch any part of his body or the bull with the free hand.

◆ **Saddle bronc busting.** The objective is to stay on a wild horse for eight seconds. Riders start with their feet held up over the shoulders of the horse. In addition to the no touching rule of bull riding, a rider is disqualified for dropping his rein or letting his foot leave the stirrup.

◆ **Calf roping and/or steer roping.** Just like its name says, this is an event that requires the cowboy to rope and tie a calf or steer from horseback.

◆ **Barrel racing.** A traditionally female event which is becoming increasingly coed, this is a timed event in which the rider must maneuver the horse through a "cloverleaf" pattern of three (sometimes four) barrels.

Although there are other events which you might or might not see at any given rodeo, a good cowboy will need to master these major events in order to become an accomplished pro.

Pay and Perks

Rodeo doesn't pay as well as other professional sports. Although race car driver Michael Schumacher gets $25 million in a single year for performing in much less risky circumstances, rodeo cowboys settle for much less money just to have the chance to compete. A bull riding champion might earn something around $125,000 in a banner year. A competitive cowboy ranking in the top 20 of his or her discipline could expect to earn around $100,000 in 2005.

How do rodeo cowboys cover their expenses, much less make a living? Simple. Professional rodeo cowboys rely on corporate sponsorship. Although cowboys don't have as many sponsorship patches on their clothes as can be found on any highly ranked tennis pro, there is always at least one. Patches advertising Resistol hats, Justin boots, Tony Lama boots, Wrangler jeans and shirts, and Dodge trucks are common sights on cowboys' chests, backs, sleeves, and chaps.

Key Attributes

Cowboys nearly all come from humble and less-advantaged American backgrounds (although there are some Australians and Brazilians). And they love to ride rodeo even though the risks outweigh the monetary gains, because at heart they are true athletes.

Regardless of what the financial gains might be (and they are relative—cowboys think $50,000 is a good living!), athletes participate because of their competitive nature and the love of their sport. The true cowboy has the soul of a competitor. Some people like bulls and horses and going for the wildest ride possible—and even more important, they like to show that they are the best at their sport.

Key Tip

Be prepared to encounter danger regularly. Every cowboy gets "throwed." Indeed, during the national finals no cowboy rode all ten go-rounds without eating some dirt, and there were several cracked ribs, sprained wrists, pulled muscles, lacerations, contusions, and concussions. But no one was killed—at least this year.

Key Resource

For information on the life of a rodeo cowboy, visit the National Cowboy Museum web site at www.nationalcowboymuseum.org.

Barnum and Bailey's Elephant Handler

Remember your first circus? The thrill of the trapeze artists, the smell of cotton candy and popcorn, and the excitement of seeing myriad wild animals? Of course you weren't paying any attention to the people behind the scenes, like the animal handlers. But they are a vital part of any event involving exotic animals.

It takes a lot of talented people to make a circus run, especially when you're dealing with animals as large and smart as elephants. And although jobs with exotic animals are few and far between, they can be exciting if you're able to land one.

Facts and Figures

At 10,000 pounds, elephants are serious business. So getting some professional training is key when dealing with such large animals.

The best way to pursue a career in this field is by attending a school that offers animal training programs where you can get a practical and solid foundation. It takes dedication, experience, and patience to enter into this exciting field professionally. Most of the knowledge you will need is learned from observing and participating in the actual handling, training, care, and maintenance of exotic animals. Animal training is an art form learned by masters in the field. It is only truly learned by hands-on practical experience and knowledge.

Keep in mind, though, that although any school can offer the basic knowledge you'll need to enter the field, some people have a special aptitude with animals, and others do not. Only you know whether you have the ability to grasp the knowledge and experience an exotic animal training program offers.

Job Description

Training elephants involves working with creatures that have 11-pound brains, the largest in the animal kingdom. They communicate with each other through a series of high-pitched and deep sounds, which can be fairly complex. They're known to nurse sick comrades and even appear to mourn their dead family members. So you'll need to be prepared to deal with some pretty tricky and intelligent animals if you decide to take on this career.

An elephant handler works long hours training and bonding with his animals. A handler does everything from supervising feedings to bathing to transporting the animals to different sites for performances. Additionally, you'll need to be able to stay on top of your elephant's health needs and grooming requirements.

And don't forget showmanship. A great elephant handler knows how to draw a crowd into his performance. The elephants fascinate, but the handler is the Johnny Carson of the arena—making sure the elephants entertain the crowd.

Pay and Perks

In general, you don't get rich working with animals. Performers, handlers, and studio trainers are not in this profession for the money—they have a passion for it. This is a profession and a lifestyle requiring a strong commitment to animals. The average exotic animal trainer earns $300 for an eight-hour day. The average elephant handler can start at anywhere from $17,500 to $30,000 per year.

Key Attributes

Generally some of the requirements for excelling at a career in handling exotic animals like elephants include the following:

- Strong dedication and commitment
- Practical hands-on experience with exotic and/or domestic animals
- Good health, exceptional physical and athletic ability
- Knowledge in zoology as well as animal behavioral and experimental psychology
- Confidence and patience, with a positive attitude when talking to the public
- Excellent communication skills
- Theater, drama, and dance experience (which is helpful in live presentation and educational programs)

Key Tip

There are many perils attached to elephant handling. Trainers get injured, maimed, and even killed by elephants that go on unprovoked rampages. Another problem for trainers is that they face a lot of heat from groups like PETA that protest the supposed cruel treatment of elephants at circuses and carnivals.

Key Resource

For more information on training to become an elephant handler, check out www.animalschool.net/FAQ.htm

The Water Cooler
According to studies, elephant handlers are three times more likely to incur a fatality than a front-line, big city police officer.

Rodeo Clown

When rodeo first began, the concept of clowns developed as a way to entertain spectators in between shows or events and to keep the children in the audience from becoming restless. The clowns' role has evolved greatly since then, and now they are an integral part of the workings of any rodeo.

Today, a rodeo clown serves many purposes, from crowd entertainment to safety mechanism. But it's one of the riskiest jobs in the business. So if you are looking for a career that will let you combine your sense of humor and appetite for danger, this might be just the path for you.

Facts and Figures

Rodeo clowns apprentice at small rodeos and at youth events and may also attend clown-training schools, which hold camps mostly in the Southwest. However, many rodeo clowns are former rodeo contestants and start off as bull riders. Clowns have to be in top physical shape, and it helps to have a high pain threshold.

The demand for rodeo clowns is somewhat limited, but there is some turnover. There are fewer than 300 rodeo clowns working in the United States, according to the Rodeo Clowns and Bullfighters Association. And the number of rodeos held each year is increasing with consumer demand.

If you're willing to apprentice and work hard, the life of a rodeo clown can lead to fame, fans, the opportunity to travel, a good amount of money, and plenty of broken bones.

Job Description

The primary purpose of rodeo clowns has become to protect bull riders from serious injuries or even death. Clowns often endanger their own lives to save a rodeo cowboy, working to distract the bull so the rider can escape to the nearest gate or rail.

Feisty, 2,000-pound bulls are very different from horses. A horse tries to avoid stepping on a downed human, but bulls actually go out of their way to attack anything that gets in their path. That's where the rodeo clown comes in—literally stepping into the path of the bull to distract it from the rider.

Three different categories of rodeo clown represent three different jobs. The bull-fighter is primarily concerned with protecting the cowboy. A barrelman remains in a barrel during the cowboy's ride and emerges to distract the bull if needed. Comedy clowns are primarily crowd entertainers.

Underneath their silly costumes, rodeo clowns wear special equipment to help protect them from injuries to their chests, ribs, thighs, hips, tailbones, shins, and ankles.

According to F. J. "Scooter" Culbertson, professional rodeo clown, bullfighter, and barrelman for the Cowboys Professional Rodeo Association, "Getting hit by a bull is like getting hit by a car going 20 mph. It's not if you are going to get hurt. It's when and how bad."

Pay and Perks

Rodeo clowns can make between $100 and $225 per show, according to Salary.com. Depending on how many jobs a clown gets per week, he or she can make $20,000 or more during the peak rodeo season, May through September.

One of the prime perks of the job, according to most rodeo clowns, is traveling and seeing America. Freelance clowns will jump from show to show all around the country. Frequently they will pay their own travel expenses, however.

Key Attributes

Athleticism. It's not easy running from an angry bull when you're in bad shape.

Key Tip

Work on your sense of humor. According to one rodeo clown, "As a funny person, you have more potential to make money." Many clowns will tell you that being funny is the hardest part of their job. How many jokes can you think of while being chased by a bull?

Key Resource

Rodeo Attitude's website is www.rodeoattitude.com/main/bullfighters.htm.

Professional Beekeeper

Most of us spend the summer months trying to avoid bees and keep them away from our picnics, but there are those who see a life with bees as a great way to earn a living.

With honey prices hitting an all-time high in early 2001, the beekeeping industry is a little-explored avenue for a career with a lot of independence.

Clearly not a job for anyone afraid of the occasional sting, some beekeepers are involved in bulk honey production or the collection of pollen; others are involved in queen bee breeding. Any way you choose to go, a rewarding lifestyle can be built among the hives.

Facts and Figures

Bees are very important. One in three mouthfuls of food you eat is produced directly or indirectly by bees. It could be the honey on your toast, apples pollinated in orchards, or even the steak that comes from lucerne-fed cattle. So the demand is there for people who are interested in this field.

Beekeeping is one of a small number of occupations that can be started on a hobby scale for a few hundred dollars and can grow into a multimillion-dollar business.

Most days you will get stung, so you'll need to get used to it. But you can develop a tolerance, and if you learn to get the stinger out immediately, the effects can be gone in 30 seconds. Most people can tolerate stings and aren't allergic.

If you're afraid of bees, and not prepared to be away from home, then this might not be the job for you. Beekeepers need to have a finger in many honey pots; they need to know about botany, insect behavior, and marketing, and they should even have basic carpentry skills. There's no doubt, though, that those involved in beekeeping are passionate about their subject and the lifestyle.

Job Description

Beekeepers work the bees within the hives and manipulate the hives, checking where the queen and the brood are. Working with smokers, bee brushes, protective clothing, and hive tools, beekeepers constantly manipulate the frames and boxes to assess the health of the colonies, control breeding, and collect the honey.

Beekeepers are constantly on the go, following the floral blooms around their area. Bees are moved at night and unloaded at dawn at the new site to ensure minimal disturbance to the colony (and to the general public!). Make no mistake, this work can be long and physically challenging. Commercial beekeepers move up to 100 hives per truck or trip—this translates to up to 6 or 7 tons being moved around every 6 weeks, and hence mechanical loading devices like cranes are a necessary part of the job.

As the availability of food and water also impacts the size of a colony, beekeepers need to know when to give bees supplementary feeds to prepare for the honey season in spring and summer. Beekeeping involves ongoing management of the colony all year round.

Honey is collected in two ways—either on site or at a plant. A good hive or box of honey can produce 55 pounds a week at the peak—making for good returns for the beekeeper.

Pay and Perks

Salaries for beekeepers vary widely depending on the number of hives kept, and whether you own the business or function as an employee. The average starting salary for a trained beekeeper is $20,000. Small owner/producers can gross up to $100,000 plus for honey and related products. But you have to be dedicated to reach this higher figure—it might take a number of years to get there.

Although beekeeping can be an arduous job, it's perfect if you like a little solitude and an outdoor lifestyle.

Key Attributes

People who want to consider beekeeping should enjoy being independent and able to run their own businesses. You'll need a good deal of self-motivation, a sense of responsibility, and a willingness to perform many different types of tasks.

A successful beekeeper must also be a good salesperson, be good at keeping track of money and accounts, enjoy hard, physical labor, be willing to work 10 to 15 hours per day at certain times of the year, and should really have a keen, alert, and interested scientific sort of mind. The beekeeper must pay attention to lots of minor details, as well as signs of changing seasons, floral conditions, beehive strengths, and potential problems with the bees (subtle indications that the hives might be suffering various illnesses, might need new queens, or need extra food reserves).

Key Tip

If you're thinking about launching a beekeeping business, find a local beekeeper and ask lots of questions. Each part of the world has very different conditions for bee-keeping. The local beekeeper will be able to advise the best time of the year to get started, whether or not the local flowers will support the bees with sufficient nectar or whether the bees will require extra feed from the beekeeper, when to put extra honey storage boxes on the hive, and other precautions. Most beekeepers are very helpful about getting someone started and might even have equipment for sale.

Key Resources

For more information on becoming a beekeeper, visit ourworld.compuserve.com/homepages/Beekeeping/startup.htm. Some other excellent online resources include the APIS Newsletter Home Page (www.apis.ifas.ufl.edu) and Tucson Bee Research Lab (www.gears.tucson.ars.ag.gov). The A.I. Root's *Bee Culture* has excellent articles and timely information. For general beginning information, try *Practical Information* from University of North Carolina, *Getting Started in Beekeeping*, from the University of Nebraska.

Llama Rancher

Combine animals that are beautiful, useful, and fascinating with the possibility of making a profit, and it's obvious why so many people are looking into owning llamas and alpacas.

Facts and Figures

For many years, demand for llamas grew faster than the animals became available, and prices went up and up. In the 1970s a breeding pair of llamas sold for around $1,500. Prices gradually rose, and then in the early 1980s, there was a plateau, with most females selling for $4,000 and most males for $500. By 1990, the starting figure for females was closer to $10,000. The fanciest show animals commanded prices in excess of $100,000. The rise in prices was at times rather frenzied, and around the time of the Persian Gulf War and the recession, prices began to decline. Today, they are under half what they were in 1990.

Because these animals are easy to raise on small acreages, some exotic-animal owners and breeders rushed into the livestock business like gold miners stampeding to mining claims. And like mining, exotic animals have both boomed and busted.

Unlike ostriches, llamas from the camelid family are raised in the United States for utility and fiber rather than meat. They serve as pack animals and guard animals, and their value varies depending on their suitability to perform certain tasks.

Job Description

Like any career involving the breeding and raising of animals, a llama rancher spends much of his or her time cultivating and caring for brood stock. The job requires going to auctions to buy and sell animals, helping females deliver their offspring in the middle of the night, and cleaning up after the herd.

For most llama ranchers, the job is not about profits. It's about lifestyle and preserving a way of life they think is worth more than gold. They have many reasons for being in the business, whether it's booming or busting.

Even though llamas are no longer the "get rich quick" investment they were in the 1980s, they can provide a lifestyle that many people envy. The job will allow you to enjoy natural resources, be outside, and help preserve the agricultural aspect of ranching that has been such a strong historical part of American culture.

And you might be surprised at the ways llamas can generate income. One Seattle-area llama owner has found innovative new ways to use her llamas to reach out to the public—she takes her geldings to all kinds of social events, from birthday parties to conventions. At around $50 (plus travel costs) per gig, it's a great merger of llamas for love and for money.

Many people are finding that the public loves llamas, too. Many therapists are starting to incorporate llamas in their work. And several bed-and-breakfasts have llamas as part of their attractions.

Pay and Perks

When the llama industry was booming in the late 1980s, show animals could sell for as much as $170,000. They still can sell in the tens of thousands of dollars, with the average price for a llama at most sales running around $5,000. However, the price of an average llama has dropped 60 percent since the early 1990s, so a good rancher will need to find alternative ways to market his livestock.

Unfortunately, the market was inundated with poor-quality llamas from three or four countries with uncontrolled importation. A lot of animals became available in the world market and the quality went from exceptional to run-of-the-mill. Success in the llama industry right now depends on marketing. The llama rancher needs to be able to develop his own market, breed good animals, and do a good job selling them.

Raising llamas can still be profitable. They can be sold as pack animals, brood stock, show animals, or even guard animals. Llamas still bring a price that makes raising them worthwhile.

Key Attributes

In addition to loving the llama life, a good rancher will know how to keep a clean establishment and will be able to assess the quality of livestock. A novice to the llama will need to spend many hours looking at animals and learning from experts in order to learn to distinguish excellent stock from mediocre animals.

To be successful in the llama business, though, a rancher needs to understand the marketplace. Marketing is the most important part of a llama business today, and without a strong marketing drive, few llama ranchers will succeed.

Key Tip

It might not be the first thing you think of when you think of a llama, but consider marketing llamas as guard animals. There is a steadily growing demand for llamas for use as guard animals. One mother living in a state riddled with coyote leases a llama to keep coyotes from bothering her children. The llama follows the kids around the yard and keeps coyotes away.

Llamas are also becoming popular as guard animals for calves, sheep, chicken, and goats. A llama runs as fast as a horse, it has a powerful neck and front feet, can turn quickly, and has a natural mothering instinct. It's a social animal and is content with a sheep herd once it adopts the sheep as its own.

Key Resource

To learn more about how you can develop a steady livelihood working with llamas, visit www.llamas-information.com/llamas-love-and-money/09-3-what-else.htm.

The Least You Need to Know

- Careers in the animal world can lead to rewarding lifestyles, if not hefty bank accounts.

- You'll need to have a natural talent and love for animals to be successful in any animal career.

- Animal-related careers can be unpredictable, but they can also provide lots of flexibility and an occasional warm, fuzzy snuggle.

- Think outside the box to turn your love of animals into a rewarding career.

Chapter 9

Sports Afield

In This Chapter

◆ The career benefits of the professional sports circuit

◆ Playing to win: professional poker

◆ Zambonis and roller coasters

◆ Diving for golf balls

◆ Becoming a professional "HotDogger"

Joining the professional sports circuit—in any venue—is a great way to perform in front of throngs of adoring fans. As Yogi Berra once said, "If people want to come out to the park, you can't not stop 'em."

So grab your jockstrap, a can of athlete's foot treatment, and hot foot it over to your sport of choice—and see if there isn't a great career there waiting for you.

Professional Poker Player

Maybe you've seen the movie *Rounders*, where Matt Damon plays a card shark who takes the big pot and saves his best friend's life at the end of the movie. Or perhaps you've seen one of the myriad poker shows on television, or sat down at a table in Las Vegas next to Amarillo Slim or Doyle Brunson.

If you did, and you liked it, you got the bug—the poker bug.

Poker is a hot commodity these days. From games in blue-collar basements and big city firehouses to bacchanal gambling weekends in Vegas or Atlantic City, it seems like millions have grown accustomed to the adrenaline rush of winning on the flop and raking the pot to their side of the table.

But can you make a living at it? Some people do—probably more than you think.

Facts and Figures

Although millions play the game, the odds of making a real living at poker—defined as $100,000 or more annually—are tough. Professional poker players estimate only one percent of poker players can survive or thrive as a professional. The payoffs, however, can be huge, even for garden-variety players. Amateur Chris Moneymaker won the 2003 World Series of Poker—and a $5 million prize—despite never having won a professional game in his life. Actor Ben Affleck, another amateur who loves the game, won a California professional poker tournament the same year. So it can be done.

Job Description

Professional poker players usually work nights—and long ones at that. Average tournament games can go 10 to 12 hours per day easily, usually ending up in the wee morning hours. After some much-needed sleep—the pros say that being well rested is key to a sharp poker mind—a tournament-savvy player pretty much bides his or her time until the action begins that night. To some, that could mean a round of golf, or a brisk workout at the gym. To others it might mean more poker, either practicing on one of the many Internet poker websites or heading down to the casino or over to a back room at the local union hall to hone their game. Drinking alcohol is frowned upon by the game's greats—Amarillo Slim said it dulled his mind and emptied his pockets, so he never touched the stuff. And he's still playing.

Pay and Perks

As noted previously, the benchmark for a professional poker player is about $100,000 per year. Anything less than that and you risk not being able to bring big money to the table to make the kind of aggressive bets that really win huge tournament poker pots. For each tournament, you'll need between $4,000 to $10,000 to get you off and running.

Key Attributes

Patience and individual discipline are keys to making it on the professional poker tour. Your boss is you, and it's up to you to motivate yourself and provide yourself with the discipline needed to hone your craft and stay up hours on end studying cards and the players who hold them. It helps to have a little psychiatrist in you. Reading opposing players is actually a laboratory study in human behavior. Poker legend Doyle Brunson once said he could "read" a player's hand by the way his eye twitched when he picked up a card, good or bad. The ability to recognize—and fleece—poor players is a key job attribute. That's tough on the professional circuit. And that's why most "professional" poker players make their living on cash games against tourists, wealthy wannabes, and other amateurs.

Key Tip

Play a lot of poker before you go to Vegas and sit down at a table. One rule of thumb is 500 hours of logged table time at poker before sitting down with the big boys. And, for financial safety's sake, have about six months' worth of living expenses saved up in case your initial foray into professional poker isn't as lucrative as you hoped. Remember that you'll be traveling a great deal and you'll have to eat, handle dry cleaning costs, and pay for lodging, too. Moving to Vegas is probably your best option to reduce those kinds of costs.

Key Resource

Your best bet is Doyle Brunson's book *Super System*. It's the bible of the poker world. The best players swear by it. Find it at bookstores or on Amazon.com. Then sit down and study the game from one of the sharpest poker minds in history.

> **On the Job**
>
> To get a feel for the game of poker, take a trip to Las Vegas (yeah, I know—it's a sacrifice) when the World Series of Poker is occurring. The tournament usually starts in June and ends in July. A bonus: for less than $50, you can enter a satellite tournament for a chance to actually play your way into the tournament.

Belly Dancer

Care to catch the elusive rhythm of the night?

One way to do so—and potentially make a living approaching $100,000 annually—is through the magic of exotic dancing. So grab your navel ring, belly up, and pay attention.

Facts and Figures

The classic, centuries-old art of belly dancing originated in the Middle East and North Africa. The art dates back to fifteenth century Turkey, where older women taught their young, pregnant offspring the art of "belly rolls"—undulating their midsections to demonstrate how to properly give birth. Culturally, belly dancing is largely a female practice, says Rosina-Fawzia Al-Rawi in *Grandmother's Secrets* (Interlink Books, 2000). "Belly dancing gives a woman the possibility to discover, learn about, and understand herself," she writes. "More than words or thoughts, it reveals her attitudes and feelings toward herself and her sexuality, toward men, children, and other women."

Belly dancing didn't make it to the United States until the late 1800s, when it finally caught the public's eye and led women to begin donning lavender, I-Dream-of-Jeanie bra tops and light, veiled skirts and taking to the dance floor. By the late 1990s, belly-dancing classes were all the rage in New York, San Francisco, and other large U.S. cities.

By 1997, over 2,348 professional belly dancers—or "choreographers" as they are known in the trade—were employed in the state of New York alone. By 2007, that number is expected to grow to 2,760.

Job Description

Many professional belly dancers are part-timers, teaching school or planning corporate marketing campaigns by day and dancing to their inner beauty by night.

Like most entrepreneurial efforts, you're pretty much on your own as a belly dancer. Nightclubs, event planners, and now teaching salons are the most common markets for belly dancers. With no professional union, it's up to dancers to negotiate their own pay, and their own benefits—if they can get them.

Most professional dancers work two to five nights per week, for about three hours or so per event. Those who practice belly dancing full time usually teach the art by day and dance professionally at night. Check your YMCA or local community arts center for more information about taking—and teaching—belly-dancing classes.

One prejudice belly dancers say they face is the perception that they are strippers and belong in low-rent clubs like Tony Soprano's *Bada Bing*. With history on their side they have a point. But do expect to work midnight shifts and be prepared to accept dollar bills tucked into your g-string when you dance.

Pay and Perks

Fees for belly dancing varies, depending on the gig you land. Belly dancers who go onsite for bellygrams and birthday parties can make $100 to $200, depending on their ability to negotiate with the buyer.

If you go the club or social event route, the money seems to be better. According to the state of New York, individual professional belly dancers earned between $22,000 and $85,000 in 2002, depending on the amount of time and effort the dancers demonstrated. Keep in mind that a good belly dancing costume can set you back $500 or even $2,000.

The perks are great if you enjoy flexibility and attention from the opposite sex. You can set your own schedule and will attract plenty of attention from men during your act.

Key Attributes

Women who can dance, have some background in choreography or gymnastics, and are fit and trim are the best candidates for belly dancing slots as professionals. It might not be fair, but private event holders and club owners frown upon dancers who are overweight or who are getting along in years. But if you can dance, you'll always have a shot.

Key Tip

Take a dance class to see if you like belly dancing and have what it takes to make it as a professional dancer. An 8- to 10-week class will show you if you have the ability and the desire to dance in front of the public on a regular basis. Also, be a real professional and have nice business cards made up that you can pass out at functions or give to your family and friends. A good website wouldn't hurt, either. It shows customers you take belly dancing seriously and plan to make a living at it.

Key Resource

A great website for all things belly dancing, from navel piercing to instructional videos, is www.bellydancingbyzamoras.com/bellydancing_links.html.

Zamboni Driver

The wheels on the Zamboni go round and round … round and round.

Um … Zamboni?

That's right. After all, what hockey fan worth a bagful of pucks hasn't wondered what it would be like to sit astride a souped-up tractor and ride around the ice at big league hockey games, with 15,000 people following your every move?

Chill, dude. It might be easier than you think.

Facts and Figures

Okay, three guesses where the mighty Zamboni machine was invented.

Toronto? No way, hoser.

Boston? Don't bet your baked beans on it.

Minneapolis? Man, you are cold.

Nope, the Zamboni was invented in sunny Southern California in the 1950s by a guy named—you guessed it—Zamboni. Frank Zamboni.

Called the world's first ice resurfacing machine, Zamboni's Zamboni was an efficient, smooth-running work of art. After demand from ice rinks in northern climes, Zamboni came up with a way to create a multifunctioning machine with blades that shave the ice surfaces, a snow tank to gather and hold the ice shavings, and a separate tank that spews out water that exceeds 160 degrees (pipes under the ice immediately freeze it), and a six-foot-wide squeegee to make the ice shinier than Wayne Gretzky's Hall of Fame credentials.

On average, a single Zamboni travels 2,000 miles each year resurfacing ice. And more than 7,000 Zambonis are in operation around the world.

Job Description

Handling heavy equipment is a key part of the job. You'll get to the rink early to smooth it out and then spend the rest of the day maintaining it. You'll clear the ice before hockey games or ice skating events, and then again during intermission. On average, you'll clean the ice four times each night.

Be prepared to work a lot of nights and weekends—even holidays. Hockey and figure skating events bow to no date on the winter calendar—so you're working a lot in-season. The good news is that when late spring and summer roll around, you'll have a lot of free time on your hands.

Pay and Perks

Beginning Zamboni drivers don't heed their Ice-landic calling for the wealth. Hourly wages for newbie drivers, usually at local rinks, start at about $13 an hour. If you work your way up to the top—a Zamboni driver at, say, Boston's Fleet Center or Detroit's Joe Louis Arena—you can make up to $50,000 annually.

But it's the perks that count. Free passes to games, good-natured jawboning with professional hockey players, and cultlike celebrity status with fans in the stands who would give their autographed Bobby Orr jersey to trade places with you.

Key Attributes

Most drivers get started at local rinks where driving the Zamboni is only one of their many job responsibilities. Many sharpen skates, man ticket lines, and handle equipment operations duties—anything to be handy around the rink.

Practice is the key. Professional Zamboni drivers say that ice cleaning is an art. Some say they have spent 16 hours a day practicing their craft. If you've ever seen a Zamboni driver at work, you know how easy it is to see their mistakes. A sliver of snow on an otherwise clean sheet of ice can ruin any Zamboni driver's day—and fans do notice.

On the job, the key is to excel in making those all-important turns around the ice and to take care to put the right amount of water down on the ice. Too much ice and you'll hear about it from hockey players—they say it slows the ice down.

Oh, it helps to tolerate cold weather, too. Ice at most rinks is kept to a minimum 17 degrees to keep it neat, clean—and frozen.

The Water Cooler

Most Zamboni drivers begin as "rink rats"—guys who play hockey and like to hang out at the rink. Aside from being able to be methodical and careful, a great Zamboni driver should have good hand-eye coordination. It also helps to know how big engines operate. You might have to operate on a Zamboni someday, mechanic-wise.

Key Tip

In general, it's tough to go to school to become a Zamboni driver. But you *can* attend college and major in Arena and Operations management studies. That's what Travis Larson, the Zamboni driver for the NHL's Minnesota Wild, did.

Key Resource

It's not a resource, in the traditional sense, but a good way to gain insider knowledge of the Zamboni business is to visit a local skating rink and ask to speak to the general manager. Chances are he is the guy who cleans the ice. Ask for 15 minutes of his time, buy him a cup of coffee or a beer, and get the scoop from someone in the know.

Roller Coaster Designer

Any recreational activity that can make grown men scream like little girls has a lot going for it. The only thing better than participating in such an activity is designing it.

That's the appeal of becoming a roller coaster designer. Sure, it has it ups and downs. But creating the kind of thrill rides that make the toughest Marine squeal like a two-year-old who dropped her ice cream has the term *career fulfillment* written all over it.

Facts and Figures

I'm not kidding when I say that roller coasters—in the United States anyway—have undergone some ebbs and flows.

In the early 1900s, over 1,500 roller coasters rose above amusement parks all over the country. Due to safety concerns, that number dropped to about 200 by the 1960s. Today, 115 or so coasters are up and rolling in the United States. The good news is that, thanks to state-of-the-art technology and some very creative (and security-minded) designers, roller coasters are bigger, faster, and more popular than at any time in recent memory. And more rides are being built every year—some as high as 300 feet tall with cars that travel in excess of 80 miles per hour.

Roughly 100 roller coaster design companies exist in the United States, most of which are near major theme park centers in Florida, California, Texas, and Ohio.

Job Description

You'll spend a lot of time on the computer, drafting architectural designs that meet rigid client specifications. And then you'll spend a great deal of time meeting with those clients. Onsite work is part of the job description, too. You'll don a hard hat and work boots and visit the site on a regular basis.

Pay and Perks

Pay varies, with some roller coaster and theme park designers easily clearing six figures annually. Others work on a freelance basis, hopping from project to project. But they command big bucks, too.

Roller coaster design is a very creative field that rewards people who know how to balance risk and safety to create the fastest four minutes in most people's lives. Some engineers are well known for riding their own coasters—and have the added benefit of being able to "buck the line" at popular resorts like Six Flags and Disney after they're recognized.

Key Attributes

The best roller coaster designers have a good combination of design and engineering (especially electrical, drafting, and structural engineers) training. Most have college degrees in those areas. If you're looking to get some hands-on training, check out any of the these fine theme park design centers:

- Art Center in Pasadena, California
- California Institute for the Arts (CalArts) in Valencia, California
- Ringling School of Design in Sarasota, Florida
- University of Cincinnati in Cincinnati, Ohio

The ability to plan is key, too. As most roller coasters are custom built, usually over a year's worth of time, a designer has to factor in timetables, budgets, design specs, safety regulations, and environmental concerns. Put it this way—if you think you had a tough time getting the zoning board to clear your back deck, imagine the red tape you'll face trying to build a 250-foot high roller coaster in Cincinnati.

Count on spending a great deal of time designing and drafting roller coaster models on your computer. CAD training really jumps off the page when a design firm is reviewing your resumé. Working with marketing to draft a quickie proposal on spec—the roller coaster business is very competitive, and multiple design firms are all involved in project bids—is a task that many newbie designers get assigned.

But if you can show some initiative, apply those math and physics skills you honed in high school and college, and feel the need for speed, roller coaster design is a good bet and a lucrative career.

Key Tip

Get a biography of Walt Disney and read it, cover to cover. Figure out how the best built amusement parks and act accordingly.

Key Resources

Get involved with professional organizations like the International Association of Amusement Parks and Attractions (IAAPA) and the Themed Entertainment Association (TEA). Get on their mailing lists, go to their conventions, and network like crazy.

Pro Skateboarder

Okay, let's get one thing straight about professional skateboarding.

It's for the young, to the young, by the young.

While 30-somethings like Tony Hawk still ride high on the skateboarding circuit, promoters and sponsors say that the riders they look for must have three key ingredients.

Youth, youth, and more youth.

But if you're young and can remain attached to a skateboard while traveling 40-miles-per-hour at 40 feet above ground level, and live to tell the tale, then you might have a future in pro skateboarding.

Facts and Figures

There's a reason that promoters look for young skaters to groom for the professional circuit. Their key demographic is teenagers—teenage boys, to be specific. Teenage skateboarders prime the skateboarding industry's pump to the tune of $1 billion worth of sales annually. That makes boarding the number one extreme sport among that most sought-after demographic.

Young males are the ones who spend the money on the equipment and, more important, the merchandise that fuels the skateboarding industry.

Overall, there are about 500 pros in skateboarding, inline skating, and BMX freestyle combined in the United States. But that's out of an estimated 12 million skateboarders, according to the U.S. Skateboarding Association.

Job Description

Pro skateboarders train hard to prepare for the events that they hope can earn them a good living. Skateboard events are usually held outdoors, in warm weather climates. Events last about two hours and you'll perform for up to 10 minutes per roll.

Pay and Perks

If you can defy the law of physics, master the ledges, rails, walls, and ramps of the skateboarding circuit—and look good doing it—you just might have a future as a professional boarder.

If so, the pay and perks are great. Pro skaters compete in weekly events where cash stakes can go as high as $150,000. Even mid-list skaters can earn $100,000 per year. Top-notch skaters can earn between $500,000 and $1 million annually. And guys like Hawk are millionaires many times over.

Actually, the big money isn't in professional events—it's in merchandising and sponsorships. Most professional skateboarders can earn up to $3,000 per month for riding a particular skateboard, $2,000 per month for using the right wheels, $1,000 or more per month for wearing a sponsor's sunglasses or shoes, and thousands more for trading cards, action figures, and—the Holy Grail for skaters like Tony Hawk—video games.

If you can stand pretty young girls begging for your e-mail address, plying your craft in warm sunshine in front of huge crowds, and becoming a cult figure—or better—before you reach age 21, then the perks in skateboarding aren't bad, either.

Key Attributes

Pro skateboarding is a great deal harder than most people might think. It's a gritty, rough-and-tumble sport, where busted ankles, dislocated knees, and badly twisted arms are as much a part of the landscape as they are to the National Football League or NASCAR. So a high tolerance for pain is essential.

That's where the youth factor comes in. Besides the demographics angle, which is huge, sponsors need young, agile, athletic types who can withstand the rigors of the professional skateboarding circuit. Usually, years of practice on the streets precede an entrance into big-time skating. The trick is to enter local contests whenever they pop up and wow the sponsors, promoters, and vendors who populate the local skateboarding circuit looking for the next Tony Hawk. Becoming a professional skateboarder is all about getting the right people to notice you—and local skate-offs are a great way to create the right kind of attention.

If you're noticed, and a sponsor appreciates the adrenaline and flair you bring to the table, you'll likely be "comped" with skateboards, shoes, and other merchandise and nurtured through the beginning stages of your career. Professional skateboard fat cats look for good presence and marketability as much as they do skating talent. So some savvy self-promoting can go a long way in the industry. You'll hit the mini-tours for free and build some experience. Maybe you'll do a training video or on-site demonstrations. To save money, you'll likely be bunking with other young skaters.

So what's the down side? Watch out for the lure of the party circuit. With access to cash and parties, it's easy to burn out. The best pros don't let that happen. Your income as a professional skater can be erratic, as well. As eight-time X Games skateboard champion Andy Macdonald said, "Certainly, if you're in it for the money, start playing tennis or golf."

On the Job

Get to know the main sponsors on the professional skateboarding circuit. Start with Vita Shoes, Element Skateboards, Quicksilver Clothing, Destructo Trucks, and Spitfire Wheels. Then approach them when you're ready to show your stuff.

Key Tip

If you crack the barrier and make yourself known on a local or regional skateboarding scene, focus on sponsorships. They're the quickest and most reliable way to a steady income. Otherwise you might struggle with travel, hotel, food, and equipment costs and event entrance fees. A good sponsor can take some of the pressure off and allow you to skate.

Key Resources

Check out the United Skateboarding Association at www.unitedskate.com or phone them at 732-790-5168. It's a treasure trove of information about the industry and how to make it on the professional circuit.

Oscar Mayer Weinermobile Driver

Okay, so maybe being a Weinermobile driver doesn't have the cachet of a professional skateboarder or roller coaster designer (of course, depending on your perspective, maybe it does).

But there's no questioning the "uniqueness" credentials of one of America's most highly visible jobs. So if you not only tolerate, but also relish, the title of "Hot-Dogger" on your business card, then read on.

Facts and Figures

To be perfectly, um, frank, it's not easy to become an Oscar Mayer HotDogger and gain access to the coveted Weinermobile. The Madison, Wisconsin-based company only chooses 12 to 20 HotDoggers each year. So the numbers don't work in your favor. The company says it gets 1,000 applications each year and takes a long hard look at just who can cut the mustard.

But here's some inside information. Log on to the company's website or write them directly (send your resumé to Hot Dog High in care of Oscar Mayer in Madison, Wisconsin). You'll receive either a direct invitation to interview for the job or information on when the company plans to visit your area to recruit HotDoggers for the job. Note that Oscar Mayer usually focuses on recruiting at college campuses.

The Oscar Mayer's HotDogger program began in 1989. Since that time over 240 Wienermobile drivers have taken the wheel, logging, on average, about 1,000 miles per week. The Weinermobile itself is 27 feet long, 7 feet wide, and weighs 10,500 pounds. Its inside décor is, naturally, relish-colored. The license plate of each of the six Weinermobiles reads *WEENR*.

Job Description

Expect to spend a lot of time in grocery store parking lots, amusement parks, and baseball stadiums. HotDoggers spend a lot of time handing out free tee shirts and

Wiener Whistles, and signing up kids to enter the Oscar Mayer jingle contest (the winner receives a $20,000 college grant and a free trip to Sea World in Orlando, Florida).

Pay and Perks

The primary reason to become an Oscar Mayer HotDogger is to get paid to travel. It's also a great springboard to a career in marketing, journalism, or public relations.

Pay is $500 per week, including expenses. Oscar Mayer will put you up in a nice hotel each night you're on the road, which is a pretty good gig for a young college student or college graduate.

Key Attributes

Oscar Mayer says it looks for outgoing types with bubbly personalities to become HotDoggers. What they are really looking for are ambassadors for the Oscar Mayer brand. Here's a real inside note. Oscar Mayer also prefers college graduates, but really likes those with a journalism degree (the company wants its HotDoggers to be good story tellers and encourages them to connect with kids and help them write new jingles). A good driving record and a love for all things frankfurter is an obvious advantage. In other words, making your preference for vegetables known at the interview is a big red flag.

Above all, the best HotDogger candidates are the ones who can convince the Hot Dog High gurus that they want to see the world through the windshield of a Wienermobile.

Key Tip

Memorize the Oscar Mayer HotDogger Oath—then recite it in your intro letter and again at your job interview. I'm serious.

It goes like this: "As official HotDogger of the celebrated Oscar Mayer Wienermobile, I salami swear to uphold the dogma set forth here … to be frank, and furthermore, to be upstanding in a line for hot dogs at ball parks, barbecues, buffets, and other bashes …"

Key Resource

If you think you can cut the mustard, send your resumé to the following:

> HotDogger Advisor
> The Wienermobile Department
> Oscar Mayer Foods
> 910 Mayer Ave.
> Madison, WI 53704

Golf Ball Diver

If you love golf, swimming, being your own boss, and don't mind fending off the odd alligator or two, then have I got a career for you: golf ball diver.

Think about it. Golf ball diving combines the best elements of some of our favorite pastimes: golf, water sports, and making money. And any career that can see you turn around and sell a product that the previous owner just hit into the water—at a decent mark-up—has a lot going for it.

Facts and Figures

The used golf ball industry is a license to print money (divers call golf balls "white gold"). It's a multimillion business that feeds on the shanks, skulls, slices, and hooks that are offered up in abundance by 18-handicappers across the globe.

Make no mistake, there are a lot of hackers. Studies show that of the one billion or so golf balls that hit store shelves each year, up to three million of them wind up as unintentional offerings to golf's Water Gods.

Job Description

Patience comes into play as you stand—or dive—for hours at a time to collect as many golf balls as possible. But the return on investment is worth it. A golf ball diver can resell the balls for anywhere from 25 cents (for driving range-quality balls) to $1 or even $2 for the top-of-the-line Nikes and Titleists.

Pay and Perks

Serious golf ball divers can make anywhere from $50,000 to $100,000 a year. Of course, that means harvesting about 150,000 balls per year—about 15,000 balls per month. Of course, any golf ball diver (or waders, there are a lot of waders, too) can bring in 1,000 balls on a given eight-hour day on a busy course.

For people who like working outside, it's a great gig. Plenty of fresh air, no boss looking over your shoulder, and you can call it a day whenever you want. Plus, good divers just don't retrieve golf balls. They can—and do—dredge up full sets of golf clubs, wallets, money clips, gold coins, wristwatches, and other valuables.

The down side is the environmental dangers that are often attached to golf ball diving. Crabs, eels, alligators, and especially snakes are real and present dangers to divers. Many divers, in fact, carry snake venom medication with them for some fast first aid in case of a bite. The chemicals that modern day courses use to make their greens green and their fairways lush also can be problematic. Many divers also get protective shots from their doctor to ward off any chance of getting a disease from the chemicals in the water.

Key Attributes

Patience, discipline, and the ability to keep a secret once a good spot is found are the ingredients that fuel a golf ball diver's success.

Most golfers arrange deals with local golf clubs and used golf ball outlets. For instance, a golf ball hunter will pay a golf club 10 cents a ball for rights to poach its ponds for wayward Titleists. Or some courses will agree to take 10 percent of a diver's daily haul for permission to keep mining the course's waterways.

High technology can help, too. Hydraulic rollers can now be used to literally comb ponds and lakes for golf balls. One North Carolina diver claims he used the rollers to pick up 600 balls in 20 minutes.

Key Tip

Use eBay to sell your golf balls. Golfers flock to the site to get good balls for a fair price, instead of paying country club prices for balls they're going to splash into the water within a week's time, anyway. You have the supply and eBay will provide the demand.

Key Resource

Like the Zamboni driver, there really isn't a tried and true organization or association for golf ball divers (hey—it's truly an "every man for himself" endeavor). Instead, visit your local golf club and see if you can shag balls there. If they say "no," move on to the next one.

The Least You Need to Know

- ◆ To get a job in the sporting field, be competitive. You're going to face some tough competition and not everyone can be a professional skateboarder.

- ◆ Many jobs are solo ventures—so negotiate. With many of these jobs (okay, Zamboni driver may be an exception), it might help your cause to live in a warm-weather state. In most of these jobs, you'll be outside a lot.

- ◆ Do your homework and bone up on your specialty, whether it's belly dancing or poker playing.

- ◆ The people who make a living at these jobs are serious about their crafts.

Part 4

The American Dream: Being Your Own Boss

Deep down inside, everyone wants to be his or her own boss. (Why not? Could you do any worse than the boss you have now?) That's why Americans are opening their own businesses in record numbers these days.

Scarred by spiraling layoffs and pigeonholed by autocratic bosses who feel threatened by anyone who deviates from the corporate party line, today's entrepreneurs are taking matters into their own hands by running their own shops on their own terms. And they're doing it matter-of-factly, with little fanfare and less chest-thumping than previous generations.

In this section, we'll take a look at some of the coolest businesses that are attracting the "do it yourself" crowd. Mainstream American business will never look the same.

Chapter 10

Sweatpants Nation: Dream Home-Based Jobs

In This Chapter

♦ Great home-based careers

♦ Writing, day trading, inventing, and more

♦ Home-based jobs that may surprise you

♦ Becoming a bed-and-breakfast operator

Well, the title says it all.

If you know someone who works out of his or her home, clad in sweatpants and carrying that good-natured, if smug, countenance that so many home office types seem to radiate, then maybe you've got a case of the Green-Eyed Monster.

After all, who wouldn't want to be their own boss, control their own destiny, and know that the money you earn is yours (save for Uncle Sam's cut)?

Not many people I know. Who wants to spend their working years shedding blood, sweat, and tears for corporate fat cats who might not really appreciate who you are and what you bring to the table?

You can end all that by running your own home-based business. And here are some great ways to do just that.

Freelance Writer

Imagine rolling out of bed in the morning, yawning, and then heading downstairs to your dream job without so much as changing out of your pyjamas or taking a shower.

No agonizing commute. No surly boss. No boring meetings to endure.

Just you, your brilliant mind, and your home office.

It's the life of a freelance writer and, trust me, it's a good one.

Facts and Figures

There are several thousand freelance writers working either part- or full-time in the United States today. And there are thousands more magazines, newspapers, book publishers, corporations, and websites starving for writing talent. In short, the work is out there if you want it. You just have to hustle.

Job Description

Freelance writers essentially are "free agents" who write articles, books, marketing copy, and even screenplays on a work-for-hire basis for magazines, newspapers, publishers, and businesses.

As a freelancer, your day is a full one from the get-go, despite the lack of a commute or annoying co-workers interfering with your work. You'll start by checking e-mail and phone messages to see if you earned any new assignments overnight (editors are famous for e-mailing writers after 5 P.M.—they're too busy to do so during the day).

Then, you'll check your calendar and see what deadline is coming up next. It might be a front-of-the-book piece on budgeting tips for *Baby Talk* magazine, or a piece on nurse-run medical clinics for *The Chicago Tribune*. If you're really clicking, it might be a book on dream jobs for a lucky publisher. After you've determined your next deadline, you dig in with phone interviews and Internet research, and begin banging out a masterpiece that you'll e-mail to your client (ideally, one day before your deadline).

After a break for lunch and the mad scamper to the mailbox to see if a check has come (a tip: never get between a freelancer and his or her mailbox. You'll get flattened.), you might spend the afternoon crafting query letters (i.e., story ideas) and e-mailing them to the appropriate editor at the appropriate publication. If you're good, the editor will green light the story, send you a contract, and you're on your way.

Also expect a lot of time following up with editors on invoices. Getting paid is the bane of existence for freelancers who are otherwise thrilled with their careers.

Pay and Perks

I already described the perks: you are your own boss and set your own hours. If you work late, the money you earn goes to you and you only—not to a faceless corporation. No dress code and no cow towing to pointy-haired bosses.

Pay varies. Many freelancers earn well over $100,000 a year. Others who don't put the time in or who are just starting out and haven't yet made a name for themselves often earn much less. Some magazines pay over $2.00 per word for stories. But they are the exception. Most pay .50 cents to $1.00 per word. Any publication that pays less than that isn't worth your time (unless you're just starting out and trying to garner clips).

Key Attributes

The ability to string a good sentence together is key. So, too, is a manic desire to make it as a freelancer writer. In the freelance game, failure is not an option—it could mean a return to cubicle nation, and no freelancer wants that. Good marketing skills and the underrated ability to work on your own are necessary, too.

Key Tip

Write about what you know. If you have a financial background, target investment and business publications. If you come from a health background, target health publications. These assignments will be your "base." They'll provide a good income and enable you to grow and expand into other areas as a freelancer.

Key Resource

Join Freelance Success (www.freelancesuccess.com). Founder and editor Jennie Phipps runs a great site for freelancers. It's filled with good job leads, a great chat room chock full of other writers, and tips on querying and breaking into new markets. It's an indispensable site for newbie writers, especially.

Day Trader

Day traders represent a fairly recent development in the investment industry. It is thought to be a reaction against traditional, old guard money management funds and well-heeled stockbrokers; and to the emergence of a renegade outlook that says the average Joe (or Jane) can, with a little street smarts and effort, get in on the market "game" and compete with the pin-stripes-and-suspenders crowd.

Although it's an appealing notion, there's nothing easy about day trading (now often known as "active trading" by advocates), despite some of the myths and the hype of recent years, particularly during the Internet stock boom of the late 1990s. Day traders don't "invest" in the traditional sense; instead they buy and sell throughout the day, relying on their market knowledge, observations, and moment-to-moment decisions to bring in a profit. But most traders find that what looks easy on paper is anything but easy in the real world of stock market trading.

Facts and Figures

Day traders work out of cubicles in big city offices around the United States—and sometimes trade from home—with small-time brokerages backing them. These are the hard-core traders, not the goofy characters from the Ameritrade TV commercials. Successful full-time day traders might execute 15,000 to 25,000 trades a year, creating huge commissions for their clearing firms. It's estimated that as many as 45,000 people have turned to day trading as a full-time profession—which is only a fraction of the more than 20 million amateurs who have opened brokerage accounts to perform some level of trading on their own. Still it remains a controversial subject, with many professional traders blaming the small pool of full-time day traders for millions of dollars in market swings.

On the Job _____

Learn the lay of the land. Your bank account and financial future may depend on it. Before you start trading with a firm, make sure you know how many clients have lost money and how many have made profits. If the firm does not know, or will not tell you, think twice about the risks you take in the face of ignorance. Like all broker-dealers, day trading firms must register with the SEC and the states in which they do business. Before you do business with any firm, call your state securities regulator to confirm their registration, and ask if the firm has a record of problems with regulators or customers. You can find your local regulator in the phone book or through the North American Securities Administrators Association at www.nasaa.org.

Job Description

A day trader spends the workday glued to his or her computer screen, monitoring the stock market continuously for stocks that are moving up or down in value. They're looking to "ride" the momentum of the stock and be sure to get out of it before it changes course. Day traders rely on their instinct and dozens or hundreds of quick judgment calls during the course of the day, buying and selling in rapid succession, and hoping their insights and speed will enable them to profit and close out by the end of the day.

"True" day traders don't hold onto any stocks overnight due to the high risk of radical price changes that can result in huge losses from day to day. Day traders usually buy on borrowed money, which can offer some leverage but obviously risks higher loss.

To stay on top of the market, a day trader has to be up with the sun, poring over newspapers and business reports, scanning message boards online, checking out new reports or analysts' research. Thanks to the Internet, individuals now have a great deal of this information at their fingertips—but it still takes a tremendous amount of time and energy just to take it all in.

Pay and Perks

There is no way to estimate annual salary, or even a range, for a business as volatile as day trading. For example, one successful trader might report having cleared $200,000 in one year—but that's before subtracting commissions of close to $40,000 to his online brokerage firms, $60,000 for taxes, plus monthly services like PC Quote, newspapers, cable TV, and other home office expenses. All told, assuming a continued strong performance (and no sudden disasters), this trader might see $85,000 in profit for the year. So it's crucial to factor in *all* your expenses before you pop the cork on the champagne.

> **On the Job**
>
> Beginners are well advised to read a few books on trading and look into a course on short-term trading to see if it's really for you. Market experts would tell anyone considering this field to start slow, with low share size and minimal trades. Learn the software that's out there, study the markets and stock charts, and create a trading plan with a list of rules (which might include a specific stop loss per trade, stop loss per day, share size you will trade, trading hours, and strategies to minimize losses). You might want to establish a maximum profit per day, to avoid the temptation of "over-trading" and jeopardizing whatever money you've managed to make.

Day trading is not unlike gambling, with a similar rush of highs and lows. You might turn your initial $10,000 account into ten times that or more, only to see it collapse back below that in further trading. Most traders enjoy the thrill of the "game" as much as or more than the actual profits. And most individual investors simply don't have the wealth, the time, or the temperament to make money and to sustain the devastating losses that day trading can bring.

Key Attributes

Discipline, perseverance, quick thinking, excellent concentration are all important to the successful day trader. You should love the stock market and be comfortable working alone.

Key Tip

Day traders have high expenses, for commissions, for training, and for computers—so having sufficient capital up front is important. Most experienced traders would advise a newbie to have at least $50,000, preferably $100,000 or more to work with before making a start. You should expect to suffer some losses in your first months of trading, so *only* risk money you can afford to lose. Any day trader should know up front how much money they need to earn to cover expenses and break even.

Key Resource

Check out Toni Turner's *A Beginner's Guide to Day Trading Online* (Adams Media, 2000).

Divorce Mediator

It's no secret that getting divorced is a painful and often a prolonged procedure, one that can reduce grown (and formerly loving) adults to bitter and churlish behavior by pitting them against one another in a courtroom to fight over property, alimony, even their children.

It doesn't have to be this way. These days more and more people are opting for divorce mediation, in which both partners come to a settlement with the help of an impartial and expert divorce mediator. It happens outside a courtroom, without a trial. The goal of divorce mediation is to preserve as much good will as possible, which is especially important when children are involved. Mediation reduces emotional stress, saves time and money, reduces the burden on courts, and makes the world a more civilized place.

Facts and Figures

Nearly 50 percent of marriages in the United States end in divorce—not a pretty statistic, but one that indicates a genuine need for the services a mediator can provide. More and more couples are turning to divorce mediators to help settle their affairs in what many describe as a more civilized and empowering process than a traditional courtroom divorce. As more couples have become aware of this alternative, demand for mediators is growing quickly. Getting a divorce mediated takes less time than going to court, and it's much less expensive. Average cost of going through a mediator to obtain a divorce is around $1,200 (which is split between the couple) and as anyone who's gone the other route can tell you, that's a bargain.

The Water Cooler

A legal background would seem like an obvious advantage here—and can certainly help you—but there are an equally large number of mediators with experience in counseling or therapy, which helps to support and guide couples through the stress and pain of a divorce. Particularly when there are children involved, it's important to have a handle not just on the children's economic best interests, but also their psychological and developmental well-being.

Job Description

A mediator works with couples to settle disputes outside the courtroom system, making arrangements for things like childcare or alimony, and drawing on both parties to come to an agreement so that a judge won't have to decide for him- or herself. Mediators don't necessarily need a law degree but should be familiar with legal rules and procedures, and they often have a background in psychology and/or mental health.

A mediator charges an hourly rate, like an attorney, and will meet with a couple usually for two or three sessions, lasting less than 10 hours. In these sessions they hammer out a contract that seems fair and agreeable to both parties, which is then delivered to a judge.

And if you find divorce cases simply too upsetting, there are a growing number of mediators hired to settle employment disputes.

Pay and Perks

Most people working in the mediation field have a genuine interest in helping others, guiding couples through an extremely difficult process in a way that will reduce their financial and emotional burden. Easing the pain of others is one of the job's great rewards; and the compensation for this type of work is considerable, ranging from $100,000 to 300,000 a year.

Key Attributes

A divorce mediator must have the following qualities: empathy, sensitivity, patience, and strong communication and interpersonal skills.

Key Tip

One of the best ways to market yourself and your services is to get on state and federal government lists of approved mediators.

Key Resource

To get more information on divorce mediation, check out www.mediation-matters.com.

> ### The Water Cooler
>
> Mediation allows the couple in question to draw up their own divorce contract, settling issues like child-raising arrangements, income and alimony, division of property, and living arrangements for the couple themselves (i.e., who gets the house?). When a divorce is filed for and accompanied by such a document, the divorce procedure becomes only a formality with the judge—which helps make it quicker and relatively painless.

Image Consultant

The recent success of wildly popular makeover shows on TV has only drawn more attention to an already burgeoning field—that of the image consultant. What once was reserved for the likes of Hollywood stars has become a much more mainstream fascination, with applications from beauty pageants to boardrooms, courtrooms, and the like. These days ordinary people are discovering the power of a makeover on their everyday interactions and state of mind.

Image consultants coach and train in everything from wardrobe and grooming to eye contact, body language, and social graces; and they are involved in broader concerns such as corporate protocol and helping with a company's visual image and public relations.

These days more and more people subscribe to the theory that "image" goes far beyond what you've got in your closet—and that an image consultant's advice can help you land a job or relationship, get a promotion, or simply feel better about yourself.

Facts and Figures

Although there are few formal programs to train you in image consulting, many people drawn to this field come from a background in beauty consulting, counseling, or some form of marketing. For centuries people have used clothing and presentation to communicate power or place within the social order, but it wasn't until the 1970s that the idea of one's personal "image" became a popular notion, as more and more people recognized that the way someone presented him- or herself could have a direct bearing on career, love life, and self esteem.

The Association of Image Consultants International offers three separate levels of qualification within the field of image consulting, culminating in Certified Image Master.

> ### On the Job
>
> Image consulting is a service business, so it doesn't require a large investment to get started, which is great news for beginners. (And you can get your start part-time while working at another job.) The first step is to decide what kind of services you want to offer—whether to specialize in wardrobe or fashion consulting, offer advice on communication skills and etiquette, or be a makeover consultant who gives feedback on "the total package."

Job Description

An image consultant advises clients on all aspects of personal appearance, etiquette, presentation and marketing, and public speaking. He or she might also work with companies or corporate clients on issues like the company's image and making contact with the media.

Also known by such titles as wardrobe consultant, fashion stylist, or makeover consultant, image consultants are paid to show people how to create a positive impression. They might recommend a grooming or wardrobe makeover, or offer advice on verbal (voice, grammar, vocabulary) or even nonverbal (posture, fitness, eye contact) communications.

Image consultants should be skilled and experienced in a wide variety of areas, such as personal grooming and makeup, dress codes and fashion trends, publicity, and the media. Hours vary widely as consultants must schedule appointments around their clients' working day. Depending on their specialty (corporate clients versus individuals, very high end versus "regular" people), an image consultant might spend a great deal of time on the road.

As with anyone who's self-employed, consultants devote a great deal of time to developing and marketing their business, building a reputation, and attracting new clients.

Pay and Perks

Most image consultants are self-employed, so earnings vary greatly, but an established consultant can earn around $50 an hour advising their clients how to present a better image. Training programs for corporations (which might entail anything from tips on professional attire to telephone etiquette and supervisor-employee communications) are a particularly lucrative way to go, as a one-day seminar can bring in thousands of dollars.

Among the perks of this field are independence, great flexibility, and a genuine sense of accomplishment, seeing a client achieve success or personal satisfaction through your work.

Key Attributes

An image consultant should be highly personable, polished, and diplomatic, with a strong visual sense and excellent communication skills. Obviously, you should present a professional image yourself.

Key Tip

If you're just getting started, the most important ingredient will be experience. You can read books or find formal training workshops, but nothing beats having a roster of satisfied clients. As a start, you can offer free makeovers for friends or family members—using the "before and after" approach with photos to document the work you have done. You can then put the photos in a portfolio or on a website to help you get paying clients.

> **The Water Cooler**
>
> Sometimes it takes a village to complete a makeover. That's why many image consultants develop a network of "strategic partners" they can refer clients to, such as hair stylists, makeup artists, nutritionists, dentists, personal trainers, plastic surgeons, and voice coaches. It's like having a bullpen of all-stars to draw from at any time.

Key Resource

Check out the Association of Image Consultants International (www.aici.org).

Team Statistician

How many times have you been watching a big game being broadcast, heard the announcers report on some player statistic or factoid, and wondered—who in the world gets paid to do that?

If you're a sports junkie (like me) with a keen head for figures (unlike me), chances are you've considered this dream gig.

Facts and Figures

For every sport at the professional level, individual teams keep elaborate information on every other team (things like scoring, injuries, salaries, and so on), which adds up to a whole lot of information. However, paid careers as a sports statistician are rather limited and don't pay especially well. All the major television networks will have one or more sports statisticians employed on a full-time basis, and these lucky few are well paid. But there are fewer than a dozen people in the country who work in this capacity and, therefore, entry is practically impossible. There are also sports data agencies that accumulate sports results and supply the leagues and media with relevant information for their clients' diverse needs.

On the Job

Because it's so highly specialized, the business of sports statistics is often combined with another related profession, such as sports journalism (in which allows you to cover games and pick up the relevant stats while earning a living at something else). Other areas to explore might be within the marketing, PR, or accounting departments of an athletic department, sports league, or team.

Job Description

A sports statistician (or team of statisticians) might be responsible for some or all of the following: recording stats in real time as a game is being played; auditing stats along with play-by-play announcement; preparing final stats for league records; serving as an official scorer for both competing teams; preparing mid-game and final summaries for the press; resolving disputed calls; and/or entering data on a computer.

Pay and Perks

Nearly all who work in this field are employed on a part-time basis, though a few people are hired full time as computer specialists or statisticians for a professional team. Most are paid on a per diem basis, at around $50 to $100 a game for sports like basketball, baseball, or football. Although this field might be very attractive and certainly a blast for a sports fan, very few people can ever earn a living; it's better viewed as an enjoyable hobby or interest. (If you're really sharp with numbers, bear in mind that top level mathematical statisticians can earn up to $65,000 a year.)

Key Attributes

Superior math skills and mental quickness are a must. You should be able to add, subtract, and divide in your head, checking and double-checking all the time.

Key Tip

Try to get some experience while you're in high school by volunteering to keep stats for any of the sports teams. Coaches and players will be glad for the support, and you'll have something for your resumé. When it comes time for college, contact the sports information office to apply for paid or voluntary positions as a statistician for any sport they offer.

The Water Cooler

A recent growth area within sports statistics is the use of hands-on computers to record the actions directly at the game site. This calls for qualified computer operators and software technicians to work the arena or field. Again, the demand for such workers remains limited.

Key Resource

Check out the statistics in sports newsletter at www.stat.duke.edu.

Bed-and-Breakfast Owner

A bed-and-breakfast is a property that serves as a private home for its owners, as well as offering accommodation (and breakfast) to paid guests. B&Bs must meet all health, tax, building, and other business regulations. A country inn might share the characteristics but in addition has a restaurant that serves dinner to guests and/or the public.

B&Bs aren't for everyone—either to stay in or to run. There's a definite "coziness" that goes with the territory, so if you're a stickler for privacy and like having your boundaries, you will probably want to look elsewhere. If, on the other hand, you are truly the "hostess with the mostest" type, who likes nothing better than meeting new people, showing off your hometown and hospitality, and creating a home that's a haven, read on.

Facts and Figures

From a small niche industry a few decades ago, the number of bed and breakfast or "country" style inns in the United States has grown to an estimated 20,000. Although it's an attractive lifestyle, owning and operating a B&B does take a considerable investment of money upfront—not to mention time, effort, and expertise. Average purchase price for an existing B&B in 2002 was just over $650,000, and the average price of a country inn was $1.1 million. If you're thinking of converting an existing residence, the typical cost of renovating rooms (for example, adding a bedroom with bath attached, which is standard in 95 percent of B&B accommodations these days) can run anywhere from $20,000 to $70,000 per room. As with most real estate and buildings costs, this is determined largely by your geographic location.

> **On the Job**
>
> If you're not quite ready to take on inn keeping full time, you can enjoy a taste of the lifestyle and earn some extra money as an "inn sitter" for others, taking care of a property while the owners are away. Pay for this service ranges from $100 to $300 a day.

Job Description

A B&B keeper gets up with the sun, rising early to put coffee on and prepare breakfast for whatever number of guests. During the day you might find yourself occupied with general house duties—changing linens, cleaning rooms, catching up on maintenance or house painting. You know that last-minute rush to clean up before guests arrive? Think of that as your full-time job now. Depending on your location (and the season) you might find yourself out in the garden, or landscaping and keeping the outside of your home in attractive shape. You can expect to be on call or available nearly all the time—because you're the front desk, concierge, and maintenance crew all in one.

Other ongoing tasks involve marketing your business through local tourism associations and other venues and publications, creating a website, helping guests find their way to local attractions, and keeping up with messages and reservations, as well as attending to guests' special needs.

Pay and Perks

The yearly income generated by a B&B varies widely, depending on your location and your average occupancy. The Professional Association of Innkeepers International quotes the standard rates in the northeast and west at $100 to $120 per night, compared to the low $90s in the Midwest and south. Corporate rates are typically about 20 to 25 percent of the standard rate.

If you rent 1 to 4 rooms at about 45 percent occupancy rate, you can expect to generate $42,000 in a year; 5 to 8 rooms at about the same will bring in $111,000, and 9 to 12 rooms at over 50 percent can bring in as much as $245,000. All the numbers, however, are gross—and don't include your outlay in renovation and upkeep, which in early years might mean running a loss. (And bear in mind that some states consider inns with more than six rooms to be hotels, with separate regulations). The expenses of running a home will become tax deductible; for example, cleaning supplies, car expenses, insurance, and so on. But unless you've got some funds to invest, don't expect to earn a living from your hospitality alone.

That said, the personal satisfaction of owning your own business, creating a relaxing and enjoyable atmosphere, and sharing your part of the world with vacationers is a great reward for many people. B&Bs are most often located in a picturesque or otherwise special location, and by default attract folks who are looking to unwind and enjoy. You'll meet people from all over the world, and your efforts to make them feel at home will be much appreciated.

On the Job

The Professional Association of Innkeepers International offers a free Aspiring Innkeeper Kit, a great resource to help you decide if this is really the life for you. For further training the association has also developed a Master Innkeeping program that includes books, workshops, seminars, and apprenticeships to get your feet wet. In addition, many regional tourism boards offer classes in areas like business management for the hospitality industry, which can be a good starting point.

Key Attributes

The B&B owner is a jack-of-all-trades: gracious host or hostess, short-order cook, concierge, and problem solver. You should be handy around the house (and certainly in the kitchen!). You'll need a positive outlook as well as a good instinct for which guests would like your conversation or company, and which guests prefer to be left alone. People skills and a good sense of humor are critical.

Key Tip

This is the kind of career that truly takes over your life, so before taking the big leap or making a major investment, it's a good idea to talk to other innkeepers about their experience. You need to know if you've got the energy and temperament required to open your home to strangers on an ongoing basis—as well as any tips they might have for keeping your own life sane and manageable in the process.

Key Resource

Check out www.paii.org, the Professional Association of Innkeepers International website.

Life Coach

Imagine having a rewarding and high-paying job helping people to achieve success in their careers, relationships, and life. You're their number one "fan" on the sidelines, helping them identify obstacles that might be holding them back from having everything they want in business or life, and you coach them to overcome those challenges.

People use life coaches for the same reason that they use sports coaches: they want someone to work with them, to encourage them, to push them, to help them see the big picture and achieve. Life coaching is something like therapy, but instead of focusing on "issues" or problems, the focus tends to be more proactive, achieving specific goals, objectives, or ambitions in your personal life or career. Are you someone people naturally come to for advice? Do you enjoy talking with people and feel genuine excitement to see them succeed? If the answer is yes—and you think you'd enjoy the freedom of self-employment—perhaps life coaching is the career for you.

Facts and Figures

Hard numbers are difficult to come by, but the business of life coaching is a rapidly expanding field—one of the fastest growing home-based businesses in North America. (It has also spread throughout Europe, Australia, New Zealand, and many parts of Asia.) By some accounts, well over 90 percent of clients report satisfaction with their coaching experience, which bodes well for the continued growth of the field. And as more evidence-based research on the efficacy of coaching becomes available, the profession will continue to grow.

Many successful companies, including Kodak, IBM, and Marriott, hire corporate coaches to help employees reach goals in a variety of areas. Corporate coaches might lead training programs on subjects like executive coaching, burnout reduction, customer service, and maximizing employee performance—for which they can receive thousands of dollars per day. In addition, many coaches augment their practice (and income) by writing and/or speaking at workshops or conferences throughout the year.

On the Job

With the right training (in coaching and business skills) and a consistent effort, you can begin to work with clients and generate income within three to six months—though landing a full roster of clients might take a bit longer. To set up a comfortable and efficient home office and create quality marketing materials (including a website), you should probably budget about $10,000 to $15,000 in your first year. You should find yourself with a profitable business in just a few years.

Job Description

Unlike a therapist, a life coach takes on "clients" rather than "patients." A coach's role is primarily as a facilitator, listening to a client's goals and challenges, asking questions, giving feedback, and helping the client determine solutions for him- or herself.

Many people who hire life coaches are already successful, but want to achieve more. Senior executives, for example, often want the unbiased feedback a coach will give them through executive coaching. Others hire a life coach to help boost their relationships, self-awareness/spirituality, time management, personal organization, weight management, work/life balance, and much more.

In addition to talking with clients in person or over the phone, your tasks would include managing the business side of your practice—aspects such as marketing, scheduling, and administrative tasks—as well as keeping on top of developments in whatever areas you or your clients are especially interested in (for example, health and fitness, corporate culture, relationships, time management, and so on). This might mean going to workshops or meeting with others who work in the field. As with all home-based or personal businesses, it's important to manage your own time so you don't find yourself swamped.

Pay and Perks

The Coach Training Institute reports that on average, a certified, established life coach earns $4,300 a month. A successful full-time life coach can gross around $7,000 a month (that's coaching 20 individual clients a month at $350 per client). And if you maintain 25 executive clients at a slightly higher rate ($500 or so per month) you'd be pulling in $12,500 a month. The good news is that overhead and expenses for a coaching practice tend to be low, running about 15 percent of your intake.

There's definitely money to be made in this growing profession—although the "breakaway" stories are still pretty rare. Approximately 5 percent of coaches earn more than $100,000 a year. The real upsides here are the tremendous flexibility, autonomy, and personal rewards. For most coaches, who face the hard work of doing the business side of running your own practice, setting up shop can be a steep learning curve. But this is also a good thing, because the more you learn, the more confident you become. Coaching can help everyone regardless of their goals, but clients need to be in the right space to want to work on their lives and make positive changes.

On the Job

To get a first-hand perspective, you may want to consider hiring a coach for yourself for a few months. Find out what you think of his or her approach to coaching. Does it work for you? What's the experience of being coached like? Are you seeing real benefits in your life, career, or business? There's no substitute for believing in what you do for a living!

Key Attributes

Life coaches are generally personable, caring, with a genuine passion for helping others succeed. On the business side, marketing know-how and the discipline to budget for and build a profitable independent practice is key.

Key Tip

If you're serious about training to become a life coach, it's important to do your homework. Look for a school or center with strong word of mouth, and one that will train you in person (versus over the phone or Internet). The International Coach Federation, or ICF, has a list of accredited coaching schools around the country, which is a good place to start.

Key Resource

Look up the International Coach Federation at www.coachfederation.org.

Inventor

The days of Thomas Edison or Benjamin Franklin making remarkable solo discoveries might be long gone. Most modern-day inventions are more likely to come from a high-powered team at Hitachi, IBM, or Sony, and revolve around some ever-more-esoteric software or computer product. Still—as anyone with an iPod can tell you—there are always new and exciting ideas that capture the public imagination just waiting to be brought to life.

That said, there's a significant gulf between an idea and an invention. Ideas, as most of us know, are a dime a dozen. If you can take that daydream to the next level, by designing a workable mock-up with real-world applications, you're one step closer to having a bona-fide invention on your hands. The odds of discovering or developing something genuinely novel in this world might seem terribly long, but for a certain type of person, the romance of being a true pioneer is enough to keep tinkering whether by mouse or by hand.

Facts and Figures

Patents, Trademarks, and Copyrights are three distinct types of intellectual property protection, each of which serves a different purpose. Patents protect inventions, and improvements to existing inventions. Trademarks include any word, name, symbol, or device, or any combination, used, or intended to be used in commerce to identify and distinguish the goods of one manufacturer or seller from goods manufactured or sold by others, and to indicate the source of the goods.

In February 2005 the Patent Office awarded the 500,000th design patent, for Daimler-Chrysler Corporation's Crossfire convertible design. (Design patents are granted for new, original, or ornamental designs for articles of manufacture; these patents provide exclusive rights to their owners for a term of 14 years from the date of issuance). In fiscal year 2004 over 16,500 design patents were issued.

Copyrights protect literary, artistic, and musical works (these are issued through the U.S. Copyright Office). Check out *The Pocket Idiot's Guide to Copyrights* for more information.

In 2004, the International Business Machine Corporation Company (IBM) topped the list of private sector patent recipients with the U.S. Patent Office for the second year in a row, with some 3,248 patents awarded to the firm. Due to the soaring costs of engineering and development, the lion's share of today's invention takes place in corporate labs and R&D departments, but 20 percent of U.S. patents each year are issued to private inventors. So a skilled inventor can still turn good ideas into a respectable sum of money, with the satisfaction of using his or her own ingenuity.

Job Description

Having a background in science or engineering is practically required to succeed in this field. Many aspiring inventors spend years working as designers for private corporations before they develop the ideas that enable them to set out on their own. To acquire the skills of a successful inventor, it helps to have several years' experience in industry or academic research, as well as some background in product design and development. Knowledge of a new product's potential market is also important.

A great idea is just the beginning; it's the crucial next step, known as "reduction to practice," that tends to distinguish the seriously inventive minds. Before you can attempt to sell or license your product, or apply for a patent, you'll need to design and build a prototype or write up a thoroughly detailed description of how your idea or product actually works.

The world of invention is too uncertain to provide a full-time living to all but the most exceptional few. The time and costs involved in developing new products is simply prohibitive; and income doesn't flow until a marketable prototype is complete. Most inventors hang on to their day jobs in engineering, corporate research, or academia. But that's not to say all those hours in the basement workshop won't pay off someday.

Pay and Perks

Because there is so much trial and error involved, often over a number of years, there's no real way to estimate salary for this career. Many inventors continue to work as research scientists and engineers while they develop their ideas, and these are the fields that most return to if they are unable to support themselves as inventors. Many return to inventing over and over again, accumulating successes and failures over many years. The first idea an inventor develops is often not his best idea, and the experience gained with each try can be invaluable to later efforts.

One breakout idea can net you hundreds of thousands (even millions) of dollars, but another might languish in the almost-ran category. The "science" of invention is part practical and part mystery—with a big dose of timing thrown in the mix. But for most truly inventive types, the problem-solving process excites them as much or more than the reward, and it's the elusive "answer" at the end of the line that keeps them sustained.

As author and highly successful inventor Raymond Kurzweil has said, "The thing that excites me the most is having an impact on people's lives."

The Water Cooler

Each May the Intel Corporation sponsors The Intel International Science and Engineering Fair (Intel ISEF), the world's largest pre-college celebration of science. The Intel ISEF brings together over 1,300 students from 40 or so different countries to compete for scholarships, tuition grants, internships, scientific field trips, and the grand prize: a $50,000 college scholarship. Science Service founded the ISEF in 1950 and is proud to have Intel as the title sponsor of this prestigious, international competition.

Key Attributes

You must be patient, persistent, and skilled at logic and problem solving. A science and engineering background is practically a must.

Key Tip

A great read for the would-be inventor is *The Age of Intelligent Machines*, by Raymond C. Kurzweil, MIT grad, high-tech visionary, and inventor of the Kurzweil 1000 computer system (among other things), a pattern-recognition machine and the first print-to-speech computer to read to the blind. Kurzweil's machine is now used in thousands of schools around the country by blind students, who scan a book into the computer and can listen as the machine reads it out loud.

Key Resource

The best place to look is the U.S. Patent & Trademark Office, which can be found online at www.uspto.gov.

The Least You Need to Know

- ◆ It takes a great deal of confidence in yourself to bid the corporate world good-bye and set up shop in your own home. Don't get me wrong—it's highly doable. But you really have to want it.

- ◆ One thing you might miss when working at home is the camaraderie of the office culture. You'll spend more time alone as a home-based business owner, and that might take some getting used to.

- ◆ To expand your network of clients—especially local ones—join organizations like the Chamber of Commerce. There you'll meet other business folks and plant the seed for future business relationships.

- ◆ Make sure you talk to an accountant about the many business deductions you are entitled to as a home-based business owner.

I'm Gonna Make It After All: Entrepreneur

In This Chapter

- ◆ A word on entrepreneurship
- ◆ Providing personal service as a concierge
- ◆ Coffee shops and juice bars
- ◆ Off course: backyard putting greens
- ◆ Opening your own restaurant or bookstore

To be honest, every job in this book has a bit of the entrepreneur in it; a piece of that "You, Inc." mindset that I talked about in the opening chapters of this book.

But the following jobs are real solo efforts—things you do on your own, with your fortunes depending on nobody but yourself.

A good entrepreneur doesn't mind that sort of pressure. He or she knows that pressure goes with the territory, but so do the rewards.

So dive in and take a look at the following careers, where the difference between success and failure is you and you alone. But I'm betting on success.

Concierge

The concierge business is all about personal service. What was once the domain of top-class hotels and resorts has entered the corporate (and even individual) mainstream, with an increasing number of opportunities for people who like to make their clients feel like VIPs.

Concierges find their services in more demand than ever these days—not just by top executives, but by plenty of regular folks who just don't have time to take care of everything outside of work. An increasing number of companies are offering their employees concierge services, in an effort to attract and maintain the best workers. A professional concierge can help these folks feel productive and organized, focus on other priorities, and find out that the star treatment feels pretty good.

Facts and Figures

The number of concierge firms serving time-starved clients is growing rapidly, as working people feel more and more squeezed. Companies from Chicago to San Francisco reported growth rates of as much as 50 percent annually during the boom years of the late 1990s. By the end of the decade, membership in the National Association of Professional Organizers (which includes those who provide concierge services) had reached 1,100.

 **On the Job** _____

Before you get started, you'll need to figure out just what your niche will be. Will you cater strictly to corporate clients? Will you specialize in certain areas or serve as an all-around "go to" guy or gal? Whether it's scoring tickets to concerts or special events, booking a table at some exclusive restaurant, or simply running everyday errands, take some time to consider what kinds of services suit your personality—and serve the needs of the clients you're most likely to land.

Job Description

There's no such thing as a typical day in the life of a concierge—which is why so many people enjoy the work. Your raison d'etre is simple convenience; the job description is essentially to take care of those tasks the client can't handle him- or herself. These might include making dinner reservations or buying a gift; going grocery shopping; making travel or relocation arrangements; picking up dry cleaning; performing housekeeping duties; or waiting in lines. The list could go on and on, depending on the type of client you target (corporate CEO versus a soccer mom).

Your days will likely be full and fast-paced; because you're helping someone else keep to their hectic schedule, it's important that you keep to yours.

Pay and Perks

There is no set range of fees here, because services and types of clients can vary quite widely. On average, a personal concierge can expect to earn anywhere from $40,000 to $60,000 a year, depending on how many clients he takes on and the range of services he offers. In addition, concierges often receive tips or gifts from grateful clients. Some professionals bill by the hour; others use a monthly retainer or charge a "membership" fee based on how many requests they tend to receive in a typical month or a year. (An annual membership for an individual or family might run $1,000 to $1,500 per year; but for a corporation with multiple employees making many requests every month, it could run as high as $5,000.) More employees, and therefore more frequent requests, could drive this fee even higher.

Among the biggest perks is the constantly changing nature of the work—a concierge will rarely have the same day twice. You'll also get to meet all kinds of people, and feel gratified to see them happier and more relaxed as a result of your efforts.

On the Job

Fortunately, start-up costs for a personal concierge business are minimal. Your main need is a computer (to print up fliers and labels for a mailing list). You'll need the services of a good graphic designer and printer to have brochures and/or business cards made. A clear, attractive website—which doesn't cost much to build these days—is also a must.

Key Attributes

You must be highly organized and responsive, possess a professional demeanor, and be able to juggle multiple tasks with good grace.

Key Tip

Word of mouth is the best way to promote this type of business, so you'll want to alert family, friends, and as many other businesses as possible about your concierge venture. In the beginning, you might even volunteer your services or offer them at discounted rates, just to get your foot in the door and obtain valuable client referrals. Those are the gold currency of this work.

Key Resource

Check out the National Concierge Association, a Chicago-based group founded in the late 1990s as a networking and resource organization for both personal and hotel concierges (www.conciergeassoc.org).

Clown

It looks pretty simple: apply a bit of makeup, find a crazy wig, oversized shoes, and a few prop balloons, and bingo! Who couldn't pull off being a clown? But the real art of this profession is something much more; it's a kind of philosophy. At its most fundamental, performing as a clown is about coaxing a smile from a stranger, making people (regardless of age) lighten up, distracting them from the everyday, even bringing out the absurd through your performance.

On the Job

Before getting started, give some thought to your area of specialty. The amount you invest in time, planning, props, and preparation will determine how successful your business is and what kinds of materials you need to run your business. Do you need to rent or purchase a curtain, magic box, sound system, or even portable stage?

Facts and Figures

There are myriad types of clowns: whiteface clowns, "classic" clowns, tramp or hobo clowns, and European clowns (think Cirque de Solei).

Clowns work on their own, hiring out for kids' parties and community events, or are hired by companies and entertainment groups, like casinos and, yes, circuses.

McDonalds, for example, is a big market for professional clowns. According to marketing experts, McDonald's employs some 250 or so Ronald McDonalds worldwide. Each major market in the

United States boasts at least one Ronald; big cities might have several. The explosion of McDonald's franchises worldwide has turned this clown gig into a steady one. An average "Ronald" might show up at a local restaurant twice a year and spend the rest of the time on the road making appearances at schools, hospitals, nursing homes, shopping malls, and so on. He might be booked a full year in advance.

Job Description

A clown is a professional who loves entertaining, and isn't afraid to act silly if it will make someone feel better. A clown is a professional mood enhancer, one who shows other people how to find the humor in life.

Professional clowning skills can run the gamut: some clowns are storytellers; some are face-painters; some are balloon artists; some are magicians; some perform skits or physical humor; some do it all. Every one of these skills involves patience and practice. As with any other type of performance, it's mostly in the details. Getting the right kind of training and staying in character are both key.

To really get this stuff down, your best bet is to attend a clown school; there are also conferences and workshops all over the country, along with a plethora of books to help with skits, face painting, balloons, and the other skills. You might also want to find a clown mentor to work with you. Developing a persona and learning new skills is an ongoing process, and in order to continue landing new gigs, you'll need to add new skits, tricks, and routines to your shows.

Pay and Perks

Pay scale for this job is all over the map, so you should check with other clowns in similar-size towns or cities. You can also figure different pricing based on your area of expertise. If you're a "birthday party clown" and in charge of someone's entire party—from bringing treats and party favors to setting up and cleaning up—you would charge more than one who simply shows up to perform. Often the clowns who work at fairs, carnivals, and restaurants are earning only tips, which makes it a challenge. If you can land a big corporate client, they usually pay a flat fee for a show.

As for Ronald McDonald, he is usually played by actors, or ex-Ringling Bros. clowns or teachers, and makes about $40,000 a year. A busy Ronald, working 400 shows a year, can make close to $100,000; the highest-paid Ronald (the one in all the national commercials) would earn more than $300,000, according to former employees.

The Water Cooler

Clowns have an interesting history, and it's well worth a bit of studying to learn the basic "types" and which one might best suit your personality. You'll need to learn how to apply your makeup, and to identify the right sort of costume—which is an essential piece of your performance. Take a look at some; study professional and/or award-winning clowns, and you'll see right away the distinct difference in their appearance.

Clowning is a fun business, and it can be successful if handled with the same discipline and care you would give any small business. It's not necessarily a lucrative field, but the perks of being your own boss, dressing in a crazy costume, and bringing joy into the lives of children and grown-ups alike is often reward enough.

Key Attributes

Be enthusiastic and outgoing, with excellent interpersonal skills. A clown must be "on" at all times when he or she is in makeup.

Key Tip

Local clown clubs sometimes have their own training classes. It's worth a look around your area, because these can help you get a solid foundation at a very reasonable price—plus you'll get an experienced clown (or clowns) at your side, ready to assist you in your development.

Key Resource

Check out the Clowns of America International website (www.coai.org).

Coffee Shop Owner

It looks like a breeze—getting paid to hang out in a place you already love, surrounded by the smell of freshly brewed coffee.

But as with any small business, there's a tremendous amount of work behind the scenes, to create a setting that's cozy and welcoming—and make it look effortless. When the product you're selling costs an average of $2 a pop, you've got to generate significant turnover to make it work. In the increasingly competitive world of big chains with well-established economies of scale, the independent coffee shop operator faces a challenge just to stay afloat in many communities.

Facts and Figures

If you live in a big city and can't start your day without a latte, this might surprise you: only 14 percent of Americans drink some kind of "specialty" coffee. This means that—although some areas seem to be super-saturated with ultra cool coffee bars—there's a great deal of market share still out there to be developed.

Starbucks spends $320,000 on average to open a new shop. You will likely be working with much less—so it's imperative to make it go far.

On the Job

To survive in the era of Starbucks, it's a must to add value to the customer. Think of ways you can attract customers in your particular market: free copy of *The New York Times* or local magazines? Wireless Internet service? Changing art on the walls? Other marketing tools are frequent customer cards or pre-paid "gift" cards, to help speed service and build loyalty.

Job Description

In the beginning, at least, you can expect to put in long hours. Customer service is the key to this business, so you'll need to do the homework on what your customers like (types, flavors, and regions of coffee), not to mention staff training, making up schedules, marketing your business, and paying bills. To compete with the bigger chains, many local shop owners spend time rearranging the interior, painting walls, moving furniture, and changing art work or décor to maintain a warm and inviting retail space. You'll need to maintain equipment and keep an eye on your set-up and work flow system to keep customers moving in and out quickly. The time commitment is serious, but the rewards can be great.

Pay and Perks

Even in the shadow of the mega chains, there are hundreds of successful independent coffee concept operators all over the country. An independent shop can bring in between $200,000 and $500,000 a year in sales—but that's before subtracting staff costs, rent, and overhead. More indie shops earn a profit of around 10 to 15 percent on their gross sales, so with a decent location and a well run shop you can expect to profit something in the range of $50,000 to $75,000, and sometimes more.

It's important to be realistic—the financial rewards of this business are hardly eye-popping, and the stress of owning your own business is ever-present, but the satisfaction of running your own place for most entrepreneurs is priceless.

Key Attributes

You should be a hard working, energetic, organized person with great people skills.

Key Tip

Customer satisfaction is the name of the game, so do your legwork and find out what other shops in your area are (or aren't) offering that people would like to see. Wireless Internet access? Late evening hours? Live music or spoken word performance? Drive-through service? More sandwiches or desserts?

On the Job

Location, location, location. Like the real estate agent said—it's the single most important factor for the success of a retail coffee business as well. Among the most prime spots are: college towns (ideally near a book shop); downtown business districts with high density and walking traffic; older neighbors being renovated or revived; unattached buildings on a high-traffic road; visible corner locations, whether in a city block or a strip mall—any place your business will stand out and be easy to reach. Also keep in mind the opportunity to add a cart or small kiosk to an existing business somewhere.

Key Resource

Be sure to check out www.espressobusiness.com.

Juice Bar Owner

Back in 1999, *Entrepreneur Magazine* called juice and smoothie bars one of the hot new trends for the future—and it appears they were right. In addition to successful franchises like Jamba Juice, Smoothie King, and Zuka Juice, a growing number of independent juice bars are popping up in local communities around the country—proving this was more than a short-lived, west coast fad.

Nearly everything about this business is appealing—you offer a healthy and colorful (and delicious) range of products. You're providing a service for customers who want to take care of themselves. It's a feel-good business with an even more attractive bottom line, for those who find the right recipe for success.

Facts and Figures

Jamba Juice, one of the most successful franchises of its kind, opened its first location in northern California in 1990, known as the Juice Club. These days the company boasts more than 430 stores nationwide, and has partnership agreements with developers in Hawaii, Florida, the Midwest, and Texas. In addition, Jamba Juice has licensing agreements with Whole Foods Markets and also operates stores on college campuses and in airport locations across the country.

Smoothie King, another leading franchiser, has more than 340 franchises in 34 states. For a $25,000 single unit franchise fee, you can join their growing family of smoothie bars.

As the industry evolves, you'll see more "fusion" concepts, combining the juice and smoothie bar model with other products such as coffee, espresso, salads, soups, and wraps.

The proper information, training, support, and connections can save you hundreds of hours and thousands of dollars and will help you be more profitable. For example, if you don't design the equipment flow correctly, you will be less efficient in the kitchen area. If you aren't efficient, you will be giving slow service or will need to hire more staff to prepare the products quickly.

> **Balancing Act**
>
> A major element of entrepreneurship is recognizing that it involves inherent risks. Failure is always a possibility. The success stories are those who do their homework to minimize risks, learn to be adaptable, and make sure to learn something from them when mistakes happen (as at some time or another, they will).

Job Description

As the owner of a juice bar (or franchisee) your start-up duties might involve site location, product development, construction, and design, as well as hiring employees, complying with government codes, banking, marketing, providing great customer service, ordering products, and much more. You'll become very familiar with the standard equipment—blenders and a juice machine—as well as with nutritional information that might prove useful to your customers (i.e., what combination of fruits or "boosts" provide specific health benefits).

Pay and Perks

Any entrepreneurial venture is a gamble, so the pay range will vary widely. Much depends on your geographic location and the amount of traffic you can attract. A successful juice and smoothie bar can bring in $200,000 (and sometimes much more) in sales per year—so if you keep things efficient, and your overhead low, you'll be looking at a comfortable living. (And if you're able to branch out to additional locations, you'll see that revenue rise even more.)

> **On the Job**
>
> If you live in an area where a franchise has a really strong name, there may be value in forking over the monthly royalty to share that brand appeal. But if no such industry leader exists in your town, it might be best to consider a juice bar consultant, who can help you get set up without costly royalties.

The perks are those of any private business; self-employment can be scary, but it gives you an enviable degree of freedom and control.

Key Attributes

You must have a strong work ethic, be persistent, and enjoy solving problems.

Key Tip

Visit as many juice bars as you can find, keeping an eye out for their set-up, customer service, and menu options. What works well in Seattle might need adjustments to succeed in Savannah. If you've already seen a juice bar that seems perfect for your market, ask around and find out if that company's franchising, and whether or not they've got one in your area. If, on the other hand, you feel you've got a unique and workable concept all your own, and would need only minimal direction, you should consider a restaurant consulting firm to help you with the details.

Key Resource

Check out the information at Juice and Smoothie Bar Consulting online at www.juiceconsult.com.

Backyard Putting Green Installer

Having your own private putting green might once have seemed like the golfer's ultimate luxury—reserved for the pros or the spoiled CEO. But these days you'll find more and more of these artificial-turf greens turning up in ordinary suburban developments. Advances in technology have made them easier to install and care for and have produced synthetic greens of remarkably high quality. Greens can be designed with any variety of breaks and sways to truly challenge putt-reading ability. Artificial greens can be installed in most spots, even indoors.

It's a booming market with no sign of a slowdown in sight, thanks to golf's tremendous surge in popularity, and to the growing number of baby boomers who are willing to spend their leisure time and their disposable income in pursuit of a par.

For landscape contractors, and for others with a passion for the game and a willingness to apply it, the installation of backyard putting greens is a fun and profitable field to pursue.

Facts and Figures

From affordable, D-I-Y projects to lavish, high-end creations, putting greens can be installed in a number of different ways. For an initial cost of around $500 you could put in a 1,000-square-foot, non-USGA-approved bentgrass putting green. Starting at $10,000, a professional company will decorate your yard with synthetic greens that require no more maintenance gear than a snow shovel or leaf blower. From basic putting greens to elaborate, par-3 courses with multiple sand traps and greens, costs can easily reach six figures as amateur duffers indulge their inner Tiger Woods.

> ### The Water Cooler
>
> Some putting green installers have reported a rise in sales of well more than 200 percent in a year. And it's unlikely that the current boom is a passing phenomenon. There are nearly 30 million golfers in the United States, and golf is one sport that consumers spend more money on as they age—so that business could very well explode in the coming decades as baby boomers age and retire.

Job Description

Putting greens are a high-end landscape offering, so landscapers that hope to get into this line need training in how to design and build them. A putting green really has two main ingredients—the best artificial turf product and workmanship, and the design of the sub-base. Good synthetic turf costs up to $4 a square foot, but it's essential for a quality product. You begin with design, customizing the shape and pitch of the green so that it "flows" with the yard you have (and can ensure proper drainage). After you've removed the topsoil—using herbicide to kill any remaining roots—you install the sub-base (which might be limestone, decomposed granite, or rock dust). Then you dig holes for the cups, and lay the artificial turf over the surface—a little bit like laying carpet. After you've cut holes for the cups, you have a putting green. The whole process usually takes three to seven days, depending on the size of the green and degree of customization.

Word-of-mouth is the ideal tool for marketing this kind of business. But you'll still want to work on some simple, quality marketing materials (brochures, a website, and so on) and stay up-to-date with landscapers in your area to see what they're offering. Many who install putting greens say they welcome others getting into the game, as it helps spread the word and supply what is a rapidly growing demand among recreational golfers.

In addition, artificial turf is increasingly being used in a variety of other applications including playing fields and country clubs, which opens up some lucrative new markets for landscape contractors. Some are even designing and building golf driving cages in addition to greens.

Pay and Perks

Salaries in this field vary depending on your experience and the size of the job, but are generally very healthy. Backyard greens typically run from 300 to 500 square feet, and take a couple of days to install. You might establish a $2,500 minimum charge, based on $12 to $21 per square foot.

Key Attributes

You must have passion, a streak of perfectionism, and an eye for detail.

Above and beyond that, you should have a passion for golf and for golfers. After all, you'll be dealing with the type of golf fanatic who sticks a putting green in his back yard. A good comfort level for landscape design is also very helpful.

Key Tip

As a landscape contractor, finding the right artificial turf company to provide materials can be an important key to your success. These providers might serve in a partnership or distribution capacity, so it's important to ask that company questions before you commit. Find out what kind of training they offer to distributors, what their upfront and ongoing costs are, and whether they provide sales leads or marketing support (in the form of videos or brochures).

On the Job

Installing backyard putting greens makes sense for landscape contractors, as it uses many of the same tools required for the contracting trade. Still, proper training is essential. Having the credentials for both can be a big asset in selling your services to customers.

Key Resource

Visit www.putting-greens.com.

Restaurant Owner

Owning your own restaurant is a dream job for so many people it's almost become a cliché. (Just think of all the celebrities you've read of lately opening up their own "joint" … and imagine how many are actually sweating it out on the fry line, or hustling to greet guests on a busy weekend night).

But as anyone who's ever worked in a restaurant knows, there's a tremendous amount of work behind any successful operation. The odds are against you, the hours are brutal, the stress can be unrelenting—and yet for some, the satisfaction of serving that perfect meal, nailing that five-star review, or just seeing a full house of grateful customers somehow makes up for it all.

Facts and Figures

According to the National Restaurant Association, this industry employs over 12.2 million Americans—making it the largest category of employer in the United States, behind the government. There are more than 900,000 restaurant locations in the country (which includes everything from fine dining to snack establishments). Their projected sales for 2005 were over $476 billion, which represents 4 percent of the U.S. Gross Domestic Product (and an almost 5 percent increase from the previous year).

Most eating and drinking establishments are small businesses, employing between two and ten people on average; and more than seven out of ten are independent operations.

> **On the Job** _____
>
> Start-up costs for a restaurant depend on the type of place you're looking to open, the facility you've chosen, how much equipment you'll need (and whether you purchase it new or used), your inventory, your marketing costs, and your necessary operating capital (i.e., how much you need to stay afloat until your business starts generating cash). Just like a house, a restaurant can be a money pit, and it's possible to spend hundreds of thousands just getting a place off the ground. On the other hand, you can start with a small-scale operation like a bakery or café, find an inherited space and equipment, and focus your funding on inventory. Think hard about the kind of commitment you're willing to make, financially as well as emotionally, before tearing down walls or installing a courtyard with fountain.

Job Description

There's hardly a typical workday for a restaurateur, but the atmosphere you inhabit will depend largely on the type of establishment you plan to run. Restaurants are generally classified into three categories: quick-service, midscale, and upscale. Quick-service restaurants (also known as fast-food restaurants) offer limited menus, quick preparation, and low prices. The atmosphere is casual, and many feature take-out service or a drive-through window in some locations.

Midscale restaurants fall somewhere in between fast food and upscale, offering full, sit-down meals at a price that most would consider affordable. Characteristics of midscale restaurants can vary widely; some offer the full dining room/wait staff experience, others have counters for ordering food. Some limited-service restaurants offer salad bars and buffets.

Finally, an upscale restaurant delivers just what the name implies: formal table service and fine cuisine with an emphasis on sophistication and ambiance.

Regardless of what kind of restaurant you plan to start, the best way to learn the ropes is to work for a similar operation for a while before striking out on your own. Doing so will give you invaluable insight into the realities and day-to-day logistics of the business. Ordering inventory, developing menus, balancing books, and managing marketing and promotions are just a few of your primary responsibilities. You've also got to keep your establishment in compliance with myriad local, state, and federal regulations. Hiring, training, and scheduling personnel—in a field with notoriously high turnover—is one of the biggest challenges by far for the restaurateur, at any level.

Pay and Perks

According to the National Restaurant Association, average unit sales in 2002 were $730,000 at full service restaurants and $619,000 at limited-service restaurants. More than three out of five foodservice managers have annual household incomes of $50,000 or more.

The Water Cooler

The National Restaurant Association reports that the overall economic impact of the restaurant industry is expected to exceed $1.2 trillion in 2005, including sales in related industries such as agriculture, transportation, and manufacturing. Every dollar spent by consumers in restaurants generates an additional $1.98 spent in other industries allied with the restaurant industry. Every additional $1 million in restaurant sales generates an additional 42 jobs for the nation's economy.

Because of the unusual hours and single-minded dedication involved with most restaurateurs, this is a job most people get into for reasons other than money. It's a lifestyle all its own—and definitely not for everyone—but for those genuinely driven foodies who relish the experience and ceremony of bringing people together over a meal, there's nothing they would rather do.

Key Attributes

You need lots of energy, enthusiasm, adaptability, and a genuine passion for food and delivering a first-rate dining experience.

Key Tip

To help lessen the intense workload of opening a new restaurant, find a suitable partner to go in with you on the business plan. You might choose someone who has financial resources and wants to roll up his or her sleeves and get involved in the business. Or you might find someone with the funds to invest but no interest in actually running the place. (Either way has its advantages.) Just be sure to draw up a written partnership agreement that clearly defines your respective responsibilities and obligations.

Key Resource

You'll definitely want to visit www.restaurantreport.com.

Computer Consultant

These days the term *computer consultant* can mean almost anything—from the tech-savvy guy down the hall who helps his neighbor install a new package of store-bought software, to the high-priced expert called in to devise a new IT strategy for a Fortune 500 firm. Computers in general—and PCs in particular—have come to play such a large role in our lives that it's hard to imagine how we'd survive without them. Hence, the need for this category of on-call experts to diagnose when something's gone wrong, to advise on the most appropriate system for a particular business or service, or to help make the best use of the technology a company already has.

Not surprisingly, the demand for these services is growing dramatically. Everyone from the blue chip companies to the mom-and-pop store on the corner makes use of computers these days—and because the vast majority of small to medium businesses can't afford a full-time tech guru, a consultant offers the perfect solution. If you've got what it takes to be a "geek for hire," you can earn a good living while enjoying the freedom of the contractor's life.

Facts and Figures

The Independent Computer Consultants Association (ICCA) is a national not-for-profit association based in St. Louis, with chapters in most major metropolitan areas representing nearly a thousand consulting firms nationwide. A recent survey of some of its active members revealed that more than 75 percent were over 30 years old and 69 percent had been in the computer field for at least five years before they became consultants. They're a well-educated bunch, on the whole, with more than 80 percent having graduated from college, and a third having earned a Master's degree (though only a quarter of their degrees were computer related).

Job Description

As a computer consultant, you're the on-call whiz kid who helps keep your clients' critical information systems up and running all the time. As a freelancer, you'll be making house calls to any number and variety of businesses, depending on your area of expertise and client base. Establishing an ongoing relationship with a few key customers will make your life (and theirs) much easier and more productive. Many companies pay their consultant a retainer good for a few hours per month so they can call up with specific questions or request equipment upgrades. You'll need to communicate to your clients how you can help them in their day-to-day operations—and be sure your own schedule allows you the flexibility to work within their parameters.

> **On the Job**
>
> You might want to supplement your resumé (and your income) by writing articles for tech magazines or publications or presenting seminars or workshops. These kinds of side projects not only bring in extra money, but they can help to expand your network for both clients and subcontractors. Having your byline in print is instant credibility.

No matter how busy you are, you should always spend some of your time bringing in new business. Only you can decide how much time is enough for this, and what will enable you to maintain an even flow of projects without getting overwhelmed. As a consultant, you might be surprised how little of your time is actually spent in "billable hours" (that's why your rates are so high!). There's just no escaping those clerical/administrative functions. A certain amount of time must be spent doing administrative functions, such as billing and taxes. Another portion of your work must be spent in staying up-to-date with current developments in the industry and with software and hardware innovations.

Pay and Perks

Because you'll mostly be working on-site at your clients' locations, you might not need an outside office in the beginning. This helps keep your overhead low as a start-up consultant. Setting up an exclusive work area in your residence lets you deduct home office expenses from your taxes, which also helps. At most, you'll be spending a few thousand dollars on advertising and marketing materials as you get started. But with the right approach and follow-up, you can break even in a short time (and certainly less than a year).

On the Job _____

In the beginning it's important to do some legwork and find out what types of customers are out there and in need of your services. Generally it's best to target mid-size corporations when you're marketing yourself as a consultant. (The bigger ones probably have someone on payroll and smaller companies may not have the money to hire you.) You should also take a good look at your strengths and expertise. Do you have a particular specialty or are you more of a jack-of-all-trades? Do you have knowledge or experience that lends itself to a specific industry (travel, transportation, accounting)? Think about what kinds of businesses are in your area and whether you can afford to stay local—or if you need to cast your net wide. Guru.com is just one of the places you can advertise you services to a national audience.

Salary range within this field is quite broad; an established computer consultant might bring in revenues ranging from $50,000 to $250,000 a year (before expenses and taxes). A small number of independent consultants will net more than $100,000 a year—but many more fall in the $40,000 to $80,000 range. Some are tempted to grow into a larger-scale operation, and take a percentage of everything earned by their employees. But growing your small business at the right pace can be tricky. And for most it's the intellectual challenge of tackling technical problems, along with the freedom of running their own firm, that's the prize.

Key Attributes

Be personable and quick thinking, with an aptitude for problem solving.

Key Tip

No one person can possibly keep up with all there is to know about computers, so it's important to have a list of "lifelines" or contacts in the industry who can help you when a question falls outside your expertise (university professors often freelance as consultants). You might want to put your subcontractors on the payroll, or simply put your client in touch with your outside expert and let them do the talking. You might not see payback right away, but the long-term karma earned can be well worth your efforts. Not only will your resourcefulness build good will with your client, but the other consultant is likely to return the favor when he or she needs someone with your expertise.

Key Resource

Read *The Computer Consultant's Guide: Real-Life Strategies for Building a Successful Consulting Career* (John Wiley, 1994) by Janet Ruhl.

Used Bookstore Owner

Are you the type who can spend hours in contented contemplation in a bookshop? Does the idea of being surrounded with objects you love, or helping some fellow bibliophile find a long-lost first edition or discover a new favorite author, seem like the ideal way to make a living? It's not easy in this age of giant chain retailers, but there is a core of dedicated book lovers just like you for whom the search is as much fun as the ultimate purchase. If you're a bookworm with some business sense, an outgoing attitude, and the energy it takes to tackle a start-up project, read on.

Facts and Figures

Ideally, a used bookstore needs a market population of at least 50,000 people to support it. Your inventory should start at around 10,000 books when you open—which means you'll do an awful lot of purchasing upfront. A good rule of thumb when purchasing is to spend no more than 25 percent of the new price for a mint condition hardcover book (and buy only those you're fairly certain will sell), and no more than 10 percent of the new price for a mint condition used paperback.

Typical start-up costs for a 1,000 to 1,500 square foot store range from $10,000 to $25,000 or more (including rent, utilities, insurance, inventory, advertising, and so on). Monthly operational costs can run anywhere from $4,000 to $8,000.

It's best to locate your store in a "high traffic" area, as near as possible to a college or university campus. Something to bear in mind is the shopping habits of the average used book buyer: first, he is a browser. He notices your shop, drops in, and begins looking around to see what kind of books you have available. If he spots something that really interests him, he'll

On the Job

Your store hours should match those of neighboring businesses. A good tip for a bookstore owner is to open half an hour or so before your neighbors, use the extra time to do paperwork, and get organized for the day. This way, all the early shoppers will stop in to your store to browse and kill time while waiting for the other shops to open.

probably buy then and there. If not, and provided you've made him feel comfortable this first time in your store, he'll be back—dropping in to browse whenever he's in the area.

Job Description

Most used bookstore owners begin with their own book collections as start-up inventory base. You might also cull donations from friends, family, and neighbors (everyone's got some old books they would love to clear out of the house). From here, you would start making the rounds of garage sales, flea markets, and so on in your area. Thrift shops, Goodwill stores, Salvation Army outlets, and church bazaars are other places to visit. Also keep an eye out for estate sales, which can provide you with valuable rarities and sometimes with "complete" libraries.

With practice and experience you'll learn to quickly assess a book's condition and what price it will command. You'll develop the intuition you need to realize a profit on every book you buy—the ultimate goal here.

On the Job

Once you have your location selected, paint the inside of your store in a warm, comforting shade. Your lighting should be indirect, and somewhat subdued, to give the store a cozy feeling. Be sure your checkout counter doesn't block easy entry or exit from your store; you want customers to feel comfortable just visiting. Do everything you can to encourage the browser, because these are the proven book buyers. Give them time to fall in love with your store and selection, and they are sure to be back.

Equally important to the used bookstore owner is hiring qualified staff. These people must be passionate about books and can provide excellent service to customers, marketing your business in a cost-efficient manner, handling invoices and accounting, and maintaining a balance of inventory, so you're never under- or overstocked.

Pay and Perks

Start-up risks can be high, with three years being the average time needed to become firmly established. After that "becoming established" stage, however, you should be able to enjoy ownership of a business without extreme market fluctuations, plus an income close to $50,000 per year or more.

Lots of used bookstores augment their income by running mail order (and increasingly, Internet) operations in addition to their "bricks and mortar" business. These days there are more and more avenues to sell your inventory through big-name websites like Amazon, Half.com, and countless others.

The risks of starting a used bookstore are high for the dreamer unaware that it's just another retail business and should be handled as such. Well organized and operated used book stores can provide a very comfortable income for the owner-operator willing to persist through the start-up period.

Key Attributes

You must love books, of course. You also must have strong attention to detail and lots of energy and perseverance.

Key Tip

More important than a fancy window display is a clean window area that allows passers-by to see into your store. You want to create an inviting atmosphere that leads people to join the others already browsing inside.

Key Resource

Go to www.bookhunterpress.com for some great information about starting your own used bookstore.

The Least You Need to Know

- ◆ Good entrepreneurs have a "failure is not an option" mindset.
- ◆ With many of these jobs, you'll need to create a business plan stating what your company is going to do, how it's going to be funded, and how you plan on attracting customers. It's a blueprint for your business that you can refer to, time and time again.

◆ In entrepreneurial endeavors, you're the boss. That means you accept responsibility for your company: hiring, firing, revenue, liability. One idea: bring good legal council aboard. You may not need legal advice all the time, but having a trusted source to go to is worth its weight in gold.

◆ Have fun. As an entrepreneur, you are your own boss. You get to follow your passion. Don't lose sight of that as you get more deeply involved in the day-to-day operations of your company.

Part

Mind, Body, and Soul

Woody Allen once said that reality has its contradictions, but it's still the only place to get a good steak.

So it goes in the spirituality sector—a marketplace with plenty of opportunities for those who are able to tap into their souls and provide spiritual sustenance to people starving for it.

In this section, I'll show you jobs that feed the mind, nourish the soul, and lift the spirit. These jobs are immensely fulfilling, emotionally enriching, and in many cases, financially rewarding.

So tap into your Zen and take a look for yourself.

Tell Me Where It Hurts: Health and Spirituality

In This Chapter

- ◆ Careers in the health and spirituality sector

- ◆ Helping others through hypnotherapy

- ◆ The growing massage therapy field

- ◆ Organizing others' living space as a Feng Shui consultant

- ◆ Magic as a profession

"My brain? It's my second favorite organ."—Woody Allen

The matter of the mind—and how it impacts all of us in ways that mental health experts are just beginning to understand—is big business these days.

Careers in the health and spirituality sector are both plentiful and rewarding in this, the information age, where knowledge is as much a commodity as widgets or washing machines.

Tapping into our culture's propensity to dwell on things we don't understand in order to improve our state of well-being isn't that difficult for people looking to make a vocation out of mind games.

As usual, you just have to know where to look.

Hypnotherapist

Check it out. On stage, a man is making out with a floor mop. Nearby, a woman squawks like a chicken, flapping her arms excitedly. The audience roars hysterically as a man with a top hat and long coattails resides over the pandemonium. Sitting his two audience participants down, he commands them to "Sleep!" and their heads flop down onto their chests. Slowly reviving them from their hypnotic state, they seem to have forgotten exactly what has just occurred.

This spectacle, most hypnotherapists would agree, is not an accurate or positive image of hypnotism and its benefits. In the practice of hypnotherapy there is no swinging clock. There is no "You're getting very sleepy." There is simply the coached mental exercise of averting one's mind from a state of consciousness to a state of partial unconsciousness.

After people can get to a deeper level of thought, they can begin to understand the root of their deep-seated phobias, bad eating habits, or even fears of public speaking.

That's the hallmark of a good hypnotherapist.

Facts and Figures

To become a hypnotherapist you have to visit a state office and put a bureaucrat into a trance. Just kidding.

Actually, no formal certification is lawfully required to practice hypnotherapy, but certainly one couldn't hurt. A hypnotherapist can gain certification from either the American Board of Hypnotherapy or the International Association of Counselors and Therapists. Further education in the form of hypnotherapy seminars usually ranges in cost between $400 and $500.

Due to stereotypes about hypnotism formed on television and in film, hypnotherapy has a certain social stigma attached to it. Contrary to popular belief, it is not a form of voodoo or witchcraft. No props or idols like wands, candles, statues, or swinging pocket watches are necessary. Instead of the watch, many hypnotherapists simply mark a spot on a wall for patients to stare at. The goal of such an exercise is simply to distract the mind from conscious thought.

Job Description

Like any form of therapy, a hypnotherapist's job is to help people work through their fears, addictions, and other issues by guiding patients as they see fit. They do this through helping the patient access thoughts, feelings, memories, and problem-solving skills.

Patients "work out" their minds through hypnotherapy, guided by the tools their hypnotherapist gives them, to improve upon pretty much any personal issue. Patients come to cut out bad habits like smoking or overeating. People sign up to overcome physical pain associated with anything from common allergy aches to the act of childbirth. Others go to hypnotherapists to conquer fears of everything from escalators to snakes to flying. More generally, a lot of people attend sessions as they would with any therapist: to work on boosting confidence or self-esteem. So it's a hodge-podge, of sorts, as far as patients go—but the market is full of people looking for the key to self-improvement.

Pay and Perks

A licensed, full-time hypnotherapist has the potential to earn up to $75,000 a year. The typical amount hypnotherapists charge per hour-long session could be anywhere from $50 to $150, but most sessions cost around $100.

Very often, much of the business a hypnotherapist receives is by way of referrals from previous patients. But seeing that a patient usually schedules a limited amount of sessions with a hypnotherapist (usually ten or under), business can tend to be erratic. Therefore you must find other ways to generate business.

Aside from the money, the ultimate perk of this work might be the very skills you learn yourself. You will know how to keep from getting overly stressed. Aside from being relaxed yourself, you will take pride in the fact that you are giving others the tools to reach within their own memories, thoughts, and feelings, and truly learn how to problem-solve and help themselves.

> **The Water Cooler**
>
> Self-hypnosis is beginning to be taught in the corporate world. With people skipping lunch to work longer hours, a five-minute hypnotic break is a way to regain focus and productivity.

Key Attribute

Put simply, you will want to have a passion for hypnosis. A keen understanding of hypnotherapy is essential. Hypnotherapists who have the greatest success maintain emotional distance while remaining receptive to their patients' needs. They should also receive some formal training and understand that hypnosis is not magic, but a psychological exercise—like meditation.

Key Tip

In summary, a relaxed hypnotherapist makes a relaxed patient. Understanding psychology, having strong communicative skills, and having a nurturing teaching method are all key.

Key Resource

There is a cornucopia of hypnotist links on the Health Care Disciplines & Education website. Find it at www.hsl.mcmaster.ca/tomflem/hypnotists.html.

Massage Therapist

Americans love to complain about their achy backs and creaky joints. Oh, the pain! But they are looking for relief, too.

Some people go for a walk or jog to loosen things up. Others take medications, either over-the-counter or by prescription. And some, unable to find a working solution for their aching necks, tight shoulders, and tired backs, simply ignore the problem.

But recently, more and more people are turning to a new solution for their chronic pain: massage therapy. Over the last decade, the number of people getting massages has tripled.

Now masseuses set up in health clubs, hotels, the local mall, on cruise ships, and even in your very own doctor's office. Regular massage has been

> **The Water Cooler**
>
> A mounting number of corporations like Pepsi, Reebok, and NBC offer massage as an employee benefit. It's been proven to boost morale, improve productivity, and decrease sick days in the workplace.

proven to reduce periods of sickness. And many corporations are beginning to include massage as an employee benefit.

Masseuses aren't just people who rub your back anymore. They're massage therapists.

Facts and Figures

The outlook for massage careers is fairly bullish. The U.S. Bureau of Labor Statistics 2000 reports that the massage therapy industry will grow faster than the average job market through 2010. Uncle Sam also reports a 25 percent rise in certifications every year since 1996.

There are many massage schools and programs out there that usually include Swedish massage, deep tissue massage, and trigger point therapy in their curriculum. On average, one year or so is spent in one of these programs (although you'll need 500 hours or so of massage therapy experience to be fully licensed in most states). They range in cost from $2,500 to $5,000.

But learning to be a good massage therapist shouldn't stop there. Volunteering one's services is always a way to further educate oneself—not to mention building one's clientele. Enrolling in new classes from time to time to improve upon one's techniques, reading books on massage, and receiving massages from other massage therapists should all help you gain experience and insight into this work.

Finally, every state has different requirements to become a massage therapist. Make sure to investigate this on your own.

Job Description

There are three key areas a massage therapist can work in: relaxation massage, clinical massage, and sports massage. Relaxation massage is mostly seen in spas and massage therapy centers. This is the most highly consumed version of massage.

Although people with serious physical problems can go to relaxation massage therapy, usually clinical massage is a better choice for people with ongoing injury-related pain. Clinical massage takes places in doctors' offices, chiropractors' offices, hospitals, and medical clinics.

Finally, sports massage is fairly self-explanatory. Sports massage therapists work with all types of athletes to both improve their physical performance and also help them recover from sports injuries. Sports massage pops up in health clubs, in sports medicine clinics, and within professional sports.

Pay and Perks

With a growing demand for massage in recent years, there is naturally a growing need for massage therapists. On average, massage therapists earn between $40 and $70 an hour. Some people start their own private practice; others, who are just starting off, might join someone else's business.

A big perk in the massage market are the very skills you learn. Assisting clients to heal from sickness and reduce tension is certainly something to feel good about. Not only this, you learn where your own major high-tension areas are and become an expert in relieving your own chronic pain.

Key Attribute

Massage is a very quiet, independent job. Usually, while working with patients, a massage therapist must maintain an atmosphere of calm. But at the same time, having good listening skills is a must to determine sources of pain and discomfort on part of the patient. Physical conditioning is helpful. First, it instills confidence in clients to see a fit, trim massage therapist. You'll also need the strength to administer to the aches and pains of 6–10 clients each day.

Key Tip

When choosing a massage program or school, do your homework. Familiarize yourself with the various curriculums and philosophies at massage schools to make sure you choose the one that is right for you.

Key Resource

Spend some time on the BodyWorker.com website (www.thebodyworker.com). It offers tips, resources, a good chat board, and recommended reading for massage enthusiasts.

Feng Shui Consultant

Nobody likes living next to the freeway or under high-tension power lines. We also don't like living inside of a building that is too cramped, doesn't get good lighting, or more simply, we get a bad vibe about. We all have these places. For some reason, no matter what we do, we just cannot seem to get comfortable. Ancient Chinese Feng Shui masters would call this feeling of confinement or negative energy *sha*.

More and more, Americans are turning to Feng Shui consultation to organize their living space. Contrary to popular belief, Feng Shui has nothing to do with any religious orientation. Instead, it works in a similar manner to horoscopes. Calculations are made based upon ancient Chinese geomancy, which is a system of probability based upon Earth's elements.

Now people are turning to Feng Shui to organize their homes, outdoor landscaping, and offices into peaceful spaces to live.

Facts and Figures

Feng Shui is best described as "4,000 years of common sense." The art of Feng Shui originated in China and in parts of India. For the Chinese, Feng Shui is both an art form and a science. One needs to make calculations based upon the I-Ching or *Book of Changes* while, at the same time, taking into account the physical relationship between four elements: building, time, person, and environment.

> **The Water Cooler**
>
> In Feng Shui, confusion is not a deterrent. It is looked upon as a positive part of an "energetic alignment process" toward solving a problem.

A genuine Feng Shui consultant, it is recommended, should practice in an apprentice role for many years, learning complex calculations and becoming aware of the fundamentals of Feng Shui before making consultations himself.

Job Description

Feng Shui has been practiced for thousands of years, and it might very well be practiced for thousands more. After all, an age-old Chinese saying states that five main factors will determine one's life: destiny, luck, accumulated goods and deeds, education, and finally Feng Shui. Think of a Feng Shui consultant as a "personal spiritual organizer."

Taken literally, Feng Shui means "wind and water." To consider this, we must realize that a Feng Shui consultant's job is to maintain the flow of a natural process in organizing one's home, office, or general property.

The first step to a proper Feng Shui consultation is visiting the property in question. At this point, a Feng Shui consultant must not only consider the environment but the property's directional orientation. He uses a compass called a *Lo Pan* to determine this. Calculations are achieved through utilizing five elements and eight trigrams and especially the principles of yin and yang. After calculations are made, remedies are prescribed in order to balance the energy of the place in question.

Pay and Perks

It depends. Some well-off clients might pay you $70,000 for banishing the clutter and letting their home breathe. Other, less affluent clients, might pay only a few hundred dollars. Either way, Feng Shui has been reported to produce feelings of prosperity, health, and well-being for both those who have had consultations and for those who practice it. So you've got that going for you.

Key Attributes

People who practice Feng Shui might have an interest in organization. They are attentive to how the organization of the external world spiritually affects their internal world. They balance a passion for interior decoration while appreciating the sensibility of maintaining open space.

Ideally, an organized Feng Shui consultant will have clients fill out a detailed questionnaire beforehand, to get a feel for both the client and the house. Then creativity and vision come into play. You'll visit the home and start to get a sense of the home's energy (or lack thereof) and begin to balance out the home's *chi*—its harmony and balance.

Key Tip

Consider yourself a "space-clearing educator." It is your job to create not only a physical space for people but also a mental space in which people can live comfortably and peaceably.

Key Resource

Read the book *The Principles of Feng Shui* by Larry Sang (American Feng Shui Institute, 1995). It offers good background on the Feng Shui culture, and is a good jumping-off point for people considering a career as a Feng Shui consultant.

Professional Magician

Abracadabra, Ala Kazam! Hey, where'd that rabbit come from?

Let's face it, everybody enjoys a good show. We go to the movies, watch stand-up comedy, and attend musical concerts. To say that we go simply because we "want to be entertained" leaves a bit unexplored. In reality, we go because music, humor, film, and other art forms inspire us. We go because there's magic.

And, indeed, magic itself is an art form. It's a stage performance. We sit in the audience dazzled at how the magician managed to pick the right card. We're on the edge of our seats as he dangles, chained up, from a rope. We're completely baffled as a woman levitates, and we simply have no explanation. We know it's a trick, but we can't quite figure it out—and this fills us with a sense of awe, just like with any other art form.

The only person it fills with more awe is the person who decides to take it on as his profession.

Facts and Figures

Scratch an entertainer and you'll find a magician. Johnny Carson, Muhammed Ali, Andy Griffith, and even Frankenstein himself, Boris Karloff, were amateur magicians back in the day. But how do you get started?

Formal education is not a necessity to succeed in the field of magic. Of course, there are many methods to learning how to become a good magician. Some train under other magicians. Others have acquired their skills secondhand simply through watching videotapes and DVDs and reading magic books. Many magicians agree that learning magic on one's own is entirely feasible.

Practice is key. A fledgling magician can get experience in many ways. He can practice in front of the mirror, in front of his friends, or even videotape himself. From here, he can move on to giving free public shows. This will also help in improving one's public speaking performance, which is a necessity for the showmanship of magic.

On the Job

Many magicians are very charitable and donate their time to hospitals and charities. This is also a good way to meet contacts and gain new business.

Job Description

When it comes down to it, there are essentially two different kinds of magicians: party magicians and corporate magicians.

Party magicians are experts in entertaining children. They are mostly hired for children's events such as parties, school assemblies, and picnics. Often, they appear in costume, sometimes as a clown. They usually list themselves in the phonebook under *Magicians* or *Entertainers*.

Corporate magicians, however, do most of their work for big companies to promote products. They are used at sales meetings, trade shows, and conventions, and even in television commercials. They can make good money but are required to travel constantly.

There are various forms of specialized magic, too. Like David Copperfield, a magician can use big props, have high production sets, music, and assistants to perform illusions. There is also theatre magic like Cirque Du Soleil that involves dramatic conventions, a storyline, and dance. A magician can also perform "up-close magic" in the very hands of an audience member. This usually involves cards, coins, or string. "Stand-up" magic is usually strictly for adults and involves humor.

Pay and Perks

A party magician usually gets between $75 and $100 per party. Magicians use many methods to draw in work, such as posting their card in local magic shops or putting ads in the phonebook.

A corporate magician earns about $500 to $1,000 a day. He gets work through putting together a professional publicity packet wherein he includes a resumé, brochure, and professional publicity photo. He can either send his portfolio to companies looking for magicians or he can get an agent to do this for him.

Key Attribute

Magic is an art form. And, like any career artist, being a magician is not a business you leave when you go home at night. Magicians are always practicing and thinking about new ways to innovate their art. They must be curious, and have a strong enough stage performance to make others curious as well.

Stage presence is key. A facility for communicating with people and making them feel relaxed is mandatory for a professional magician. A sense of humor is a boon, too. People like to laugh while being amazed.

Key Tip

Every magician makes mistakes. But the magicians who practice enough find ways to cover up their mistakes and continue the show unfazed.

Key Resource

For tips, job opportunities, and chat rooms on magic and magicians, hang out at MagicWebChannel.com. The site is well worth bookmarking for would-be magicians.

The Least You Need to Know

- You don't need to find your inner Zen to be a professional magician or Feng Shui consultant. You just need the proper training and the fire in your belly to make it to the top of your profession.

- In most cases, the money in the spiritual field won't make you a millionaire. But you can still make a good living at it.

- One potential market—a huge one—in the spiritual field is the baby boomers. Always looking for an edge or a way to stave off old age, boomers will take to massages or hypnotherapists who can help them feel and look better.

- The spiritual field presents many opportunities to help others, so it can be very rewarding.

Chapter **13**

Weird Science: How to Turn Your Eighth Grade Science Class into a Career

In This Chapter

- ◆ Turning your love of science into a profession
- ◆ Nurture orchids as an orchid grower
- ◆ Can you dig it? Dinosaur hunting
- ◆ Helping Mother Nature as a professional ecologist
- ◆ Blowing things up: demolition as a career

The world of science is wonderful, mysterious, and magical, full of questions just begging for a skilled individual in a white lab coat to answer—or at least look busy while he or she does so. As Werner von Braun, father of space travel, once said, "Basic research is what I am doing when I don't know what I am doing."

What do you know? Even scientists have a sense of humor.

So if your mom and dad bought you a chemistry set as a kid—and you still have it—a career in the sciences might be right up your alley.

Professional Sports Trainer

Is stitching up an NFL quarterback so he can get back into the game your idea of a good time? Is helping superbly conditioned professional athletes make the most of their talents and keeping them healthy a big priority in your life?

If so, then you might have the stuff that a professional sports trainer is made of.

Facts and Figures

According to the National Athletic Trainers Association, there are about 25,000 trainers working in the United States today. Of course, not everyone can work for a professional sports team—there are only 150 or so of those jobs available. The good news is that, in the burgeoning world of what is now called sports medicine, there are plenty of other hats you can wear in the business. That list includes orthopedic surgeons, sports medicine physicians, physical therapists, dietitians, exercise physiologists, and sport psychologists.

Job Description

As a professional sports trainer these are your top priorities, in descending order:

1. Prevention of injuries
2. Clinical evaluation and diagnosis
3. Immediate care of injuries
4. Treatment, rehabilitation, and reconditioning of injuries
5. Organization and administration
6. Professional responsibility

Keeping top athletes healthy and available to play at their peak performance is what a professional sports trainer's job is all about.

Typically, your day begins early, whether it's in season or not, or whether you are on the road or not. During the season, you'll spend a great deal of time treating athletes before practice begins. You might be rehabbing a banged-up knee or taping an ankle or two before practice starts. You'll attend all practices and games and will be expected to be ready in the event of an injury. There's a great deal of paperwork involved, too. Keeping up-to-date medical records and dealing with insurance record keeping is part of the job, as is maintaining training logs and writing up progress reports on treatment sessions.

You'll be communicating directly with team coaches and players—even the odd hands-on owner or two—so good communication skills are a must. Your tools of the trade include rolls and rolls of athletic tape, whirlpools, heat packs, exercise equipment and gear, and, of course, a first-aid kit.

Pay and Perks

Professional sports trainers can make as much as $100,000 per year. But if you are just starting out, you can expect about $30,000 to $40,000 in annual salary. You'll also get playoff shares and per diem expenses, and you'll receive world champion rings just like the athletes if your team goes all the way. Plus, you'll get to rub elbows—literally—with professional athletes and have a front row seat for games.

Key Attributes

Your fastest path to a professional sports trainer gig is through academia, preferably internships, graduate assistantships, and advanced degrees. A major in sports medicine or exercise science is a good addition to your resumé, as is any certification or coursework in areas like human anatomy, nutrition, and exercise physiology.

You must be certified by a state-sponsored board that monitors athletic trainers. Athletic trainers must be great organizers, have solid communication skills, be able to handle stress, and have good nurturing skills.

> **The Water Cooler**
>
> According to the latest figures from the National Athletic Trainers' Association (NATA), 14,459 of its 30,207 members are women (47.9 percent).

Key Tip

One way to get a leg up on the athletic training market is to first work at a professional sports medicine clinic. Plenty exist, and virtually all professional sports teams have affiliations with such clinics.

Key Resources

Check out—or join—the National Athletic Trainer's Association. Visit the website at www.nata.org.

Orchid Grower

"When you get down to it, as sooner or later you must, gardening is a long drawn-out war of attrition against the elements, a tripartite agreement involving the animal, insect, and bird worlds, and the occasional sheer perversity of nature." —Author and humorist Alan Melville

No doubt Melville had his finger on the pulse of the gardening world when he wrote those words.

In fact, rumor has it that Melville was an orchid lover; a man who saw infinite beauty in what many consider to be the quintessential merger between God, nature, and the human element.

The thing about wanting to be a professional orchid grower and trader is that you know already that you want to be one. By that I mean orchid enthusiasts are so passionate about their flowers that many rank them right up there with their children and spouses (probably above the latter) in terms of life's joys. So if an orchid fanatic can find a way to make a living growing the flowers, he'll do it.

Facts and Figures

Wild orchids date back to the days of the Ming Dynasty in China, where emperors were known to favor the indigenous species of Cymbidium for their fragrant odor and beautiful colors. The famed Chinese philosopher Confucius was known to love orchids, as well.

A little farther west, the ancient Greeks were known as orchid aficionados, too. Greeks, and later the Romans, valued hardy terrestrial orchids not just for their beauty, but for the medicinal and healing elements found in orchid leaves and roots. The term *orchid*, in fact, is derived from the Greek word *orchis*, meaning testes, referring to the tubers found in some orchid species. This analogy is instructive, if only for the mistaken belief that the orchids posses aphrodisiac properties and eating of underground tubers might "provoke Venus" and enhance a couple's prospects of giving birth to desirable male heirs.

> **The Water Cooler**
>
> Eight percent of all flowering plants are orchids.

Orchids are defined as flowering plants categorized in the family Orchidaceae, which contains an estimated 600 to 800 genera and about 25,000 species. The Orchidaceae family is believed to contain more species than any other plant family in the world, with the possible exception of the Asteraceae family. Orchid taxonomists can only estimate the species numbers due to the huge magnitude of the family as well as the relative inaccessibility of many species that are hidden high in the canopies of tropical forests.

Job Description

Orchid growers buy, grow, and nurture their favorite plants in backyard gardens and hothouses. They might grow their own from seed, or they might even buy unique orchids on the black market for resale. They might also create decorations with flowers and greenery for parties, weddings, and other occasions based on the customer's order. Orchid growers who own their own shops might do everything from growing and purchasing flowers to keeping financial records.

Many orchid growers double as floral shop owners or employees. So a good part of their day is spent nurturing their orchids—that means growing, cutting, cleaning, and repotting fragile flowers. So it helps to think of your vocation as a small business; not only are you growing and trading flowers, but you're keeping tabs on receipts and transactions, and marketing your orchids on websites and in industry trade publications. You'll spend a great deal of time on eBay, too, looking for the next profitable orchid.

Pay and Perks

It's hard to quantify a pay scale for orchid growers, but statistics show that your garden variety orchid can earn you $50 and up per flower. In the trading market, the old

Wall Street standby of "buy low and sell high" really applies. So the more orchids you sell at a profit, the better you do. Just like any small business.

Key Attributes

You have to immerse yourself in the orchid culture to succeed as a trader. In other words, you must become a master of botanical matters like seed germination, stem characteristics, monocots, endosperms, and plant biology. You must also have a good eye for a plant that could bring in a hefty profit. So, for instance, knowing the difference between monopodial and sympodial orchids is job one.

A good sense of design and color are important. Having the patience required to buy a good flower and sell it might not happen overnight. The good news is that there rarely is a bleak market for orchids. Followers love them so much that there is always a bull market for orchids.

Key Tip

Looking for a great way to start out in the professional orchid grower's world? Here's a tip: get a job at a floral shop as an apprentice. You'll learn a lot about the proper caretaking of flowers and you'll make some useful contacts for use later when you are out on your own. If you live near a college or university, chances are they have a good orchid lab where you can volunteer or work there part or full time.

Key Resource

Get a subscription to *Orchids: The Magazine of the American Orchid Society*. Find it at www.orchidweb.org.

Dinosaur Hunter

Remember *Jurassic Park?* Sure you do.

After all, the 1993 film, based on the best-selling novel of the same name by Michael Crichton, earned $360 million at the box office and changed, through its mind-boggling special effects, the way we viewed movies. Steven Spielberg, who produced and directed the film, recognized (as did Crichton) that dinosaurs—especially, large, hungry and mean ones—sell.

Anyone who spent their childhood years playing with toy T-Rexes and going on imaginary fossil hunts in their backyard can dance to the same siren song of paleontology that Spielberg did. The actual field is hard work in tough conditions, but the chance to recreate dinosaurs out of bones buried in the dirt for one million years is too good to pass up.

Facts and Figures

Dinosaur hunters, more formally known as paleontologists, study the history of life through the excavation of fossils—history's first draft of life on Earth. What are fossils? Simply the remnants of life forms such as plants or animals that once thrived on Earth but were buried and preserved in the earth's crust for centuries. Lots of centuries.

Not to get too egg-headed, but paleontology, as far as dinosaur hunting goes, comes in different forms:

◆ Vertebrate paleontology (the science of fossils of animals with backbones)

◆ Invertebrate paleontology (the science of fossils of animals without backbones)

◆ Micropaleontology (the science of fossils of single-celled organisms)

◆ Paleoecology (the examination of ancient ecosystems—not exactly gunning for T-Rex, but the surroundings he thrived in)

Universities are the best place to get hired to study dinosaurs, although science and history museums often have paleontologists on staff, as do private foundations interested in preserving and studying the past in ecological terms. Governments also employ paleontologists, but usually to help in geological mapping efforts. Oil companies might have one or two paleontologists on staff, and they're paid very well for their expertise.

A great way to start your Jurassic journey is through a major in geology at a good college or university. You'll study fossil excavation there and, if you're good and you are lucky, you can get an internship that will get you out on the field and on to the site of a big dig.

But be realistic—there are only about 3,000 jobs in paleontology to go around. So you have to make a big effort to succeed.

Job Description

Paleontology is an interesting blend of research and paperwork. Unfortunately, many archeological digs are privately funded through government and private grants and outside contributions. So there is a lot of paperwork involved in just getting a dig off the ground. But after you have the money and you are out in the field, you'll spend your time doing the research into prehistoric dinosaurs you love. And, if you make a discovery, you'll get credit for it and your name will be attached to the discovery forever.

Pay and Perks

A fresh-out-of-the-gate paleontologist, working for a university, earns about $23,000 in annual salary. The good news is that, as times marches on, the pay scale goes all the way up to about $90,000. Plus, there's plenty of fresh air, you're recreating creatures that walked the earth millions of years ago, and you'll get to travel to far-off lands for your fossil-hunting adventures. Imagine August in Mongolia!

Key Attributes

A good digging technique and lots of sun block.

I'm serious. The physical labor that goes with the fossil-excavation terrain calls for a hardy disposition and the patience of a saint. I mentioned the academic training required—usually at least an Master's degree in geology or paleontology to get you into the industry—but a minor degree in biology won't hurt, either. You'll also need about a year's worth of chemistry and calculus courses. So any undergraduate or post graduate school you consider should have a great reputation in science.

> **The Water Cooler**
>
> Academic training is key to becoming a dinosaur tracker. On average, a Master's degree in paleontology or geology takes up to three years to obtain. A Ph.D. takes longer—about four to six years.

Solid computer skills are also a must, and I don't mean just balancing a laptop on your legs in a driving sandstorm, although that helps. The job calls for some significant statistical analysis on fossils and the terrain they're likely to be buried in.

Key Tip

Visit a nearby museum and let them know you're pursuing a career in fossil hunting (only don't call it that—say "paleontology"). Offer to volunteer. And, believe it or not, fossil clubs have popped up all over the globe. Just go to www.Google.com and type in "fossil clubs" and your zip code and see if you don't get lucky.

Key Resource

Check out Project Exploration at www.projectexploration.com. The site has loads of information on dinosaurs, paleontology, and geology.

Professional Ecologist

If you're in harmony with Mother Nature and care deeply about the preservation of Earth and all its inhabitants, plant, animal, and otherwise, why not put your talents and enthusiasm to use as a professional ecologist?

Okay, you won't get rich (at least in the financial sense) but you'll be doing important work, get a chance to hone your keen, analytical mind, and help keep nature clean and healthy for future generations of Earthlings to enjoy.

Facts and Figures

People who become ecologists stay ecologists. Studies show that over 80 percent of college graduates with environmental science degrees who enter the field are still working there five years later.

The hours aren't too strenuous. Industry data shows a 40-hour-per week average on the clock. And opportunities to work in the industry are reasonable—over 13,000 professionals are employed in the ecology sector. The majority of those are scientists with chemistry, environmental science, geology, biology, climatology, and statistics experience. Like a paleontologist, an ecologist will spend a lot of time writing reports and summarizing data. When you do go out in the field, you'll camp out near active volcanoes or sleep in a makeshift hut near the scene of a natural disaster. And if you're a true naturalist, you'll love every minute of it.

Job Description

There's a myth about ecologists that portrays them as grape-nut-crunching Grizzly Adams clones, chaining themselves to trees and hugging bunny rabbits all day long.

Hogwash. Although many ecologists do go to the sites of eco-disasters like the Exxon Valdez oil spill in Alaska or the tsunami disaster in the Far East, ecologists don't have the time or inclination to do much of either. Professional trained ecologists spend most of their time studying the relationship between the environment and the people inhabiting that environment and how the two impact each other—and what that means to Mother Earth.

Consequently, you'll spend a great deal of time in the laboratory or in an office studying issues like rainfall, pollution, temperature levels of icebergs inside the polar cap—things like that. So be warned that you'll be as likely to wear a lab coat and work on a sophisticated computer as you will be to wear L.L. Bean's gear and trudge through the Everglades or the Alaskan tundra. It's a data-cruncher's dream job, assembling mathematical models and analyzing the data those models project. How much time will you spend indoors and outdoors? Overall, you can expect to be in a lab or an office 8 to 10 months a year and out in the field the rest of the time.

Pay and Perks

Again, you won't threaten the Vanderbilts or the Buffetts on any list of the wealthiest people around. Beginning pay for a professional ecologist is about $22,500. After five years that number slides up to about $40,000 and, after ten years, you can expect to be paid in the $60,000 per-year range.

You're most likely to be hired by universities, private foundations sympathetic to eco-causes, or by the federal government, by far the largest landowner in the United States. So think Environmental Protection Agency (EPA), the Natural Resources Defense Council, the University of Colorado, or the Sierra Club when you're filling out those resumés.

Key Attributes

It's no secret that it helps to be a real nature lover to make it in the ecological field. Most people there spend their time studying big ecosystems and then saving them. So it helps to be totally dedicated to that cause.

That said, you'd also do well to grab an undergraduate or graduate degree in some combination of biology, chemistry, meteorology, math, computer science, and geography. To go far in the field, a Ph.D. is just about mandatory. Surprisingly, to me, anyway, is the fact that the ranks of professional ecologists are filled with people who come from the education sector—particularly teachers. That's because ecologists not only have to know how to absorb information, they have to know how to help the general public learn about it, too.

That said, anyone who loves nature and shows enthusiasm, intelligence, and the ability to be highly productive can make it as an ecologist—just like in any industry.

Key Tip

Many private foundations interested in the field of ecology spend a great deal of time in Washington, D.C., lobbying for tighter restrictions on industry and more favorable legislation to protect the environment. So one doorway into the industry is as a volunteer or an intern for an organization like the Sierra Club or the National Resources Defense Council. You'll learn, you'll lobby, and one day you'll leave for a laboratory job as a professional ecologist.

Key Resource

Try EnvironmentalCareer.com. The site has a host of data on finding work in the field and gobs of good educational tools, as well.

Demolition Expert

Things that go "boom!"

That's what demolition experts like. Skilled at blowing things up, but in a safe, responsible manner, demolition experts are in demand as urban communities—dynamic by nature—change their landscape on an ongoing basis.

Old buildings go down and new buildings go up. In between, demolition experts are called on to make sure the transition goes as smoothly and safely as possible.

Facts and Figures

The term *implosion* was coined by demolition industry legend Mark Loizeaux back in the 1960s. It is meant to describe the series of small explosions that, combined together, cause a building to collapse down upon itself. A common misconception about demolitions is that a blockbuster supply of explosives is needed to take a 25-story skyscraper down. Not true. Actually, a small quantity of explosives, expertly positioned, can do the same thing better and safer.

Explosives go off at intervals because the demolition expert wants it that way. Buildings are designed to fall one way or another, or straight down, depending on the objectives of the hiring contractor. It's the demolition expert's job to ensure the building falls the way it is supposed to.

The job outlook for demolition experts is fairly bright. The U.S. government estimates that over 128,000 Americans make a living in the demolitions contracting field. By 2010, that number is estimated to rise to 144,000.

Job Description

Demolition experts specialize in the structural dismantling of buildings, often in urban environments, that must be demolished to give way to new construction projects. Such experts don't exactly "blow up" buildings—they bring them down with explosions positioned at key points and underpinnings.

The idea is for the building to collapse into its "footprint" instead of explode outward, thereby ensuring maximum safety and security and leaving a debris site that is much easier to clear and manage. The last thing you want in demolishing a building surrounded by other buildings is to cause damage and endanger lives by having a demolition go awry.

That's where the demolition expert and the "destruction team" come in. The expert assesses the structure with his or her team of demolition specialists, and figures out how to bring a building down with absolute safely and minimal cost to the paying construction firm. They know that the fewer holes that need to be drilled, the less expensive the cost of labor, and the less likelihood of a major explosion causing damage to external structures and people nearby.

Demolition specialists review building blueprints (if available—often they are not), test building conditions (often by detonating smaller "test" explosives to see how the building reacts), decide which walls and surfaces are load bearing and what are not (the latter need to be removed for a cleaner implosion), and handle the drilling and drywall removal that needs to be complete before an implosion can be triggered.

Pay and Perks

Demolition experts are well compensated. Many earn as much as $100,000 annually. Median starting salary to work on a crew is about $31,000. Hourly rates range anywhere from $11 to $27 per hour.

You don't need any specific experience to climb aboard a demolition team. Just an eagerness to learn and a willingness to get the hands-on training you need to succeed.

Perks? That's an easy one. Imagine a box seat view of a 25-story tower collapsing in front of you. Anyone who liked to stack blocks as a kid and knock them down again can relate.

> **The Water Cooler**
>
> Hollywood loves demolition jobs. Often, big-budget movies whose plots require a building to be destroyed will film an actual implosion. The movies *Mars Attacks*, *Lethal Weapon 3*, and *Telefon* all used real building implosions on film to wow movie-goers.

Key Attributes

Knowledge of explosives is essential on demolitions projects. A building with concrete underpinning, for example, might require traditional dynamite to do the job. But steel-columned buildings are much harder to topple. There, knowledge of stronger explosives, like cyclotrimethylenetrinitramine, called RDX for short, comes in handy. Instead of imploding the entire column, the high potency RDX slices right through the steel, splitting it in half. So knowledge of explosives, electrical detonators, and blasting caps to detonate those explosives is a big issue in the demolition industry.

Key Tip

So what's my best advice? Try to hire on with a well-established blasting company. About 20 top demolition firms exist across the globe. The more jobs the firm has done, the better the firm. In this field, experience counts.

Key Resource

A great book for beginners on the subject is *Demolition Experts: Blowing Things Up* (Rosen Publishing, 2001) by Suzie Nightingale. For more advanced reading try *Demolition: The Art of Demolishing, Dismantling, Imploding, Toppling and Razing* (Blackdog Publishing, 2000) by Helene Liss.

Taxidermist

Take this job and stuff it.

Okay, I was dying to say that.

Speaking of dying, there's a huge market for taking animals, prized pets or otherwise, and reconstructing them for posterity.

It's called taxidermy. If you know all about antler-mounts and bearskin rug techniques—or if you want to—then a career in taxidermy might be the right stuff for you.

Facts and Figures

Taxidermists are in big demand by museums, private clubs, and private pet owners.

Job Description

Is taxidermy a pastime where you're up to your arms in, well, icky animal innards?

Not really, although it's not a career for the decidedly squeamish. Taxidermists take deceased animals, birds, and fish and "reconstruct" them into a representation—monument, if you will—of their living, breathing selves.

This process is completed by removing the animal's skin, preserving it through sophisticated "tanning" techniques, and then mounting it on an anchor device—like a pedestal, wood or granite base, or picture frame—for display.

Some study in the animal sciences is required, as knowledge of anatomy is a critical part of the job. You need to gather all the information you can on the animal's behavior, motor skills, and appearance. To handle the big stuff, like large African game, you'll need to be physically fit—some animals weigh in at 500 pounds or more and are difficult to maneuver.

A good taxidermist also has to know how to "sculpt" a model based on the same animal that he or she is working on. That's done using a sequential combination of wire, wood, wool, paper mâché, and clay. The tanned skins go on the finished "model." Some touch-up work in the form of enhanced skin coloring and the creation of natural habitat displays (okay, that one is more than just a touch-up job) is used to authenticate as much reality in the presentation as possible.

Much of this work is done in the taxidermist's own workshop. Most are self-employed but some taxidermist companies do exist and they are always on the lookout for good tanners, skinners, painters, and sculptors.

Your workplace must also include a good computer to practice renderings on, along with an online logbook to keep client information and records up-to-date.

Pay and Perks

The pay scale for taxidermists is wide-ranging, depending on the job in question and the reputation, skill, and experience of the taxidermist in question.

Some can earn as much as $6,000 for mounting big game, like a bear or a lion. You can earn $600 or so for mounting a falcon or $300 for a shoulder-mounted deer. A good rule of thumb if you're just starting out is $30 or so an hour, and that includes use of your equipment and workplace. Work your way up from there based on the quality of your work and your good reputation.

Oh, and make sure you always get 50 percent of your fee up front. The last thing you want is to do the work but have Mrs. Feebleman's pet kitty Snowball hanging around because she changed her mind at the last minute.

Key Attribute

Anyone with good knowledge of animal anatomy (someone who has worked in a zoo or pet shelter, for example), experience in the tanning industry, and a good feel for modeling and sculpting techniques has a good leg up on a career in taxidermy. Good vision and artistic skills help, too.

Industry apprenticeships are possible, but they can take three years to complete. So you have to be a bit patient.

Knowing the tricks of the trade helps, too. One taxidermist specializing in bird reconstruction "cleans" his birds in a soft-cycle washing machine.

One thing you should not have is allergies to dust, animal skin or dander, or bird feathers. That would be a drawback.

Key Tip

Market your wares to professional artists and sculptors. It's a great side business for taxidermists. For instance, you can earn $6,000 or so on a sculptor's finished work, using your "model" for a model. Watercolor paintings and other art works based on your animal model can earn even more.

Key Resource

A list of good taxidermy schools can be found on Taxidermist.com. Find it at www.taxidermy.net/learn/schools1.html.

The Least You Need To Know

- ◆ The natural sciences is a great venue for a career. If you're curious about how life works and what makes humans (or animals) tick, that's a great place to start.

- ◆ Let's lay it on the line. To get hired and have a successful career as a taxidermist or paleontologist, you're going to need some serious training on themes like human anatomy or the earth sciences. You're easily talking four years of college here.

- ◆ One shortcut to a career in the life sciences is through the U.S. government and academia. They, along with private foundations and oil companies, are the biggest recruiters of life sciences professionals.

- ◆ The jobs in this chapter provide many options for the inquisitive mind.

Chapter 14

Food and Drink as a Career

In This Chapter

- Careers in the food and drink industry
- Get paid to eat: food critic
- Providing healthier food: organic farming
- The increasing demand for the personal chef
- Hop to it: beer tasting
- Nothing to whine about: sommelier

"Please sir … I want some more." —Charles Dickens, *Oliver Twist*

When it comes to food and drink, who doesn't want more?

That's the real beauty of a career in food and dining. People love what you do. They go out of their way to give you their business. And they will pay top dollar to sit at your table or shop at your store.

Ultimately, a career in the food and dining sector is the ultimate in self-fulfillment. People preparing food for people who love food—what a concept!

Food Critic

In the comedy classic *Monty Python's The Meaning of Life* one unforgettable scene involves a fat man at a restaurant, wolfing down serving after serving. Then, forced to finish the meal with one thin mint, the diner explodes.

That's kind of like the life of a food critic. Without the explosion, that is.

Facts and Figures

The United States has over 900,000 restaurants serving $476 billion worth of food to hungry diners. Picking which ones are the best is at the core of a good food critic's job.

Job Description

A food critic's job is to eat food and get paid for it. Lots of food. Restaurant reviewers visit restaurants, usually incognito, and sample as many different dishes as possible. They furtively take notes and then write a critique of the restaurant. Food critics might also branch out and write feature articles on the newest fad diet or an interview with a wine maker or celebrity chef. Count on writing at least one review per week.

Your best bet for a food critic gig is at a daily newspaper—every reputable paper has a restaurant reviewer. With the ascent of the Internet, plenty of online jobs are also available for gifted food writers.

Pay and Perks

The perks are obvious—all the tasty, rich food you can handle and the knowledge that you hold the future of a given restaurant in the palm of your butter-covered hands. The pay isn't great—about $35,000 a year for a full-time newspaper food critic. A handful of critics—those who write for *The New York Times* or for *The Washington Post*—can easily earn six figures.

Larger newspapers also regularly send their food writers to different cities and even different countries to sample the food culture in far-off venues. Imagine dining on stromboli at a Venice café or sampling wine at a comfy Napa Valley inn. Nice work if you can get it.

Key Attributes

Newspaper editors who hire food writers value great writing skills, an open mind (you'll be eating a lot of exotic food), and a passion for good food and drink. Previous clips in the food and dining arena are your best ticket to a reviewing job. Any training in the culinary arts is a big help, too.

You'll also be expected to comment knowledgably on a restaurant's décor, ambience, and service quality, and conduct plenty of research on the restaurant dishes you'll be sampling before hand. In other words, it helps to know the difference between Portobello mushrooms and white button mushrooms.

The hours are flexible, and some late hours might have to be factored in. An ability to stomach bad, ill-prepared food is a good attribute for a food critic. You'll be tasting your share of below-par dishes.

You'll also be expected to write negative reviews when the dining experience calls for it. This is tougher than you might think. Most people are not predisposed to deliver bad news, and the prospect of a bad review hurting a restaurant's business and possibly putting people out of work is difficult to overlook. But the credo of the food critic is "the people deserve the best."

Key Tip

Never tell a restaurant beforehand that you're a reviewer and that you'll be dining there tonight. Professional food critics say that you can't get an objective view of a restaurant if the workers and owner know you're coming. The restaurant help might fawn over you, the reviewer, whereas if you were an average Joe, they might not.

Key Resource

Belly up to the Association of Food Journalists (AFJ) at www.afjonline.com/rcrit.htm.

Organic Farmer

Remember President H.W. Bush's famous proclamation, "I'm President of the United States and I'm not going to eat any more broccoli!"?

But doesn't the president know it's good for him? In fact, all organic foods are good for him—and of the rest of us, too.

Thus the need for organic farmers to bring fresher, healthier food to our nation's tables.

If you've shopped at a whole foods market or health food store, you've seen organic products. More recently they've been looking better and better; watch for the grapefruit-size oranges. But these products don't just grow on trees … not without help, anyway. Organic food is quickly becoming a preference in the world, which means organic farmers are going to be doing well.

Facts and Figures

Farmers, ranchers, and agricultural managers held nearly 1.4 million jobs in 2002, with about 84 percent being self-employed. Though these were not solely organic farmers, it does show how many jobs are available in the farming industry, with organic farming taking a larger percentage of those jobs each year.

Job Description

Organic farming, on the most basic level, is farming without the addition of artificial chemicals. But before you go selling the tomatoes from your backyard garden, you should get your farm certified as organic. This means you have to apply for certification and go through a special process, which includes a visit from an inspector. Because of chemical residue often found in soil, your farm must run organically for about two years before it can be certified.

If you don't like plants, you can also keep organic livestock. Though this market isn't growing as rapidly as produce, it can still be profitable. Your organic livestock must be freerange, must not be treated with any chemicals (such as steroids), and must be fed healthier food than conventional livestock.

Ultimately, as an organic farmer you would be responsible for preparing, tilling, planting, fertilizing, cultivating, and harvesting the crops. You'd also be in charge of packaging, storing, and marketing the food. In the case of livestock, you would feed and care for the animals, and keep the barns, coops, and pens clean and in good condition.

> **The Water Cooler**
>
> Recent Economic Research Service (ERS) research shows that three key demographic trends will shape the U.S. food market in the next two decades: more mature consumers, more diversity, and more people to feed.

Pay and Perks

For anyone who enjoys it, a major perk of organic farming is working outdoors. You'll also be self-employed, which can be very gratifying. Many people would also love working the land, and living in a rural area. There is also independence, as you'll farm hard for one or two seasons, but have more time in the off seasons while you plan for the next crops.

Income for both farmers and ranchers varies from year to year because the prices of the products change depending on weather conditions and other factors that affect the quantity you and other farmers put out. You can receive government subsidies or other payments that will supplement your income for the lower-output years.

Key Attributes

You need some fancy learnin' to become an organic farmer, preferably a Bachelor's degree in business with a concentration in agriculture. Most state universities have agricultural programs where you can both gain hands-on experience as well as a degree. It is important that you gain that experience, whether from school, growing up on a farm, or interning at one; any time spent on a farm will be helpful. You can also become certified as an Accredited Farm Manager by the American Society of Farm Managers and Rural Appraisers. This requires several years of farming experience, a Bachelor's or Master's degree in agricultural science, and courses relating to the business, financial, and legal aspects of farming.

You should be strong as an ox, and willing to work long hours outdoors; you will have few days off during planting, growing, and harvesting seasons. You will also have to be strong mentally, as you will have to keep up on modern advancements, government regulations, and any environmental changes that will affect your business.

> **The Water Cooler**
>
> Studies show that not only is organic food good for us—it's good for our plant and animal friends, too. The organic food industry reports that there are five times as many wild plants in arable fields, and 57 percent more species on organic farms than on traditional farms. That's biodiversity for you.

Key Tip

Though certifying your farm as organic isn't currently a requirement, it will be eventually. So one thing to remember is that certifiers are not only looking for the absence of chemicals, but an organic and positive outlook and way of growing. Organic farming goes deeper than just the soil—it goes to your roots.

Key Resource

Try these websites on for size:

Center for Rural Affairs: www.cfra.org

National FFA Organization: www.ffa.org

Personal Chef

"Can I have it with some blue M&M's on top?"

That's a typical question a personal chef might get from a client. It's an interesting, creative, and demanding career, but if you love food, a personal chef post is a good deal.

In fact, a career as a personal chef will give you just as much freedom (if not more) than a professional chef, and a comparable paycheck.

Facts and Figures

The personal chef industry is about 17 years old and growing quickly. *Entrepreneur Magazine* has called the personal chef industry "one of the twelve fastest growing businesses in the country." There are over 5,000 United States Personal Chef Association-trained personal chefs working in the United States and Canada. The USPCA has also trained chefs in Australia, Ireland, England, and Puerto Rico. Overall, personal chefs are currently serving over 100,000 households, and are predicted to be serving over 300,000 in the next five years.

Job Description

As a personal chef, you will prepare meals for several clients. With input from your clients, you will plan menus for them to experience on the days you agree to cook for them. You'll do the grocery shopping necessary for the meals, the meal preparation, and the storage and cleanup.

A personal chef first interviews the client to gain insight into his or her likes, dislikes, and allergies. Then the chef travels to the home of his/her employer to cook. Typically, as a chef, you will cook many meals (anywhere from one week's worth to one month's) and then store them in the client's refrigerator and freezer—leaving instructions for reheating as well as a clean kitchen.

Usually, personal chefs begin their careers with recipes from an association, and don't develop their own until after they've worked for three to four years. But you should be open to trying new things should your client make a request.

Pay and Perks

The salary of a personal chef is similar to that of a chef in a hotel or restaurant. On average you can get $13 to $17 per hour; but for more experienced chefs in the New York Area, you can get $20 to $25 per hour. This works out to be about $40,000 per year for beginners and up to $70,000 for chefs who have been working for a number of years.

The main perk for this career is the flexible schedule. You can choose how many clients you want to take, which can leave your schedule open for other things you want to do, whether it's a second job or family life. There is also a lot of independence; you will provide a good deal of input when it comes to the food you are cooking, and you will probably be cooking without supervision. It's also a great career that can serve as a creative outlet and mode for personal growth.

Key Attributes

The number one desired quality for a personal chef is good culinary skills, as well as a love for cooking. However, because it is generally a personal business, you should also have experience in marketing and management. More specifically, you'll want to be familiar with bookkeeping, scheduling, and the ins and outs of the food service industry. Time management will also prove to be helpful as you will have more than one client and will be cooking a large amount of food at one time.

There is no formal training necessary, though any experience in food service will help. You can gain this experience at a culinary institute or while working at a restaurant. This experience will familiarize you with portion control, pricing, cooking skills, and food service standards.

Key Tip

Personal chefs are currently high in demand, but to better your chances you should live in an area where they are needed and can be afforded. Major cities are one option, as more people tend to work longer hours, necessitating meal preparation.

You also might consider working one night a week in a restaurant to stay fresh, so to speak. You'll have access to new ideas and be more challenged than if you were just working on your own.

Key Resource

Try the *Personal Chefs Network*, founded by Sharon Worster and Wendy Perry. Find it at www.personalchefsnetwork.com.

For recipes and seminars, check out the American Personal Chef Association's (APCA) website (www.personalchef.com), based in San Diego.

Professional Beer Taster

Ahh … the sheer joy of bellying up to the bar and asking for a cold, frosty one with a good head on it.

Sound good to you? Well, one way to turn your hops and barley hobby into a career is to be a professional beer taster—a position open to all who have a keen sense of taste and a high tolerance. A note of caution, though: you might be thinking, "I've found it! My dream job!" but it might be trickier than you think.

Facts and Figures

China recently surpassed the United States as the world's largest producer of beer. But even so, Anheuser-Busch alone rolls out 102 million barrels of beer each year. Not to say you have to drink all that beer, but it gives you an idea of the size and scope of the worldwide beer industry.

Job Description

Okay, this is not rocket science—or is it? The main job of a beer taster is to do just that: taste beer. More specifically, you must be able to measure how pleasurable a beer is, or how unpleasant, if that's the case. To do this you must be sure you taste it properly, as there are a number of factors that affect the way a beer tastes. These factors include the time of tasting (early afternoon is best because you'll be less tired), temperature (it's that warm beer we all hate that has the most flavor), glassware (all beers must be in the same size glass—larger glasses make the drink more aromatic), lighting (you have to be able to see all beers clearly, or see none), pouring (the head, or lack thereof, is always important), and the smell (sniff quickly and strongly or you'll miss it).

You should evaluate three criteria when tasting beer: Is the beer true to type? Can it be reproduced? And is it defect free? You should base your judgments on taste, carbonation, color, and overall quality. In tasting the beer, you have to remember you aren't a wine taster: swallow! Beer tasters must also take into account the importance of the sensation of carbonation. But don't worry: most beer has three times less alcohol than wine.

> **On the Job** ___
> Want a list of the 100 top beer sites on the Internet? Find one at:
>   http://chef2chef.net/rank/beersites2.shtml

Pay and Perks

As a beer taster you can make roughly $30,000 per year. This amount varies with experience and the company you work for. A large corporation when compared to a small brewpub will be more likely to provide higher pay.

Other perks? You're a professional beer taster.

Key Attributes

As a beer taster you must have a discerning palate. You have to be able to distinguish the mix of sweetness and bitterness on a daily basis. Although everyone has the ability to recognize and evaluate the changing elements and tastes, it does require some discipline.

Other qualities you should have include a high tolerance of alcohol (remember: you're swallowing), sharp sense of taste, large appetite to hold all the liquid, knowledge of beer (i.e., composition, brewing process, and so on), and, of course, you should enjoy all types of beer.

Key Tip

Try to find a seminar or course that teaches you some tricks of the trade. You might also want to check out a wine tasting seminar, as it will show a possible employer that you do have a discerning taste.

This might be one dream job that you want to keep to a time limit. The health benefits of beer are not many, and one brewery lost a lawsuit from a beer taster they employed due to the development of alcoholism.

Key Resource

Pour a cold one and hop over to RealBeer.com. It has everything you ever wanted to know about beer and the brewery industry. You'll enjoy reading lots of tips and articles directly related to beer tasting.

"Professor" at McDonald's Hamburger University

Super-size me—at least when it comes to my knowledge of all things hamburger.

What better place to learn than at McDonald's world famous Hamburger University? Or better yet, how about teaching there?

Yep, it's boolah-boolah time. McDonald's is one of the largest corporations in the world with over 27,000 restaurants in 119 countries on six continents. So where do McDonald's employees go when they want advancement within the company? That's right, Hamburger University. Hamburger University was the first corporate college, starting in 1961, and it continues to teach the hamburger-connoisseurs of the world the ins and outs of McDonald's corporate management.

Facts and Figures

The American Hamburger University stands on 80 acres in Oak Brook, Illinois; there are also universities in England, Japan, Germany, and Australia. The average class size is 200 students who come from 119 countries, who are taught by 22 full-time international resident professors. The high-tech facilities include 17 teaching rooms, a 300-seat auditorium, four team rooms for interactive education, and translators and electronic equipment that enable professors to teach in 22 languages at one time.

Job Description

"Professors" at Hamburger University are responsible for conveying both technical and soft skills. Communication, leadership, time management, conflict management, and team building are just some of the soft skills professors coach. Hamburger U. is a believer in team teaching, so instructors, as well as the students, have the opportunity to learn.

Instructors go through a three-month training period during which they take part in a buddy system, mentoring and coaching sessions, and a certification process.

Although other professionals are responsible for lesson plans and deciding how the classes are taught, the professors must study the information for each class, create outlines, and complete a dry run in front of other professors. Occasionally instructors are asked to join the instructional designers, operations people, and target audience representatives to develop the curriculum.

Pay and Perks

As a professor you will teach for a period of two years in a highly academic and modern setting. As one of the largest corporations in the world, McDonald's makes no qualms about providing ample opportunities to its employees. With classes that can be small or large in size (depending on the subject matter), the instructors have the opportunity to teach self-motivated students with the specific desire of holding management positions within McDonald's. Salary ranges are in the mid-five figures but, as I say above, professors tend to move on up into the burger behemoth's management hierarchy. Then you're talking the really big bucks.

Key Attributes

Most of the instructors are experienced workers—those people who have ascended the McDonald's corporate ladder through hard work and discipline. Hamburger University looks for those people who have years of experience in a variety of areas, including training, supervision, and business consultation. You must be able to successfully articulate your experiences and what you learned from them. Problem solving and analytical skills are also helpful in the classroom. Just as McDonald's looks for ambition and enthusiasm in their crew workers, professors must have the same.

In addition to experienced in-the-field professors, Hamburger University also has a need for degreed professionals. For some of the soft skills courses and those courses designed for mid- and executive management, the university employs adjunct faculty. These professors have expert knowledge in the desired field. However, the corporation still believes it is the experience of McDonald's employees that is the best device for teaching.

Key Tip

Hey, 90 percent of success is just showing up, right? So go work for McDonald's and see what it is they love in employees. You can then either choose to work your way up within the corporation or seek out higher education and then return to McDonald's in the executive branches.

Key Resources

Check out these key resources:

www.media.mcdonalds.com/secured/company/training/index.html

www.mcdonalds.com/corp/career/hamburger_university.html

Professional Sommelier

You might have seen them on cruise ships, in classy restaurants, and even in romantic comedies, such as *French Kiss*. They are professional sommeliers, and they like wine— a lot. The job has been compared to cycling by one sommelier, but your legs won't get as much of a workout as your tongue will.

Facts and Figures

The number of working sommeliers, on a worldwide basis is about 10,500. A sommelier works, on average, about 40 hours per week. It's not easy to reach the top of the profession—there are only 56 or so Master Sommeliers.

Job Description

Though described as a "wine waiter" by sommelier Ralph Hersom, the job requires a bit more definition. As a sommelier you must not only serve wine, but manage the selection process, purchasing, receiving, storage, and sales for the institution you work in, which can include restaurants, cruise ships, clubs, and hotels.

Ultimately, you can look at your job as a sommelier as tasting wine and then selling it. You not only have to be a salesperson but a manager and bit of a social butterfly as well (so you can sell more wine).

Pay and Perks

The average starting salary is $14,000 per year, moving up to about $40,000 after ten to fifteen years. Although the pay might not motivate you toward this career, there are some perks that might. The possibility for travel is great, as the best wines are found in Spain, Italy, and France. There's also a great respect for the person who serves and suggests the perfect wine.

Just the information gained might drive you to take sommelier classes, as you will be one of few people to have global wine knowledge including tasting, theory, practical and dining room application, as well as an understanding of spirits, beers, and cigars.

Key Attributes

Though experience with wine is necessary, higher education can be important too. There are three levels to becoming a Master Sommelier. The first is a two-day introductory course where you learn the basics strictly on paper, no wine tasting yet. In the advanced course you'll find yourself immersed in more detail. You should prepare for the exam before you attend the course, which includes a blind tasting, and ends with a demonstration of your skills at a restaurant. For the last (Master Sommelier) level, you must not only be the best, you must be invited. Though similar to the advanced level exam, the Master Sommelier exam is much more complicated and graded more difficultly. Just a hint: the test has been around for 26 years and only 113 people in the world have passed.

Putting the daunting task of test-taking aside, there are also some personality traits that might come in handy. First, and most obviously, you must have a taste for wine; not everyone does. Second, the job does require physical work as well as personality and passion for what you do, so be in shape both physically and mentally. And last, while you don't have to turn into a hater of Trader Joe's $3 bottles, you do have to attain some level of sophistication, as people will be looking to you for answers as an authority on the subject.

Key Tip

Take initiative. There are countless wines out there, so work them as much as humanly possible, without drinking so much that you forget what you've learned. After you think you've learned enough, find more to know. To become a Master Sommelier takes hard work, and lots of time. Set goals; after you achieve them you know you've earned the haughty attitude you might find you've adopted upon completion.

Key Resources

You should read *The Wine Spectator* and *Food and Wine* magazines. Also read *Windows on the World Complete Wine Course* (Sterling, 2003) by Kevin Zraly. For more information on training, check out The Court of Master Sommeliers by calling 707-255-7667 or visiting mastersommeliers.org.

The address of the Sommelier Society of America is …

> 666 Greenwich Street
> Suite 02440
> New York, NY 10014
> 212-679-4190
> sommeliersocietyofamerica.org/

The Least You Need to Know

- ◆ Turn your love of food into a career by training hard and learning all you can about fine cuisine and drink. Start by working at a restaurant, food distributorship, farm, or high-end grocer.

- ◆ Prepare to work nights. Most people in the restaurant business do. Weekends, too.

- ◆ The beauty of a career in fine dining is that you can work where you want. If you love French food, and can prepare it, you can work in Paris or in one of New York's fine restaurants. It's your call.

- ◆ Take your dream to another level by opening your own restaurant.

Part 6

Finding Coolness Where You Work

This part of the book is about harnessing your favorite pastimes and passions in life to your professional career. There's nothing cooler than turning your hobby—especially an unusual one—into your job.

What if your passion is making a difference in the world? Some say that the best you can do in politics is to rearrange the deck chairs on the Titanic, but that's a cynical view. Whether it's shepherding key legislation through congress or running a nonprofit that helps people better manage their lives, a life in public service is truly a life well-lived.

When it comes to identifying the dream jobs of the future, it would be best to be the owner of a really first-rate crystal ball. In lieu of that, I'll try to pin down some of the hottest trends today and see what jobs will emerge from them. If I'm right, remember, you heard it here first.

Chapter 15

Making Your Lifestyle Your Career

In This Chapter

◆ Making your passion your career

◆ A labor of love: pub owner

◆ Low risk and low start-up costs: professional eBay seller

◆ Matchmaking and wedding planning

◆ Unpredictability and adventure: treasure hunting

We've all heard the mantra, "Do what you love and the money will follow." Yes, it's a tad trite, but it makes sense, doesn't it? If you stop worrying about money and just do what you love for a career, you'll be so happy at your job (if you can even call it that) that you'll be great at it. Ergo, and ipso facto, then you'll be compensated well, just as others who are good at what they do.

Come to think of it, just about every dream job in this book is a good example of following your passion and making a good living out of it. But the jobs in this chapter, above all, seem to offer career-seekers a chance to do what they love and get paid to do it.

That's what it's all about, isn't it?

Pub Owner

If you've ever traveled to Europe, Ireland especially, and settled down in front of a warm, crackling fire, your hands comfortably wrapped around a hearty ale, and you let yourself get lost in the easygoing ambience of a good pub or café, chances are, the prospects of running your own pub crossed your mind.

And why not? In Europe (and in many towns and cities in the United States) the local pub is as much a part of the community fabric as the post office, coffee shop, or barber shop—maybe even more so.

People go to pubs to forget about their troubles and slap their neighbors on the back and share a brew and maybe a nice club sandwich or a hot bowl of soup. They visit, they commiserate, they congratulate each other on recent accomplishments, among friends and family.

In short, they're happy. So you, the owner, get to bask in all that happiness and be a real difference maker in the community.

That said, running a pub is like running any small business. There's paperwork, bills, employees to hire (and occasionally fire), and a constant need to market your pub to customers.

Owning a pub is a real labor of love. But if you are up to it, there are few better ways to make a living as far as I'm concerned.

Facts and Figures

What does it cost to buy your own pub? It depends. Each pub you consider is likely different. Some are older, some newer, some in good locations and some in not-so-good locations. You get the idea.

On researching this career I found a slew of pubs for sale on the Internet. The price tag for most exceeded $500,000, a good chunk of which is transferal of the all-important liquor license. Such license can cost between $100,000 to $200,000.

The number of actual pubs operating in the United States fluctuates wildly. There are somewhere between 300 and 500 true "brew pubs" in the United States today, but there are many more depending on your definition of *pub*.

Job Description

You might start your day in the late morning hours, although some of your employees—especially your cleaning person—will have already shown up. You'll check what is commonly referred to as "the book"—the ledger from the night before—which gives you a "heads up" on any issues, shortages, or potential problems.

As your lunch crowd comes and goes (there's no rule that says you have to offer lunch—many pubs don't open until 3 or 4 P.M. or so), you'll check inventories, order supplies, field customer and employee complaints, peruse the menu, check the beer lines (for cleanliness), and make out employee schedules. You'll pore over daily sales receipts and store them in a computer database for easy access.

As your customers start to wade in, you'll be dressed neatly and cleanly, greeting them as old friends. Expect to give—and receive—lots of banter from your customers, especially your regulars. Nobody likes a thin-skinned or reticent pub owner. You'll spend the rest of your time acting as host and proprietor, chatting up regulars, and helping staff with food and drink orders.

It's a busy day. But you won't notice, because it's your pub.

Pay and Perks

Like your mother always told you, what you'll get out of something depends on what you put into it. In the pub business, that means the money you make depends on how hard you work to make your pub a great place to visit. The good news is that if you find the recipe for success, you'll likely clear six figures easily. If you don't, you might join the ample list of pubs and restaurants that went under for one reason or another.

One tip to make more money: offer a good food menu. About 65 percent of your revenues will come from food sales. So whip up a creative and fun menu on your own or bring a good cook or chef to come in and do it for you. It's also worth noting that the U.S. beer market is valued at $1.3 billion annually. So you've also got that going for you.

> **The Water Cooler**
>
> The U.S. restaurant industry is huge—it's a $476 billion market in 2005.

Key Attributes

To be successful as a pub owner, a firm handshake and the memory of an elephant helps. (You'll want to memorize customers' names—they love it when you do that. Makes 'em feel special). As a pub owner, that is as close to a magic formula for success as you'll find—making customers feel special and thus generating that all-important repeat business. Make no mistake, repeat business is what fuels the restaurant industry.

Pub owners are a varied lot. Yes, many come straight from the restaurant industry (as chefs, restaurant managers, bartenders, and so on). But many more are successful business people who have always wanted to own their own pub. In the latter case, some are strictly "nonactive financial backers" who might not want to get involved in the day-to-day operations of the pub—they might just want to bask in the limelight as proprietor. The financial benefits are better that way, too. Financial backers are the first in line to get paid from restaurant profits.

Key Tip

Have a bottle of good house wine on each table, before your customers are seated. The idea is to make them say "no" to the wine to have it removed from the table. Many customers, looking to relax, might opt to keep the wine—and pad their check amount.

Key Resource

Bone up on pub ownership at the U.S. National Restaurant Association's website at www.restaurant.org.

Professional eBay Seller

"Sold ... to CutiePie911@aol.com for a bid of $417.50."

If those are the words you are longing to hear, not as a buyer, but as a seller, then a career as a professional eBay seller might be worth bidding on.

If you think about it for a moment, an eBay gig, part time or full time, is a low-risk, low-start-up cost business with upward of 50 million customers. (That's the number of people worldwide who have bought something on eBay.)

Facts and Figures

eBay reports that it has about 50,000 registered eBay sellers operating on the company's mammoth website. Of the 50 million eBay customers around the globe, the real bread and butter market is the United States, where 35 million eBay buyers have logged on and bought everything from old B. B. King records to five-bedroom homes in Connecticut. eBay moves over $5 billion worth of items on an annual basis.

Job Description

Like any sales-oriented venture, the idea is to find merchandise at low enough prices to sell at a profit on eBay. As I point out in the "Key Tip" section, yard sales and bankruptcy auctions are a good place to start. Also reach out to consignment operators—people who will let you sell excess inventories of particular products for a cut of the profits. The good news is that if consignment items don't sell, you can simply return them at little cost (just shipping charges) to you. You're not stuck with the inventory.

What do you need to start? A good computer, a good digital camera, and some free time. Start with about 10 hours a week putting items for sale online and see how you do.

If you succeed, eBay will love you. Its PowerSellers program offers free vacations and even paid health insurance for big sellers. The program starts at $1,000 in sales each month and scales up from there.

Pay and Perks

Compensation varies for eBay sellers, depending on the time they put in and the demand that their products generate. But eBay does provide some telling numbers on seller compensation from the site. The company says that profit margins average between 10 percent and 40 percent on items that sell for less than a few hundred bucks. So if you sold about $25,000 in eBay items per month, at a 25 percent profit margin, you'd gross $6,250 per month. Of course, some big-ticket items will generate even more money. One eBay seller sold a piece of real estate online and earned a $1 million profit.

Key Attributes

Some experience in sales is helpful to eBay sellers. Of particular value is the fine art of calculating an item's true value and setting a price tag that will ensure you make a profit.

Another good attribute is discipline—you really have to stick with online auctions if you want to put your kids through college via eBay sales. eBay does make it easy on you. They offer a user-friendly getting started tutorial, charge small fees to place your wares on the sprawling site, and charge a minimal commission on items sold. A middleman system allows customers to pay you via credit card transaction, so payment is easy, too. That leaves you time to hone clever pitches and create attractive photos of your 1963 baseball card collection.

Key Tip

Haunt bankruptcy auctions and yard sales and look for values. If you have an eye for antiques, collectibles, and such, then you might be able to spot a hand-tooled horse saddle that you can buy for $200 and sell for $500. Do that enough and you can retire early.

Also work on your customer service skills. Deliver when you say you are going to deliver, and keep your word at all times. On eBay, your reputation is everything.

Key Resource

Take a gander at eBay's getting started page for sellers. It tells you all you need to know about getting the ball rolling as an eBay trader. Find it at pages.ebay.com/sellercentral/newsellers.html.

Matchmaker

> I get no kick from champagne
> Mere alcohol doesn't thrill me at all,
> So tell me why it should be true,
> That I get a kick out of you?
>
> —Cole Porter

A wise guy once said of marriage: "It's sex with the same woman the rest of your life, and if it doesn't work out, she gets half of everything you own. Gee, where can I sign up for *that?*"

Ah, love and marriage. The thing is, most people do want to meet their soul mate but are either (pick one) too shy, too busy, too confused, or too reluctant to do so. That's where a professional matchmaker comes in.

Matchmaking has been around forever. Twelfth-century astrologers looked to the stars to discover people's soul mates. Shakespearean-era tarot card readers shuffled through cards to discover a person's true love. Going to a town dance in the 1850s, you'd be directed by a local matchmaker to possible suitors.

These days, things are a little more complicated. The divorce rate is up. Many people are dating again later in life. We find dates in Internet chat rooms, over hotlines, and through want ads. Above all, we're in over our heads in our careers and work more hours than we used to.

Marriages these days (in America at least) aren't arranged. Meeting someone in a bar is becoming cliché. What options do we have left? Well, because we're subcontracting all other services in our lives to financial advisors, personal trainers, and even life coaches, why wouldn't we turn again to the matchmaker to give our dating life a whirl? Indeed, we are—so much so that matchmaking is becoming a burgeoning industry.

> **The Water Cooler**
>
> Everybody is capitalizing on matchmaking through the process of referrals. Partnerships are being forged between health clubs, clothing stores, and even plastic surgeons to help us find that special someone.

Facts and Figures

Annually, Americans spend a combined $500 million on personal ads in newspapers, magazines, and now through the Internet with sites like eharmony.com and match.com. These online matchmaking sites are the newest addition to the American dating service industry that totals over a billion dollars.

The problem with many online matchmaking sites is that they don't verify facts about those participating. Men are known to lie about their height, women about their weight, and some even lie about their marital status.

Where online matchmaking is still an inaccurate science, many companies (or self-employed matchmakers) are helping people meet without a dotcom attached. They are known to scour malls and other venues handing out brochures to single women who fit specific profiles. Men, usually more comfortable in viewing their dating futures as an investment (in time and finances), are the ones who end up paying between $1,000 to $1,500 for "introductions." In an introduction, participants are offered a meeting with a potential dater, usually in the form of a lunch.

Job Description

Matchmakers—as with any business person—handle their work professionally. The self-employed matchmaker has clients, an office, an assistant to help with scheduling, and so on.

A common misconception about matchmakers is that they are coddling salespeople who cater to the egos of a clientele. Yet very often a lot of the people who seek out matchmakers are successful, well-rounded people with good careers. They simply don't have the time or resources to meet people who match their criteria in terms of age, background, ethnicity, religion, beliefs, personal interests, education, or even a similar sense of humor.

On the Job

Working as a matchmaker in an area of regional sprawl will produce a larger clientele. Work-minded professionals between ages 25 and 55 usually have fewer resources to network.

A matchmaker usually starts with a prescreening process. A license or other valid form of identification is needed to prevent people who would abuse the matchmaking service (e.g., someone who is married, or a person with questionable criminal activity) from doing so. At this point, a one-hour interview with the client is standard practice to determine his or her interests, personal background, and what he or she is looking for in the perfect suitor.

Pay and Perks

The self-employed matchmaker only works with people she likes—but she makes them pay through the nose for the chance at matrimonial bliss. Often clients are charged between $1,000 and $5,000 per year for professional matchmaking services, with no guarantee they'll meet the love of their life. But money isn't everything. When it comes to complicated decisions, a matchmaker can choose against taking on ethically compromising situations or clients she just does not trust to do the right thing. Beyond this, she gets to interact with people and understand what each is searching for. She gets to learn about people's romantic wants and needs. Ultimately, when things work out and a connection is made, a matchmaker can feel she has made a difference in people's dating lives. The ultimate? Dancing alongside the bride and groom at a client's wedding.

Key Attributes

A professional matchmaker has a way with people. She might have worked as a social worker or a psychologist, or maybe she simply has a good track record for setting friends up on dates. You must be a good listener and be able to discern from clients' nonverbal cues what they're really looking for. It's like solving a puzzle, in a lot of ways.

Key Tip

Make sure to advise clients that having a "wish list for the perfect person" will not guarantee anything. Being overly picky without having even met a person first will inevitably inhibit potentially beneficial matches. The important thing to remind clients: "The one thing I can't control is chemistry."

Key Resource

The Matchmaking Institute offers an 11-course certification, which includes classes in dating and relationship coaching as well as matchmaking skills. Check out www.matchmakinginstitute.com.

Wedding Planner

Many newlyweds say that their wedding day is the happiest day of their lives. Why not? Surrounded by your best friends and family, celebrating in elegant surroundings, cutting into a cake the size of a Buick. Good times.

For true romantics, who love weddings so much they'll get involved with them over and over again (no, I'm not talking about Liz Taylor), a true career calling might be as a wedding planner.

After all, today, weddings are becoming an American industry. With the average wedding costing $19,100 for an average of 186 invitees, no wonder weddings draw about $45 billion dollars worth of revenue a year.

On the Job _____

An aspiring wedding planner can get experience by offering service to friends and family for free, then having them write reference letters on his or her behalf.

It makes sense that whenever a couple decides to tie the knot, someone needs to handle all of the intricate details, from selecting a wedding date to booking a band to planning the dinner menu. Whether you call them bridal consultants, wedding consultants, or wedding coordinators, wedding planners manage to make a profession out of helping us walk down the aisle.

Facts and Figures

With over 2.5 million weddings taking place in the United States in 2004, there is an ever-increasing amount of opportunities in this field. An aspiring wedding planner needs no special education or experience to break in and succeed.

Many learn by attending as many weddings as possible. They read wedding magazines, visit bridal shows, and interview recently married folks, members of clergy, other wedding planners, florists, caterers, and anyone else connected to weddings. They also assemble a portfolio consisting of a collection of photographs from previous wedding work.

If the desire for additional education appeals to you, you can enroll for additional training at one of many wedding consultation associations. These lessons and sessions can run around $1,000.

Job Description

Instead of getting into business for oneself, wedding planners often choose to work for companies. Bridal stores, gift registries, florists, caterers, department stores, and anywhere products are sold have all been known to hire wedding planners as another resource to their customers. Additionally, various wedding locales such as hotels, country clubs, and cruise ships have on-site wedding planners. Wedding planners can find work in nearly any location, especially at major attraction locations like the Caribbean, Las Vegas, and Disney World.

When wedding planners do decide to go into business for themselves, very often they decide to set up office from home to save on expenses. To set up a business in this field, you need a computer, a fax machine, business cards, and marketing materials. Finally, in this day and age, an Internet site is a must. Today's brides and grooms are Internet-savvy and willing to look online for the best options possible.

Networking is everything as a wedding planner—so focus on making and keeping connections. That includes vendors who can refer you to clients. These suppliers of wedding-related material range from limousine companies to musicians, bridal stores to photographers, and party suppliers to invitation printers. In addition to providing new business leads, good vendor contacts will keep you from getting into too many binds.

Pay and Perks

How much a wedding planner makes depends upon the individual. An hourly rate for planning could rest around $50 or there could be a flat salary. It is estimated that planners can earn between $50,000 and $100,000 a year for their skills.

In addition, many aspects of organizing a wedding can be pleasurable. Finding good musicians, tasting cakes, and helping couples explore meaningful marriage vows can all make a wedding planner's job a lot more fun. Tying all of your strides together will be the feeling that you've helped make one of the most enjoyable (and potentially nerve-racking) days in two peoples' lives come off flawlessly. This is a wedding planner's ultimate personal reward.

Key Attributes

Wedding planners are creative people who are masters of social skills. They get people to be where they need to be and things where they need to go. Above all, a good wedding planner will maintain checklists, time schedules, and have general organizational tools to plan and make everything run smoothly. You should be a master problem-solver as well; you'll certainly run into plenty of snags and screw-ups while planning your client's perfect day. Even better than problem solving, come to think of it, is problem-anticipation. Knowing what could go wrong and preventing it is wedding planning talent at the highest level.

Key Tip

Any skills in business management, marketing, or food and hospitalities fields are all pluses. Work on negotiation skills; do your research (for example, know that the price of floral arrangements in May is X amount of dollars before you begin talking turkey with the flower arranger) and know to dig your heels in when you absolutely must get what you want. Your client will appreciate it and recommend you highly to her friends.

Key Resource

Check out the wedding planner section of About.com's careers website. It's full of great articles on setting up a business and succeeding in the field. Find it at careerplanning.about.com/od/occupations/a/wedding_planner_2.htm.

Treasure Hunter

You know what they say: "One man's trash is another man's treasure." What will be next? A coin? A bottle? Toy, ring, watch? At any moment, you could be scanning your metal detector over a 1960s Coke can or a nineteenth century half-dollar. It's this sense of unpredictability and adventure that keeps the treasure hunter going.

But that's not necessarily so with the professional kind. More and more, people are going out with cutting-edge metal detectors in hand trying to find new sites to search for the big treasures. They scour railroad stops, roadside parks, and especially the beach to discover treasures.

On the Job

Access to nautical records is a good way to plot out potential crash sites for ships. If a ship has sunk nearby, a find is more likely.

Even the weather impacts a treasure hunter's life. Whereas hurricane season is considered a time of disaster to most of us, professional treasure hunters consider it a time of opportunity. Big tropical storms rake pre-existing dunes left and right, dramatically altering the architecture of the beach. What they leave exposed could very well be rubbish. Then again, it could be a bona fide treasure find.

Facts and Figures

For the most part, treasure hunting is done with metal detectors on land. They're fairly inexpensive at $1,500 or so. Pouches, headphones, and batteries will set you back another $25 or $30. Like I said, not that expensive. Unless you can afford an underwater surveillance submarine for a nautical salvage operation, metal detectors are your main option. The odds of finding buried treasures (given you have a good metal detector) are high, considering that there is rumored to be more American coins lying buried in the ground than currently in circulation.

Not only is American currency to be found; gold, silver, and various gems have been reported found deep within the coastal dunes of the United States. Many missing ships have gone unfound. Untold amounts of treasures have washed ashore in the continental United States, and many more remain unexposed.

Job Description

"Finders, keepers" is the first rule of treasure hunting. If you find it, it's yours. Beyond this, it's hard to exactly identify the ins and outs of the secret art of treasure hunting. Most treasure hunters guard their secrets as they would their lives. The practice is a craft honed from understanding which places have already been scoured and understanding which methods have been used in that locale.

The main method treasure hunters utilize in their searches is a metal detector. When it comes to detecting metal, you have three options. The first is a pulse metal detector that can be used on the beach, especially in wet sand. It can detect the deepest, yet also detects every piece of metal in the ground. The multi-frequency detector is similar to the pulse except that it can eliminate trash like bottle caps, pull-tabs, and gum wrappers from its scans. Finally, the single-frequency is your best shot, where trash is rampant.

Another instrument worth utilizing is a long range detector. These units can detect larger items and treasure chests as far as 20 feet beneath the surface and 2 to 10 blocks away. These metal detectors, which range in cost between $2,000 and $30,000, are often used by professional treasure hunters.

> **On the Job**
>
> Metal detector use in State and National Parks is prohibited. If you're uncertain about using a detector in a given plot of land, always get permission from the authorities.

Pay and Perks

Although marine archaeologists would label treasure hunters as "plunderers," very often they end up giving their find to museums, which reward them sums of money to go on to other finds.

Aside from this, discovering artifacts in itself can be considered a reward. Cashing something in might not be worth the special significance it holds to the treasure hunter.

Key Attribute

To be a treasure hunter, you must be driven by the search. If, every time you find an old bottle, you sigh and wonder why it wasn't an eighteenth century Spanish doubloon, then maybe treasure hunting isn't for you. Not all items you find will be of monetary worth. But maintaining your curiosity about all of your finds will keep you from burning out.

Key Tip

Being patient and continuing to scout out new territories is what separates a true treasure hunter from a beach-combing tourist.

Key Resource

Take a look at Goldmap.com. It's got plenty of tips and advice for would-be treasure hunters. Find it at www.goldmaps.com/metal_detecting_treasure_hunting_resources.htm.

The Least You Need to Know

- Think like a small business owner. By that I mean create a plan of attack; identify the resources you need to do the job (and how you're going to pay for them); and set goals for business growth.

- When you're on your own, professionalism is paramount. You'll be judged by … you. So cultivate a professional, knowledgeable image.

◆ Attend conferences and seminars and network. Wedding planners and restaurant owners, for example, have no shortage of professional events where they can meet and greet.

◆ Start with an office from home—and expand later. It's just basic economics. If you don't have a great deal of start-up capital, open your business at home. In a year or two, if you do the job right, you'll have enough customers and enough income to open a commercial office.

Chapter 16

Don't Pigeonhole Me: Offbeat Careers

In This Chapter

- ◆ Why being different sells
- ◆ The big business of dolls
- ◆ Writing greeting cards
- ◆ Going once, going twice: auctioneer
- ◆ Just do it: motivational speaker
- ◆ Normal and paranormal investigative work

So you don't run with the herd? Good for you!

In the career market, a little bit of variety can be a good, marketable asset. Maybe IBM doesn't know what to do with a maverick like you who doesn't go for the cookie-cutter, lockstep approach that corporate America seems to value so highly.

But many other employers do. They value and appreciate the enthusiasm and passion that marketplace mavericks like you bring to the table. As Benjamin Disraeli said, "Every production of genius must be the product of enthusiasm."

So find a way to bottle that enthusiasm and that penchant for doing things a bit differently and sell it in the career marketplace. Keep the following careers in mind as you do so. One might have your unique stamp on it before too long.

Doll Doctor

Do you have a calling to plastic surgery, but hate the sight of blood? Have you always thought that being a mortician would be interesting, but don't like the idea of "seeing dead people"? If so, doll doctoring might be the career for you. This career combines artistic restoration with some of the qualities you would use in those other two, more stressful, jobs. Plus you get to work with toys! What could be better?

The American Girl Doll series has dozens of different models, and all are popular with young girls, which is sure to provide you with plenty of work.

Facts and Figures

Doll are big business in the United States today. The more expensive dolls, like the famous American Girl line—a favorite of young girls across the globe—are big sellers.

More than 10 million American Girl dolls have been sold since 1986, making over 95 percent of girls between the ages of 7 and 12 familiar with the series. They have also sold over 100 million books. With the price of such dolls so high, the incentive for parents to have their daughters' dolls fixed if a part happens to fall off or the doll is accidentally flipped out a window by a little brother is quite high.

Job Description

Your work as a doll doctor will include careful repair and restoration; the dolls must not lose any value as collectors' items. Some dolls might need large repairs, but it is your responsibility to leave the doll looking like it was never worked on.

In repairing and restoring the doll you will have a variety of jobs. The first is repairing and replacing missing or broken parts. You will have to determine what materials to use to create the new parts. Second, you might be asked to clean and/or repair the surfaces of the doll's body. This is when you must remember to stay away from harmful materials. The solvents you use should be safe and effective. And last, you might have to replace or fix clothing or accessories. The American Girl dolls have endless closets of clothes and accessories. You should be able to replace these things if you cannot repair them.

On the Job

Doll doctor "kits," including materials to fix broken dolls, aren't that expensive. Most go for between $20 and $45.

Pay and Perks

As a doll doctor, your prices will vary according to the size and difficulty of the job and age of the doll. Typically, prices for simple jobs such as cleaning wigs or resetting eyes can cost anywhere from $20 to $75. More difficult services, including full restorations, can cost from about $100 to $500. These prices depend on whether the client wants antique replacements for clothing and parts, how the doll is put together, and the material it is made of.

If you are working as an independent doll doctor, you will have freedom to look forward to. If you are working for a larger company, you will have the ease of not running your own business, and you'll also receive a regular salary. While working with dolls you will gain experience in art restoration as well as antiques and collectibles, which will be helpful in some circles.

Key Attributes

First and foremost, you should enjoy working with dolls and/or collectible items. As a way to gain experience and authority you should also look into obtaining a degree in visual arts; whether it is in restoration or a more general degree in fine arts, it will be helpful. There are certificates and diplomas available from smaller institutions also; these include the Certificate for Professional Doll Restoration from D & B Antiques, the Certificate for Professional Restoration Course from MacDowell Doll Museum, and the Diploma in Doll Repair from the Doll Hospital School in Lifetime Career Schools.

There are also doll restoration/conservation courses available from the United Federation of Doll Clubs. Working in a museum, doll or otherwise, will familiarize you with conservation standards as well as provide you with contacts.

Key Tip

Before you launch your career, do a local search to see if there are other doll doctors in your area. If there are, see if there are job opportunities within the already established company. If not, you know you will have little to no competition in the field.

Key Resources

Check out the Doll Doctors' Association at http://gmdollseminar.com/ DollDoctorsAssociation.htm and G & M Doll Restoration at www.gmdollseminar. com for more information.

Greeting Card Writer

"Dearest Brother / You are like no other / I've looked one after the other / But just can't find another ... Happy Birthday!" If you can do better than that—and I'm sure you can—you can have a career in greeting card writing.

Facts and Figures

According to the Bureau of Labor Statistics, about 210 salaried employees wrote and designed greeting cards in 1999. This number does not include freelance writers, who make up a large population of greeting card writers.

Job Description

As a greeting card writer you have some options. In the career market, options are a good thing.

You can choose to write for paper-based cards or for online greetings. For paper-based cards, you should first contact card companies of your choice and request their submission guidelines. Each card company has its own personality, so it is important that you know for whom you are writing; this will raise your chances of getting published. If you are working as a freelance writer, you can send ideas to any number of card companies. There are three basic categories for cards: traditional, contemporary, and alternative. Currently, companies prefer conversational cards rather than lyrical, rhyming ones. Humorous cards are the largest sellers, so if you have a good punch line, use it. Other types of cards that are popular celebrate birthdays, friendship, and religion. The more alternative cards can offer congratulations on new jobs or promotions, as well as sympathy for divorce or illness.

For online cards, editors like the writers to have a visual plan for the card as well as lyrics. You don't have to be an artist, but you should have the visuals prepared and be able to describe them. Ideas for online greeting cards are generally submitted through e-mail or web page. The response time after submission is often shorter for online cards as well; this is because the editor gets them faster and has an easier time viewing them on the computer.

Pay and Perks

Those 210 employees in 1999 earned an average of $36,620 for the year. If you choose to work freelance, you can make, on average, from about $25 to $150 per verse or idea. For online greetings, some companies pay as low as $10 per idea, but that usually goes up with the number of ideas they accept from you.

The greeting card industry has been deemed the easiest to get into by some writers. They also find the writing easier; of course writing a few lines is easier than a novel. This is another dream job that you won't need extra schooling for. There is no degree required, just writing ability. You'll also find this career helpful because it can help you branch out. While writing greeting cards you can easily find your way into the novelty business. Many people writing for card companies also design t-shirts, mugs, buttons, and other items for the card company or for other novelty companies associated with the card company.

Key Attributes

The number one trait necessary for this job is creativity. It helps if you are unique. Greeting card companies are not looking for cards like the previous example, nor clichés. They are looking for innovative, attention-grabbing ideas. You should keep on top of current events and trends also; there have been many cards designed around such things as Viagra ("No hard feelings? Take Viagra.").

As far as your writing goes, it should be tight. You have limited time to grab a shopper's attention with a card; your writing has be either entertaining or sentimental, and to the point. You also have to be able to write in voices that

> **The Water Cooler**
>
> About one-third of all greeting cards each year in the United States are written by freelance writers.

are not yours. Remember, you are responsible for conveying others' feelings. This might mean you have to write in a child's voice, or that of another gender.

Key Tip

When you start you should focus on submitting to smaller card companies. They are more likely to work with you personally, giving you tips and feedback. You should also try to write every day (as any writer should), build a portfolio, and be persistent. If you are interested in online greetings, learn graphics programs so you can better visualize your ideas. And, this advice goes for any writer: don't be afraid of rejection. It is inevitable, and it does not mean you can't make it in this career.

Key Resources

To find a list of greeting card companies you can look into, check out the following books:

> *Writer's Market* from Writer's Digest Books published in Cincinnati, Ohio (Writer's Digest Books, 2005).

> *The Writer's Handbook* published by The Writer, Inc., in Boston, Massachusetts, 2003.

You can also write to the Artist and Writer's Market to get the same information without buying the books. Just make sure you include a self-addressed stamped envelope for them to send the information back.

> The Artist and Writer's Market
> The Greeting Card Association
> 1356 New York Ave NW
> Suite 615
> Washington, DC 20005

Motivational Speaker

Have you seen the film *Magnolia*? Everyone watching it was gripped by Tom Mackey, played by Tom Cruise, just waiting to see what he'd say next. You can be Tom Cruise, too, or at least the motivational speaker he plays in the film.

If you, as they say in the motivational market, "B-E-L-I-E-E-E-E-E-V-E" in yourself.

Facts and Figures

The National Speakers Association's membership has increased by 20 percent in the last 10 years. The NSA currently has 3,500 members, who most often find engagements with corporations and associations. Four out of five of these members own their own speaking businesses.

Job Description

As a motivational speaker your goal is to inspire your audience to take action on a given issue or subject. What you motivate them to do, however, is up to you. Motivational speakers help people in a variety of areas, including business, relationships, and health. Depending on what topic you choose to talk about, you can find yourself speaking at conferences, schools, colleges, adult learning centers, corporations, cruise ships, and more. If you'd rather not be out on your own, you can find placement at a seminar company; otherwise you can be your own boss and present your own seminars.

After you've made up your mind to become a motivational speaker, there are a few key steps you need to take. First you have to decide what you'll speak about. You can do this by examining your own life and finding what you have to offer others. The more unique experiences you can draw upon, the greater success you have. When you have ideas, you should choose one general topic that can encompass any number of stories or experiences. The topics should be more general so that you can advertise yourself as an expert in, for example, relationships and not try to sell yourself as the man who once had a tough break-up. Next you'll have to write your speech. You can also have someone write it for you; you can find speechwriting services online. Obviously, you'll need to be an entertaining speaker. You can develop your skills by practicing yourself or by taking classes. When you begin you will have to approach companies, groups, and institutions to find work. After you have experience there are ways to get employers to approach you. When you finally have a speaking engagement, make sure you have materials to pass out. Get your name out there!

Pay and Perks

Motivational speakers who are NSA members make between $75,000 and $150,000 per year, with 10.2 percent making over $200,000 per year.

Motivational speakers often travel for speaking engagements. You will at least get to see much of the United States. Another perk is that there is a great deal of freedom. The deeper you delve into a speaker's career, the more contacts you make, the more gigs you get, and the more money you make. Then you have the leverage to call more of your own shots.

Key Attributes

Anyone who has the desire (and motivation) can become a motivational speaker. There is no extra education required. Your main concern should be your own unique speaking ability. You should be entertaining while also providing the information your audience is paying for. We've all had teachers whose monotone voices put us to sleep; you should have something new to add as far as the way you speak and what you speak about. There are many people out there who have seminars on dating; find something that few people are experts on.

Key Tip

Before you are a well-known speaker, there are some things you can do to get people to approach you to speak. Get interviewed on the radio or television. You can do this by putting ads out for producers to find (see "Key Resources"). Getting published will also help. If you write an article for a local or national paper, millions of people will read what you have to say. Putting up a website will raise your visibility too. When people are searching the internet for a speaker, your name will be there. You should also look into giving free speeches in the beginning of your career. You can gain contacts, references, and experience this way.

Key Resources

Use these sites to find information on advertising yourself: www.rtir.com, www.authorsandexperts.com, www.yearbook.com, and www.guestfinder.com.

Contact the National Speakers Association (NSA) at nsaspeaker.org or by phone at 480-968-2552.

Auctioneer

When most people think of an auctioneer, they picture a slick-talking, confident chatterbox poised at a podium, gavel in hand, whose nearly indecipherable patter will wind up with: "going once, going twice … sold!" This might be the most visible part of the job, but there's much more work that goes into closing that sale.

Auctioneers work behind the scenes, planning, organizing, and scheduling auctions—which are essentially live, public sales where items ranging from property to paintings and livestock to automobiles are offered for sale to the highest bidder.

The use of telephone and Internet bidding has expanded the reach of many auctions to far beyond the audience gathered there in the room. Even with the advent of eBay, live auctions remain a lively and popular means of commerce—and there remains a demand for qualified auctioneers to organize and oversee these events.

Facts and Figures

The National Auctioneers Association (NAA) boasts a membership of 6,400 in the United States, Canada, Australia, and several other countries. Its members specialize in the sale of everything from antiques and residential items to real estate and business equipment. With such variety, there's no such thing as a typical auction—sales figures can vary enormously at various events. You might be facing a crowd of 50 or 10,000 people, conducting sales anywhere from a few thousand dollars to several hundred million.

The Water Cooler

Unlike most fields, auction houses and auctioneers tend to do some of their best business during a recession. In hard times, people look to liquidate assets and get hold of some cash. Auctions remain one of the most efficient ways to do this, while earning the most for heirlooms and treasures.

Job Description

In addition to their "chant" at the podium, auctioneers handle a variety of tasks from inventorying the items for sale to promoting the auction via the Internet, newspaper or magazine ads, and old-fashioned personal networking. To market well, you need to know the products you're selling—the value, the demand for the merchandise, and the best way to present it. Many choose to specialize in three or four types of auctions (for example, real estate, autos, art, and antiques). Successful auctioneers have some understanding of the "psychology" of the auction—how much an item is likely to sell for, in addition to its actual worth.

More than 75 percent of auctioneers work as independent contractors for a daily fee or a percentage of sales. As a contractor, you're responsible for marketing and drumming up sales, so good people and business skills are important. Auctions can take place anywhere—from a barn to a parking lot to a large convention center—and travel is often required.

As an auctioneer, you represent the seller but should also be able to work with buyers. The many hours of public speaking and working the crowd call for a strong voice, a good sense of humor, and an agile mind.

Many auction companies continue to be family businesses, but if you don't happen to be "connected" the NAA has a list of auction schools across the country—which run anywhere from a couple of weeks to a full college semester. There you'll learn the trademark auctioneer chant, plus how to market your services and sales and how to get started in the auction business.

Pay and Perks

Although auctioneers can earn good salaries working for an auction house, in order to earn the really big bucks your goal should be to start your own firm. This business relies to a great extent on networking, so you'll need to make solid connections first by working for somebody else, or by freelancing extensively.

Beginning auctioneers generally start out part time and work on commission, so early incomes can be quite low. (They also fluctuate, due to the seasonal nature of much auction work.)

Over time, your income will largely depend on the amount of time and effort spent marketing and making a go of your business. Top auctioneers with a solid client base and a good reputation can earn $100,000 a year.

Key Attributes

Personality is key for an auctioneer, as your primary job is to connect with your audience. You should work well with a variety of people, be adept at sales and public speaking, and be comfortable juggling a number of tasks at once.

Key Tip

Before enrolling in an auction school, you might want to gain some hands-on experience as an apprentice under an experienced auctioneer. Apprentice auctioneers assist in organizing and running sales, and might act as "ringpeople"—taking bids from the audience and passing them on to the auctioneer. You'll learn the day-to-day operations of running an auction business, which will give you a taste of the life.

Key Resource

Visit the website of the National Auctioneers Association at www.auctioneers.org.

Private Investigator

Got a bit of the bloodhound in you?

Have you always been jealous of Magnum PI or Inspector Gadget? Get their job! Okay, so you might not be a hit with the ladies like Magnum was or have all the tools that Gadget had, but you will have a respectable and very cool career.

Facts and Figures

PIs and detectives accounted for about 48,000 jobs in 2002. About one fifth of those jobs were in investigation and security services, with another fifth in retail stores. The rest worked in a variety of venues including insurance agencies, government, legal firms, and banks.

Job Description

Private investigators don't always chase bad guys—it's a more legitimate business than you might think. As a PI you can work for attorneys, insurance companies, corporations, retail stores, or the general public. Whether you are working for a company or yourself, your responsibilities might include gathering client information, locating missing persons, performing surveillance, or doing background checks. You might also be hired to protect celebrities.

Most investigators have specialties. You can focus your work on any criminal act, from property theft to computer fraud to adultery. General duties can include surveillance, interviews, computer searches, telephone calls, and some travel.

On the Job

The best private investigators specialize—just like good lawyers and doctors do. Good places to look? Missing persons; background investigations; computer crime; or insurance fraud.

Pay and Perks

The average salary of a private investigator in 2002 was $29,300. This number is higher for corporate investigators, and lower for retail investigators.

Though private investigators might work long or irregular hours, there are some perks. For one, you're a PI and that's just cool. Depending on your client, travel might be necessary. You'll also be working closely with your clients. You'll get to meet a variety of people and have more than superficial conversations with them.

Key Attributes

Though you don't need it, experience in the military, law enforcement, or government agencies will be helpful. If you are interested in working as a PI within a bank, business, or law office, a degree in the corresponding field will also be helpful.

You will probably need a license. This depends on the state you will be working in, but most require some kind of certification.

Private investigators must be physically and mentally strong. You also must be persistent and assertive. You need to have the ability to gather information when others cannot. You'll also find good communication and interrogation skills helpful. PIs cannot be afraid of confrontation. There will always be someone who does not want to provide the information you need; you'll have to not only be able to get it but get it without much trouble.

Key Tip

Though this might be your dream job, be honest about your qualifications. Being a private investigator requires a strong, independent, and assertive individual with a mature, logical mind. You should not get started in this business if you are not sure, as it might cause harmful mistakes. Also, move on to another page of this book if you've been convicted of a felony; you won't be eligible for a license.

Key Resources

You can look online to find your state licensing information. Each state has its own requirements and its own website, so you can do a Google search using the name of your state and "private investigators and license" in the subject line.

Cryptozoologist

Are you captivated by the idea that there could be a never-before-identified aquatic creature lurking in the depths of Loch Ness? Does the idea of a monster under your bed give you thrills instead of chills? Then life as a cryptozoologist, or hunter of unknown species, might be just the ticket to career bliss for you.

If you're a fan of watching grainy video footage of hairy, stooped men loping into the forest, or if you find yourself wondering about the origins of monster legends like the yeti, cryptozoology can provide you with a professional outlet for your curiosity. Not a field for everyone, cryptozoologists run the gamut from professional psychologists to respected zoologists to nuts with no training. However you choose to approach this field, there's no doubt you'll find it fascinating.

Facts and Figures

Cryptozoology is the study of animals that have not been recognized by Western science. In many cases, it's the study of animals that have only been seen fleetingly from a distance, and some that have never been seen by the human eye at all.

The search for new creatures, or creatures believed to be extinct, has attracted serious investigators despite its quixotic nature. Coined by Belgian zoologist Bernard Heuvelmans from the Greek word *kryptos*, meaning hidden, unknown, or secret, cryptozoology is still a relatively unexplored field, although it's developing increasing interest. The International Society of Cryptozoology boasts 900 members, including a number of distinguished zoologists, naturalists, and other professionals.

As you can imagine, some monster hunters came to the field by way of science fiction. Movies and books about beasts like the yeti and the Loch Ness monster have captivated many an inquisitive mind. The lure of exploring the unknown can be thrilling and enticing, inspiring some to pursue career opportunities seeking out a reality not normally taught in the standard biology or natural history texts.

Job Description

Cryptozoologists do not have a formal job description, per se. Various educational backgrounds (anthropology, linguistics, zoology, biology, and so on) are helpful. Training with an established cryptozoologist can help get a novice into the field more quickly.

Some cryptozoologists teach at universities, consult, research, and write. But all of their work is centered on the notion that there are creatures out there that science has not yet identified.

Monster hunting is not all excitement and intrigue, though. There is lots of important but boring work—such as searching through newspaper files, tracking down witnesses, and double-checking witness backgrounds—but the ultimate goal is thrilling. Investigating extraordinary incidents that happen to ordinary people and chasing unknown creatures can be very rewarding to anyone who enjoys a good mystery.

Pay and Perks

Pay varies widely depending on educational background and professional associations. Some cryptozoologists are respected academics at fine institutions of higher education earning salaries in the low six figures. Others are novices operating out of their basements or garages with very little financial reward. You'll have to get some serious education under your belt in a related field like zoology or anthropology to earn a good living as a monster hunter.

The perks are obvious—who else can say they're spending their time tracking down the Abominable Snowman? The same perk can be a down side as well, because cryptozoology does not always get the respect of other academic disciplines.

Key Attributes

An ability to ferret out the truth clearly is a crucial skill for a Cryptozoologist. Some monster hunters estimate that only 20 percent of the reports they investigate prove to be genuine; the others tend to be cases of mistaken identity or outright hoaxes.

Key Tip

Take advantage of seminars, conferences, and symposia open to the public. There are several events every year that have a cryptozoological theme. Bigfoot gatherings in Newcomerstown, Ohio; Vancouver, British Columbia; and Washington State occur annually. In 1999, the first ever International Cryptozoology Symposium was held at Loch Ness.

You can also join the International Society of Cryptozoology (see the following section).

Key Resource

For the best information on a career in monster hunting, check out the International Society of Cryptozoology at www.internationalsocietyofcryptozoology.org.

The Least You Need to Know

- ◆ "Offbeat" doesn't necessarily mean "underpaid." Offbeat is just another way of saying that you specialize in a given craft. And specialists tend to be in demand, especially with the jobs listed in this chapter.

- ◆ Offbeat jobs also tend to gather likeminded people who share the same passion you do. Take advantage of that and attend conventions and join associations. The annual dues aren't much and you'll meet people who share the same enthusiasm you do over dolls or detective work.

- ◆ Since you're working on your own, consult a tax attorney for any tax breaks you can get as a sole proprietor. The IRS is getting more generous toward individual business owners.

- ◆ Write a book! That's right, write a book on your job passion and become an instant expert in the field. Self-publishing, especially books on-demand, is fairly inexpensive. And your own book can be a great marketing tool.

Chapter 17

My Country Tithes for Me: Careers in Politics and Public Service

In This Chapter

♦ Learning about politics and public service

♦ Fundraising, event planning, and lobbying

♦ The FBI and the CIA

♦ The pathway to a career in politics: congressional intern

♦ Using your diplomatic skills

Mother Theresa, the fabled caregiver and champion of the afflicted, often advised donors "to give until it hurts." Evidently, the line worked, because Mother Theresa raised millions in charitable donations for her noble social works.

But it might not work all the time. There's a story attributed to Scottish humorist B.C. Forbes that goes something like this:

A lady called on a businessman to give money. She handed him a card that read: "Charity Fair—Give 'Till it Hurts." The businessman read the card carefully and soon tears welled up in his eyes as he handed her back the card, saying, "Lady, the very idea hurts!"

Ah, the wonderful world of politics and public service, where people do well by doing good—most of the time.

The good news is that, yes, you can make a living working in public service. And you can make a big difference in the bargain.

All that it takes is a passion for an individual cause and the gumption to follow through and dedicate your career—or at least parts of it—to making sure that your voice is heard and your cause is recognized.

The following careers give you cause to do just that.

Professional Fundraiser

Can you get on the horn and convince perfect strangers to cut you a check? Can you buttonhole the swells at swanky parties and get them to crack open their wallets for you?

If so, then you have a bright future in both used car sales and in professional fundraising. Fortunately, it's the latter career we're focusing on here.

Facts and Figures

Of all the varied areas in the fundraising market, educational, environmental, and religious groups are usually the top fundraisers in the United States. Larger organizations—groups that raise more than $1 million annually—are the fastest growing nonprofits.

One trend coming out of the cyber-world is online giving, which has grown by leaps and bounds via the Internet. Almost 50 percent of all charitable groups report using the Internet to raise funds today.

Job Description

Fund raising is big business in North America. In 2004, Americans gave $241 billion to charitable organizations. For a professional fundraiser, the key to getting a slice of that money is to make sure your voice is heard above the din and ensuring your charitable group gets noticed.

That means spending a lot of time on the phone making the case for your charity or nonprofit. It also means getting out and meeting donors face-to-face, at social events, business functions, Chamber of Commerce events, and other public functions.

To be a good fundraiser it helps to have good public relations skills and have that hard-to-peg talent for influencing people and making them part with their money. But it's not just schmoozing—you'll have deadlines and goals, and you are expected to lay out good strategies to meet those goals. You also must be detail-oriented; identifying good prospects and keeping files on them, for example, is a big part of the job.

In fundraising, you have a choice of career options. For-profit companies, such as Ford Motor Co., hire professional fundraisers to work at their foundations. That's called "commercial" fundraising.

Volunteer groups that hire fundraisers are more common. Work can be found at foundations, nonprofits, industry and trade associations, think tanks, educational groups, political parties, and social and cultural services organizations. Fundraisers in that group spend their day on the phone or even canvassing communities looking for financial support.

Pay and Perks

Starting salaries for professional fundraisers start at about $25,000 annually and gradually move up the scale to $50,000 after five years. Salaries in the six-figure range are not uncommon, especially at the larger, more successful nonprofits.

To get a better sense of what you can make as a fundraiser, reach out into your local nonprofit community and get some face time with a fundraiser. Ask him or her about ways to advance in the field and keys to raising money.

Key Attributes

Expect your first few years in the fund-raising business to be extended training for your future. Be patient and keep your ears open. It is possible to gain professional certification as a fundraiser. It helps to have had a career in sales or in retail—vocations where the ability to pry money from people is highly regarded. Contacts are key, as well. It's not enough to generate potential donor lists (although that certainly helps). You have to get out and press the flesh with the people most likely to cut your group a check.

Key Tip

To garner the kind of deep experience you'll need to succeed in the field, and to determine what kind of organization you want to work for (e.g., a college or university, a church or religious group, or an environmental group) be prepared to work at several groups before you find your footing.

Key Resource

For a summary of helpful nonprofits and professional fundraising groups, visit the LISC Online Library at www.lisc.org/resources/links/fundraising.shtml.

Also, check out the National Society of Fund Raising Executives for more information on certification: www.nsfre.org.

Event Planner

Some people like to party, and some people like to plan parties.

Hey, viva le difference, right?

For the latter group, a career in event planning is a great way to flex your people-pleasing muscles and preside over fun, important, and often glamorous events.

Facts and Figures

In the event planning market, the best planners understand that people pay for experiences. They want you to capture a particular moment in time and to put a bold, vibrant, memorable face on it.

The average event planner can do just that. According to industry reports, the average planner handles about eight events a year, with about 200 people attending each one. Of course, each event planner will have different experiences. One that caters to individuals and handles things like bah mitzvahs, family reunions, and birthdays might handle 20 or more events per year. Someone who handles the Kentucky Derby will, obviously not have time for 20 events.

Job Description

Event planners do just that—they organize events, often for corporate parties and conferences, fairs and festivals, charitable galas, grand openings, trade shows, even birthdays and weddings. At the top of the field are the planners for high-profile events like the Super Bowl or Mardi Gras. Heck, even funerals need to be planned.

Event planners have myriad employers looking for help in planning their events. Corporations, theme parks, casinos, cruise lines, country clubs, and convention centers are just a few of the markets where an event planner can get hired and make his or her mark on the professional party circuit.

Why is event planning such a great career? For starters, there is a huge market for event planners. In this day and age, where time is just as much a commodity as gold or silver, people don't have the time to plan their parties. Many gigs are "one-offs," things like fiftieth birthday parties or new product launches for businesses, so clients just need someone to come in and handle the one-time party and move on.

Clients will be counting on you to pull off a high-profile event while keeping an eye on costs—all while making the client look great in the process. You'll book bands and orchestras, hire fireworks specialists, argue with thin-skinned chefs, and mull over table settings and floral arrangements. And you'll be expected to make lots of decisions on the fly.

It's not a nine-to-five job but, in most cases, you are your own boss and you'll have the power (and the responsibility) to make critical decisions.

Pay and Perks

If you plan one or two events a month—that's steady work in the event planning game—you can easily earn more than $60,000 a year. That's up from $54,000 a year in 2000. The perks aren't bad, either. You'll often jet to plush resorts (on the client's or the resort's tab) to "test" out the resort's event-handling capabilities. Free food, free lodging, and all the

The Water Cooler

Special event planning is an $800 billion industry in the United States. In addition, profit margins for event planners have risen in recent years from 15 percent up to 40 percent.

trimmings. Not bad. Actually, in many cases, hotel, resort, or cruise line directors "court" event planners for the business they can bring to the table. So you can milk that attention for all that it's worth.

Key Attributes

A sixth sense for seeing problems ahead of time and squashing them before they can rear their ugly head is perhaps the most prized attribute of a good event planner. Crisis management skills are great, too, because you can't always stop problems from occurring. But you can manage them and minimize their impact.

Of course, you'll need to possess superior organizing skills as well. Think of it as being the CEO for a day—a day where all eyes will be on you to shine and create the ultimate affair to remember.

Key Tip

Negotiate a deal with clients that says the more money you save the client on a given event, the higher your commission. A good event planner can always cut some financial corners and shave a few bucks off the bill. Make sure that, when you do so, your fee reflects your ability to keep an eye on the bottom line.

Key Resource

For a good look at the event planning industry, visit the Dallas, Texas-based Meeting Professionals International website at www.mpiweb.org. Or try the International Special Events Society at www.ises.com.

Professional Lobbyist

"Hey brother, can you spare a millionaire a dime?"

Okay, maybe that's an exaggeration. But professional lobbyists are well known for massaging politicians on behalf of, how shall we say, filthy rich clients.

Of course, those filthy rich clients often stand up, in turn, for the little people, like schoolchildren, blue collar workers, the disabled, and aging Americans.

So if you have the Rolodex and the access—or want to learn how to get them—and want to learn the ways of the professional lobbyist, by all means, read on.

Facts and Figures

Lobbying is a big-money game—about $1.5 billion is spent on lobbying efforts in Washington, D.C. annually. For all that money that clients pay to lobbying firms, they expect results. And they get them.

Typically, lobbyists ply their trade in four major areas: association lobbyists, who represent industry and trade associations, such as the American Association of Retired People (AARP) or the Teamsters; corporate lobbyists, who represent individual firms like Microsoft or Proctor & Gamble; foreign lobbyists, who hold great sway in Washington, D.C., acting on behalf of foreign governments and overseas companies; and nonprofit lobbyists, who work for charities, volunteer groups, and other nonprofit organizations.

If you accept payment from a client to lobby on Capital Hill, you have to register with the government. It's the law.

Job Description

Can you handle three-martini lunches with stuffy old U.S. senators? Maybe that, too, is an exaggeration, but not much of one.

Professional lobbyists target political decision makers because those are the folks who decide where Uncle Sam spends his money and how he legislates. Like horse to water, lobbyists need to go to where their clients' financial thirsts can be slaked, and for the past 200 years or so, that place is Washington, D.C.

Simply put, a lobbyist attempts to influence public policy and make gobs of money in the process. Lobbyists will tell you that their craft is just good citizenship in practice, and that's probably true. But lobbyists do charge fat fees for clients to get that access, often provided by ex-congressmen and -women who are hired by lobbying firms after they retire or after they fail to be re-elected and hold office.

If you want to break in, here's the deal. Expect to move to Washington, D.C. to be where the action is; spend lots of time on your cell phone; break bread with congresspersons and their staffers; and attend high-cachet social events where you can see and be seen. Oh, and get ready to pick up a lot of bar tabs, too.

It's not all steak dinners and Super Bowl outings. Lobbying has changed over the years. Congress, after pressure from public interest groups, has limited the power and impact of lobbyists over the years. Gone are the days of the free travel junkets, the all-expenses-paid golf vacations, and the lavish lobster dinners with champagne and all the trimmings. Congress, too, has forced lobbyists to officially register their names with the government so the public can see who is trying to influence whom.

In the end, though, access is king. If you have it, you can thrive as a Washington lobbyist.

Pay and Perks

Washington, D.C. is the poster child for having to start low and work your way up to the top. So it goes with the lobbyist world. In 2003, the U.S. government reported that the starting salary for a clerk was about $12,000. But experienced lobbyists could earn $150,000 or more. Median salary was pegged at $49,000 by the U.S. government.

> **The Water Cooler**
>
> The Oxford Dictionary pegs a lobbyist as "... someone who seeks to influence members of the legislature, attempts to get Bills through by interviews in the lobby and solicits the support of influential people ..."

Perks are good, but only if you like being in close proximity to power. You'll dine with senators, have drinks with congressmen, and play poker with executive branch staffers. It's a lively and extremely social lifestyle.

Key Attributes

It really helps to know somebody important in Washington, D.C. to get you in the door. That's the quickest path to a cushy lobbyist post. Short of that, a willingness to start off at the bottom of the ladder as an issues analyst or public relations staffer will at least get you learning the basics.

Also helpful are ties with individual lobbying clients. Lobbyists love to hire young college graduates who can speak foreign languages (for overseas clients) or who have experience working with congress, with advocacy groups, or with trade associations. Primarily, though, you won't find many "help wanted" ads for lobbyists firms. Vacant posts are filled by networking and word of mouth.

Key Tip

Go to Washington, D.C. and get a job somewhere in government. Don't worry, most jobs in Washington are linked to government. Then make connections, learn a specialty (auto industry legislation or homeland security issues, for example). Then use those connections and that experience to wiggle your way into a good lobbying firm. Again, don't worry. In 2000, over 280 lobbying firms spent $1 million or more on special interest efforts. And about 17,000 people are employed in the city at lobbying firms. So the jobs are out there—you just have to dig for them.

Key Resource

Try out the American League of Lobbyists (ALL) at www.alldc.org.

Political Blog Writer

What can you say about the political media industry except that it's gone to the blogs?

This is a good thing.

Blogs—short for *web logs*—offer the common man and woman a solid grip on the media megaphone.

It doesn't make traditional media organizations too happy, but that's their problem. With the advent of high-profile blogs like Daily Kos, Instapundit, and Wonkette, web log pioneers are proving you can thrive as an online political guru and make a big difference in the process.

Just ask Dan Rather. The political blogging community is widely credited for taking him down after airing a faulty report on CBS' *60 Minutes*.

> ### The Water Cooler
>
> According to the Pew Internet & American Life Project, 32 million Americans say they have read a blog.

Facts and Figures

One count of total blogs operating today totals up to four million. Of course, most of those are not political blogs. One company, Pyra Labs, which crafts blogging software, says it has over 970,000 users alone.

Most blogs are free, meaning bloggers don't charge readers for visiting their sites. That's a problem from a financial point of view. How do you make a living if you don't charge people for accessing your blog? The answer, straight out of the television and radio handbook, is advertising. More and more blogs are selling advertising to sustain some level of financial stability. Fundraising is also a common form of revenue generation. Competing, but popular, blogs from both sides of the political spectrum, FreeRepublic.com and DemocraticUnderground.com, survive largely on member donation drives, which they run once or twice a year.

Job Description

Bloggers are expected to post early and often, commenting on recent news and trends and giving people the ultimate reason to visit their web log time and time again— fresh news and opinion. Blogs are amateur websites that publish political commentary, news, and links to major media venues and other bloggers. Audiences are big and getting bigger.

As a blogger you're expected to entertain as much as inform. Fast, funny, and biased sells in the political blog market.

If that sounds like you, get started by visiting a blog-hosting site like typepad.com or blogspot.com and setting up an account. After a brief HTML tutorial that will teach you how to write, link, post graphics, and generally behave like a blogger, you're up and running. Some blog hosting sites are free and some are not. Expect to pay anywhere between $20 and $50 a blog per month for a decent looking blog that will offer visual, as well as intellectual and entertainment, appeal to readers.

Pay and Perks

The people at Weblogs Inc. say that bloggers can make between $1,000 and $5,000 a month, depending on the diligence they display in marketing the site and their ability to offer something truly unique and different. The political field is pretty crowded, so the best way to earn that kind of money is by building a blog with your personal stamp, linking the heck out of it to other web logs, and running a fundraising effort once a year or so. The reality is that you won't get rich writing a web log, but, through fund drives, word of mouth, and some advertising, you can make enough to cover costs. If you love politics that might just be enough.

Key Attributes

Be witty and original. Be timely and topical. Be opinionated (without bloviating). And be a good marketer. Create a blog with your own voice and personality. Take a stand, too. If you lean to the political right, take your blog in that direction and build an audience that way. Ditto if you skew to the political left. As one wag says, the only things in the middle of the road are white stripes and dead armadillos.

Key Tip

If you start a web log, don't operate it at your day job. It's grounds for dismissal at many firms. And whatever you do, don't complain about your company online. Recently, employees have been fired for casting a negative spotlight on their employers. Keep it restricted to politics and leave your company out of it.

Key Resource

Check out these great political web blogs to see how it's done: Andrewsullivan.com, written by political pundit Andrew Sullivan; wonkette.com, run by journalist Ana Marie Cox; and instapundit.com, run by college professor Glenn Reynolds. Each has got the format down pat and boasts sizeable audiences as a result.

Peace Corps Volunteer

Let's get one thing straight about Peace Corps work right up front. As noble as an endeavor it is, you won't be cashing big paychecks from the Peace Corps.

That's not the idea. The Peace Corps isn't about anyone getting rich. It's all about helping the less fortunate, often in far-off countries that are unsanitary, politically volatile, poverty stricken, and sometimes hostile to Americans.

It might be the most fulfilling job you ever take, but it will also be one of the hardest and least financially rewarding. But if you don't define happiness as having a dollar sign attached to it, the Peace Corps is a gig you'll never, ever forget.

Facts and Figures

Signing on with the Peace Corps (it has an annual budget of about $315 million) is a lot like signing on with the U.S. Army, from a time standpoint. You're expected to serve a 27-month stint. You have to be 18 years old and a U.S. citizen. Other than that the Corp is filled with diverse workers from rich and varied skills and capabilities. The Peace Corps is well stocked with recent college graduates looking to do something useful while they figure out their career plan. High school graduates who want to travel and help people out are

> **The Water Cooler**
>
> The Peace Corps was founded by President John F. Kennedy in 1961. Today, over 7,000 volunteers serve the Peace Corps in 78 countries.

also good candidates for the Peace Corps. Medical school students or education school majors (teachers-in-training) often join the Peace Corps to get a break on their onerous student loans and have a chance to practice medicine where they are needed most. One thing all Peace Corps workers have in common is a sense of adventure and a desire to help the less fortunate.

Job Description

It depends on where you go and what your area of expertise might be. Peace Corps workers do everything from teaching poor Brazilians to cook rice and grow new crops to teaching Savannah tribesmen computer skills.

The pedigree of former Peace Corp volunteers is rich and varied. The list includes:

- Taylor Hackford, movie producer of *Ray, An Officer and a Gentleman*, and *The Devil's Advocate* (Bolivia, 1968–69)

- Robert Haas, chairman of Board for Levi Strauss (Ivory Coast, 1964–66)

- Michael McCaskey, chairman of the board, Chicago Bears (Ethiopia, 1965–67)

- Chris Matthews, host of NBC's Hardball (Swaziland, 1968–70)

- Christopher Dodd, U.S. Senator, Connecticut (Dominican Republic, 1966–68)

Pay and Perks

You'll earn a modest monthly stipend (which varies depending on where you are sent) and are given $6,000 when you finish your stint. You've also got a stellar addition to your resumé and can likely get a good break on your student loans, if you borrowed from the U.S. government.

Key Attributes

Successful Peace Corps members have patience, a kind heart, and a strong desire to make a difference. The best Peace Corps workers are the ones who give a lot and expect very little in return. Good problem-solving skills and the ability to pick up foreign languages fairly quickly come in handy, too.

Key Tip

Not sure if you're Peace Corps material? Check out the Corps's website at www. peacecorps.gov. It spells out in real terms what the Corp is looking for—and what can be expected after you sign on the dotted line and travel overseas in the name of Uncle Sam. If you're still not sure, contact the Corps and ask to speak to former volunteers. They'll arrange it. Be specific when you talk to former volunteers. Don't ask if they liked it or not. Ask if they had a strong support network and what they learned from the experience.

Key Resource

The best resource is probably former volunteers who have served with the Corps. Start your search at the Peace Corps's index website at www.peacecorps.gov/ index.cfm?shell=learn.whatispc.notable.

Nonprofit Director

For people who really want to forge a career from their passion, an executive directorship at a good nonprofit is a worthy goal.

It's a job where you'll wear different hats, but you'll be directly involved in a cause that you, in your heart of hearts, believe in and are committed to.

Whether you pursue a director's post at the Salvation Army, the American Red Cross, or the American Cancer Society, or just the little nonprofit art center down the street, if you have a good sense of community spirit and the desire to help a cause that you embrace, you've already got a leg up on the competition.

Facts and Figures

Nonprofits and other nonbusiness groups account for 20 percent of all economic activity in the United States. Altogether, there are about three million registered tax-exempt nonprofits operating in the United States today.

So there are ample opportunities for advancement in the marketplace. Some people go into nonprofit management as a lifelong career occupation. Others do it to burnish their professional credentials. That's up to you. But no matter what, you'll earn plenty of experience as a decision maker and a responsibility taker. You're the bottom line at your nonprofit, and all eyes will be on you. If you like the limelight—and can handle tough decisions—you'll make a fine nonprofit director. The best opportunities, on an industry basis, seem to come from the hospital and university sectors. Both are in competitive markets and could really use some significant marketing help.

Job Description

A nonprofit director has to know a lot about everything. It's reminiscent of a small business owner that way. You'll be involved in marketing, fundraising, accounting and payroll, hiring help and recruiting volunteers, and writing grant proposals, for starters.

Expect heavy hours as a nonprofit director. Much of the burden of running a foundation or nonprofit falls upon the shoulders of the executive director. You are the face of the organization so, even when you leave the office, you'll be expected to represent the organization at local events, meet with potential donors, speak at board of director's meetings, and prime the organization's public relations pump through media appearances. You should be willing to do anything to cast a bright light on your cause.

Pay and Perks

Like most jobs in the nonprofit sector, entry-level positions don't pay all that much. But the opportunity to earn much more is there as you work your way up the nonprofit food chain. Starting salaries range from $15,000 to $25,000. But some posts, like event co-coordinator and marketing director, can earn you anywhere from $40,000 to $100,000 at upper level nonprofits or charitable foundations. Directors of nonprofits and foundations—the larger, more reputable ones—can earn $350,000 or more per year.

Key Attributes

Great people skills are at a premium for nonprofit managers. You need to lead people and make them buy into your program. Sales skills are important, too. Selling the organization is job one. Ideally, you're a creative, analytical type with great communications and problem-solving skills. A fat Rolodex full of wealthy would-be donors is a big advantage, too. That will open some eyes at your job interview.

Key Tip

The Chronicle of Philanthropy offers a menu of nonprofit and foundation management jobs that is refreshed each month. See it at www.philanthropy.com.

Key Resource

Guide Star is a national database of all U.S. nonprofits. Check it out at www.guidestar.org.

Federal Air Marshal

Fly the friendly skies? Okay, but can we have Clint Eastwood on board?

In a post-9/11 culture, where airline security is one of the uppermost issues in travelers' minds every time they board an aircraft, federal air marshals offer a sense of safety and security to the traveling public.

The job is an adrenaline junkie's dream job—a tough, risky, pressure-racked post where you are the first (and probably last) line of defense between murderous terrorists and your terrified fellow citizens who are flying on the plane.

Facts and Figures

There are about 2,200 air marshals patrolling the nation's skyways—they can "sit in" on up to 10 percent of the nation's commercial air traffic every day.

Essentially, air marshals are "sheriffs in the sky," charged with making America's skies safer for the traveling public, most of whom were sorely shaken after the events of September 11, 2001. The U.S. government, working in concert with the airline industry to restore confidence in air travel, implemented the air marshal program in 2002. The goal, as stated by the U.S. Transportation Security Administration, is "to protect the nation's transportation systems to ensure freedom of movement for people and commerce."

Most air marshals are ex-cops or ex-soldiers—usually "type A" personalities. All are in great physical shape and all well-trained in weapons handling and usage. Training includes rigorous physical conditioning including wind sprints, three-mile runs through foul weather, karate, and even Pilates.

Job Description

Who are these guys, and what do they do?

As a Federal Air Marshal, you'll pack heat and be expected to know how and when to use it. You'll train hard with FBI and other law enforcement specialists on ways to anticipate and thwart terrorist attacks 30,000 feet in the sky.

You'll attend the Federal Air Marshal Training Academy in Atlantic City, New Jersey. Expect about 11 weeks of training in terrorist simulation drills, firearms practice, kidnapping and hostage situations, and other safety and security procedures. You'll wear a gray tee-shirt, black cargo pants, and black boots during training, but when you hit the sky as a fully-trained federal air marshal you'll be in plain clothes, the better to keep you incognito if any bad guys strike. Tests include killing a "target" seven feet away within three seconds. Trainees who can't do so could flunk out of training school. Surveillance is also a big issue—you'll be expected to know whether a traveler's wristwatch is actually an explosive device designed to bring a plane down. The good news is that the academy training will help. The Atlantic City facility is state-of-the-art, with mock airplane cockpits and a $400,000 gym that any NFL linebacker would be happy to work out in. Come to think of it, air marshals are a lot like professional football players. It's a macho, gung-ho culture where, as one air marshal trainer puts it, "If you're lying in your own pool of blood at 30,000 feet, it's your own fault."

The Water Cooler
You can be no older than 40 years of age to apply for a Federal Air Marshal post. In comparison, the maximum age for an FBI applicant is 37.

Upon graduating from training school, you'll be assigned to 1 of 21 flight offices spread out across the United States. After you're in flight you're pretty much on your own. Like a cop walking a beat, the 750-odd feet of aircraft is your patrol zone—and there is no backup. The lives of everyone aboard are in your hands. If that's not pressure, I don't know what is.

Pay and Perks

Normally, federal law enforcement agents start off at about $22,000, but Congress is trying to do better than that, starting Federal Air Marshals off at $31,000 to $45,000 annually, depending upon prior law enforcement or military experience. Some high-level hires are clocking in at $100,000 per year (although Congress has made noise about lowering that amount).

Key Attributes

Uncle Sam likes tough, no-nonsense air marshals who don't panic under pressure, know how to use a firearm, and are well-schooled in terrorist attack techniques. As I said previously, a background as a police officer or in the armed forces is a big advantage.

Key Tip

The best advice the pros give is to trust your instincts. If something doesn't appear on the up-and-up, go to the cockpit and report it. The pilots will bolt the door and land the plane. Better safe than sorry.

Key Resource

Learn more about the Federal Air Marshall program at the U.S. Immigration and Customs Enforcement web page. Click *Careers* to fill out an application. Find it at www.ice.gov/graphics/fams.

Congressional Intern

Because of the Monica Lewinski scandal, congressional interns spent much of the late 1990s in the news—in a not-too-flattering light. And they didn't get much positive press in the years that followed. That's unfortunate.

For young Americans bursting with political passion and idealism, a congressional internship can be a critical first step to fulfilling that dream about making a successful and sustained career in the political big leagues.

Internships provide excellent opportunities for networking and boning up on how the political game is played in Washington. It also enables young Americans to give something back by serving in the public interest.

The Monica issue aside, a congressional internship is still the pathway to a career in politics. And it's well worth pursuing if you'd like to be a U.S. senator someday.

Facts and Figures

Congressional internships—or most jobs in politics, for that matter—are not 9 to 5 jobs. Because you'll be attending all sorts of meetings, hearings, lectures, and other congressional functions, you'll find that you won't have enough time to get your office work done. But it has to be done. So you'll spend some time working late into the night stuffing envelopes or keying voter information into a computer. It's all in a day's work.

Ideally, spring and fall are the best times to grab an internship. Other college students and college graduates are either in class or launching new careers during those months. Apply for an internship about six months ahead of time to make sure you have a good shot. What's the best tip? Get a letter of recommendation from a local or state politician; it's a big help. A letter from a big political donor is even better. As a student intern you'll be expected to work at least 180 hours during the semester, and will receive, on average, four credits toward graduation.

To apply, visit the congressman you have in mind via the internet at www.house.gov or www.senate.gov. Find the office you want to apply for and contact the office for the right paperwork. You can apply online at any congressman's website.

Job Description

First, some good news: congressional offices are fluid and dynamic. People are moving up and out all the time. So there are plenty of openings for good, young civic-minded professionals looking to kick-start their political careers.

That's not to say that you'll be jawboning with the prime minister of France or writing history-making legislation as an intern. You'll actually be doing some drudge work like making copies, delivering documents to other offices, answering phones, and fielding complaints from irate citizens who want a traffic light built on their street and who say there will be hell to pay for anyone who doesn't make that happen. And forget about lunching with a senator or congressman. Their schedules are packed so tight you'll hardly see them (although most elected officials will meet with interns at least once a semester—it's sort of a Washington ritual).

But remember, schmoozing with Senator Blabbermouth isn't why you are there.

You're there to listen, learn how the public policy sausage is made, keep your lip buttoned, and help out where you can. Some of the more interesting things you will get to do include background research on legislative issues, some first-draft speechwriting (if you're a skilled writer), and reading and reviewing media articles on your senator or congressman and filing them for other staffers to read and report in on. Whether your work is drudgery or not, consider it the price you pay for getting a step up on the political ladder.

Pay and Perks

Sorry. All perks and little or no pay. Congressional internships pay very little, although the opportunity to get hired into a staff position straight from your internship is a real and valuable possibility. And a reference from a U.S. senator is gold in Washington political currency.

Key Attributes

Congressional offices place a high priority on interns who can think creatively and are enthusiastic about the culture and operational aspects of congress. An ability to conduct good research and analyze data is also a key attribute, as is the ability to keep your ears open and mouth closed. The best interns, Washington insiders say, are the ones who are seen but not heard. If you do your work, you'll get noticed.

Key Tip

If you can't manage to wangle an internship in Washington, check out your senators' or congressional state offices. They need interns there, too.

Key Resource

If you want to shoot for the big enchilada, the White House, contact the White House Fellows Program at 202-606-1818 or www.whitehousefellows.gov.

FBI Agent

If you're older than 40, or know your law enforcement history, you've heard about guys like Elliot Ness and Frank Nitti.

These FBI agents brought mobsters from Chicago to New York to their knees, and brought cold-blooded killers like John Dillinger to their final justice. Or maybe you watched the Hannibal Lecter movies, where tough-as-nails agent Clarise Starling, played by Jodie Foster, saved the day.

Either way, the FBI has a long and illustrious pedigree in the international law enforcement arena, and a job at the agency is considered a plum post for anyone looking for a career putting bad guys in jail—or in the morgue.

Facts and Figures

Age is the first hurdle for becoming an FBI agent. The agency only takes applicants between 23 and 37 years of age. And you must retire at age 55 or after 20 years of field service (whichever comes first).

But that's just for starters. According to the agency, an FBI agent must …

◆ Be a U.S. citizen, or a citizen of the Northern Mariana Islands.

◆ Be completely available for assignment anywhere in the FBI's jurisdiction.

◆ Have uncorrected vision not worse than 20/200 and corrected 20/20 in one eye and not worse than 20/40 in the other eye.

◆ Pass a color vision test.

◆ Meet hearing standards by audiometer test.

◆ Possess a valid driver's license.

◆ Be in excellent physical condition with no defects that would interfere in firearm use, raids, or defensive tactics.

◆ Possess a four-year degree from an accredited college or university.

Agents who pass those tests aren't through yet. If you want to get in to one of the FBI's entry programs in law, accounting, language, or "diversified" you have to meet higher requirements relating directly to those programs. To get into the law program, for example, you must have an advanced degree from a resident law school.

Oh, one more thing. You've got to be good. The FBI hires only one out of every fifteen hundred applicants.

Job Description

The FBI website says it best: FBI Special Agents come from a variety of backgrounds, educational disciplines, and employment histories, "but the one thing they all have in common is a desire to fight crime and pursue a meaningful and rewarding career."

FBI agents are the chief investigating officers operating on behalf of the United States of America. They investigate federal criminal acts and violations and conduct national security investigations. That could mean placing wiretaps, tracking the flow of stolen goods, rifling through computer files to catch white-collar criminals, or gathering evidence of possible espionage or terrorist operations by criminals both inside and outside the United States. Investigating kidnappings, mob activity, fraud, bank robberies, and drug trafficking are all part of the puzzle for FBI agents.

If you're accepted into "the bureau," you'll spend about 17 weeks training at the U.S. Marine base in Quantico, Virginia. Following that, you'll be assigned to an FBI field office for a two-year probationary period before being hired on a permanent basis. Chances are you, as a newbie agent, will be paired up with an experienced veteran who can show you the ropes.

Above all else, the FBI is an unpredictable business. Agents say that one day they'll be digging up dirt on a cyber-criminal; the next day they'll be called upon to investigate a bank robbery. So expect the unexpected.

Pay and Perks

The U.S. Bureau of Labor and Statistics says the FBI pays a base salary of $68,000 to $80,000 for supervisory, management, or executive slots. Opening salaries are lower, in the $22,000 to $36,000 range. But there's a bonus: even though you might earn north of $80,000 before you retire, you retire with a full pension and as a valuable commodity to other law enforcement agencies like the CIA or the U.S. Secret Service, or to private security and investigations firms. In that instance, many retired FBI agents name—and often get—their own price for a "second" career.

Key Attributes

In addition to having the right educational credits as described above, and being in the right age bracket, the FBI highly values applicants who are fluent in a foreign language such as Arabic, Farsi, or Chinese (among others). Military experience or previous experience as a police officer will also get your resumé to the top of the pile. The agency also likes people who can work alone and produce the goods. Although you'll have a partner in many cases, just as often, you won't. That's especially true if you're working undercover.

Key Tip

Learn how to handle a gun. Out in the field, all FBI agents wear—and sometimes use—them.

Key Resource

Visit the FBI website to apply. Find it at www.fbi.gov/employment/employ.htm.

State Department Diplomat

"I say, old bean ... perfectly ghastly business, that Sudanese civil war affair, don't you think?"

If that line of conversation fits you like a snappy tuxedo, a career as a state department diplomat is waiting for you.

State department diplomats work all over the world on behalf of the U.S. Foreign Service. They usually serve two- to four-year terms but often come back to Washington for a stint at the home office before being sent back out for another assignment.

If you have a case of serious political wanderlust, then a career as a foreign officer is for you.

Facts and Figures

The average starting age for a U.S. diplomat is about 30—people often get into the diplomacy game as a second or even third career. You have to be a U.S. citizen, and you cannot be older than 59.

You'll have to pass a written aptitude test given by the State Department to measure your knowledge and understanding of world affairs. If you pass that you'll rank among the 30 percent of those who move on to take an oral test, which digs deeper into your skills and character capabilities. From there you'll move on to a security and background check (if you have a criminal record or bad credit, don't bother to apply) and, assuming all goes well, will be offered a position as a foreign officer.

Your first two-to-four-year stint is always overseas in a foreign embassy or consulate. Could be Athens or Tokyo or South Africa, depending on the government's needs and your unique capabilities. You could even wind up in a hot spot like Haiti teaching the locals English. That's the downside of a foreign service job—U.S. consulates in foreign trouble zones such as Iran or Columbia are often the targets of first choice for terrorist bombers. So risk is definitely a factor.

Job Description

First and foremost, don't confuse a diplomatic post with an ambassador post. The latter are appointed and serve at the behest of the President of the United States.

Diplomats are typically careerists, in it for the long haul, whereas ambassadors usually cap off an illustrious career in politics, academia, or business and (thanks to some healthy political donations) can sail off to Great Britain or New Zealand as a full-fledged ambassador.

Not so for the career diplomat. In that post, you'll spend your time issuing visas for American tourists, watching over those citizens overseas, sharing tea with local dignitaries to discuss policy, and holding press conferences. You'll also attend many social events and hobnob with the political and cultural elite from the country to which you are assigned.

Pay and Perks

The ability to travel and see the world is the most significant attraction for a foreign officer career. You'll see your host countries up close and personal. And the dispatches you send back to Washington will be read by some very influential policy makers—even the president! The pay isn't too bad. You'll start at about $30,000 annually and work your way up to $100,000 as a senior officer. And, in most cases, you'll have a living allowance that can pay some or all of your housing costs while representing Uncle Sam overseas.

Key Attributes

A college degree is a must, preferably in a field such as foreign languages, government, economics, or commerce. Fluency in multiple foreign languages is helpful, as is a familiarity with good etiquette and social protocol. Patience is key, too. Even if you pass all the tests and are put on the State Department's appointee list, you'll have to go back to the end of the line if your name isn't picked within 18 months.

Key Tip

Note that a diplomat post can be tough on raising families. It's not impossible, but having a spouse and young ones adapt to being uprooted again and again to posts in foreign lands isn't easy.

Key Resource

A great book on foreign service culture is *Inside a U.S. Embassy: How the Foreign Service Works for America*. It's published by the American Foreign Service Association (AFSA) and edited by Shawn Dorman.

CIA Agent

"Bond. James Bond."

Cue the cool 007 music.

If you grew up in the 1960s and '70s, the heyday of the Bond films, chances are you caught the bug. The spy bug, that is.

Ian Fleming's famous creation, played pitch-perfectly by actor Sean Connery in the early Bond films, probably launched the careers of thousands of CIA agents.

> ### The Water Cooler
>
> You'll have to do more than pee in a cup and take a polygraph test to pass CIA muster. Testing for CIA agents is intense. Among other things, the agency will test your intelligence aptitude, and your physical condition; they'll evaluate your heart rate, body temperature (to see how much you sweat), sudden movements (they like their agents calm under pressure), voice analysis, and even the way you make eye contact.

But in the real spy world, the good guys don't always win and get the girl at the end. So there's danger afoot—and you're just the tough, talented CIA agent to handle it.

Facts and Figures

The best way to become a CIA agent is to apply online at the agency website (www.cia.gov/employment/apply.html). Be patient—the entire process from application to acceptance takes over a year, on average. Also be prepared for some intense scrutiny from the agency if they are considering bringing you onboard. They'll talk to former employers, former lovers, and former co-workers to check you out. You'll also undergo significant polygraph, drug detection, and physical training tests. Something as seemingly minor as a temporary bad credit rating is enough to disqualify you from consideration by the CIA. So it helps to be squeaky clean.

Job Description

The Central Intelligence Agency, located in Langley, Virgina, doesn't actually call its agents *spies* or even *agents*. The proper term is *clandestine service operations officer.* But that's a mouthful—even for the government—so let's just use the term *agent*.

To succeed as a CIA agent, you have to be smart—both book-smart and street-smart—and you have to possess the physical skills to undergo a great deal of training and field exercise.

As an agent, your mission is the CIA's mission: to find, collect, analyze, and disseminate information that could be useful to the interests of the United States government. You might well be engaged in covert actions, or decoding communiqués from foreign powers, tracking down terrorists in strange lands, and spying on individuals considered to be potentially harmful to those same U.S. interests.

Although technology has certainly improved the CIA's data collection capabilities (satellites can read the bylines in a newspaper laying on a café table hundreds of miles below), the need for on-the-ground operations officers remains high. To uncover terrorist plots or to infiltrate a foreign government's ringleaders, human intelligence is still the key.

Pay and Perks

It's a government job with government pay. You'll start out making about $47,000 annually and move to the Washington, D.C., area to begin training. The CIA training program alone takes three years to complete. A big part of that training takes place at "The Farm"—the agency's training center in northern Virginia. You'll bond with fellow agents—bonds that will surely last the rest of your life, because the one thing you'll have in common is the willingness to risk your life for your country. The prospect of being poisoned in Afghanistan or facing a firing squad in Somalia tends to bring agents together.

Key Attributes

The most important thing is smarts, smarts, and more smarts. And the physical toughness of a Golden Gloves boxer counts for a great deal, too. Fields of expertise are varied. The agency hires lots of chemical engineers and computer scientists for lab and study work. It hires plenty of translators (especially those skilled in Chinese or Arabic, these days). It hires mathematicians, geologists, and meteorologists, too.

Minimum requirements include having a Bachelor's degree with a GPA of 3.0 or higher, being age 36 or under, and being a U.S. citizen.

The agency especially likes agents with advanced military experience. A Green Beret or Army Ranger has an inside track for an agency post. Foreign nationals with language, computer, and information-gathering skills are highly sought after, too. Having a family member in the agency can't hurt, either.

Above all, the ability to keep your mouth shut is the most prized—and expected— commodity by the CIA. You literally cannot tell anyone about your job—not even your family members.

Key Tip

Review the CIA Factbook on the CIA website: www.cia.gov. It tells you everything you need to know about the agency. It will be an immense help in your interview process if you study it closely.

Key Resource

For a good look at life as a CIA agent read *Inside the CIA* (Pocket Books, 1994) by Ronald Kessler and *The Company: A Novel of the CIA* (Penguin Books, 2003) by Robert Littell. You can find both at www.amazon.com. Type "CIA" into the search bar.

The Least You Need to Know

◆ In politics, who you know is as key as what you know. Connections really count in the public sector. A good word from "connected types"—a judge, lobbyist, or state senator—can mean all the difference in the world in getting on the public payroll.

♦ Embrace the nonprofit life—but don't expect riches. You might just get all the fulfillment you need by representing organizations that help people improve their lives.

♦ Public service types tend to retire early—and move on. The public pension system is fairly generous, allowing for government workers to retire early, get a monthly pension check, and move on to the private sector. A former FBI agent, for example, is a great candidate for a consulting gig at a security company or private corporation looking for security help.

♦ You can make a living working in public service. And you can make a big difference in the bargain.

Chapter 18

A Glimpse into the Hottest Jobs in the Future

In This Chapter

- ◆ Trends in the new millennium
- ◆ The infiltration of wireless technology
- ◆ Video games and smart homes
- ◆ The future of genetics
- ◆ Global warming issues

I just hate predicting the future.

To paraphrase Woody Allen's quote about death, there's just no future in it.

It's hard. And those who try to gaze into their crystal balls and tell us what they see are just kidding themselves. As Peter Drucker once said, "We know only two things about the future: It cannot be known, and it will be different from what exists now and from what we now expect."

Translation—predicting the future is for suckers.

But making your own reality in the future, now there's an idea I can get behind.

For the dream job seeker, making your own reality should be a top priority. But first, you have to know where the issues are and what trends should gain strength as the new millennium progresses.

Here's my stab at what dream jobs will really matter in 2010, based on what trends, themes, and issues might gain strength in the next five years.

WiFi Guru

Cell phones that work like movie projectors, letting you watch whole movies. Digital cameras that not only take pictures but also act as translating machines. A robot that does your household chores for you. Think these ideas sound like something out of a sci-fi movie? Think again—think WiFi instead.

Wireless technology is evolving at a rapid pace, and so is the industry. More of our technological gadgets and gizmos are advancing to perform multiple functions—MP3 players that also take pictures, cell phones that enable you to surf the web. Wireless technology isn't just for personal use. It's infiltrated the workplace, allowing more people than ever before to telecommute and conduct business from just about any-where in the world—from their living room to a bus in Bangladesh.

> **The Water Cooler**
>
> By the end of 2005, U.S. con-sumers will spend more than $375 billion on wireless devices.

Positions will open up in development of new and evolving personal and business products. Technicians will also be needed to assist individuals and busi-nesses with setup, consulting, and tech support. And marketing and publicity for such products will also grow, to ensure that consumers buy these products. WiFi is a sector of technology where you can't go wrong.

Genetic Scientist

Your aunt Grace had cancer. So did your grandfather. And come to think of it, so did your great-uncle Kevin, and your cousin Ross. Does that mean you'll likely suffer the same fate? Every body is different, which means every person is prone to different health problems. But although some health problems are caused by environmental factors, many of them stem from genes. It's not always easy to remember—or even know—if your uncles were prone to hypertension or if you had a few cousins suffering from diabetes. The more people know about their genetic history, the better prepared they'll be to protect themselves from and deal with hereditary health problems. Enter genetic scientists.

Genetics is a growing field of science, and it's affecting many areas of life, from the way we grow disease-resistant crops to the way we solve crimes. Every day, scientists are learning more and more about genes, DNA, and heredity, and as the field grows, so does the need for more scientists and researchers.

Another job is that of genetic counselor. These people help patients assess their health risks by delving into the family's history of diseases and medical problems, leading to increased early detection and even prevention of many medical conditions. It's also helpful for couples trying to conceive high-risk babies. These counselors don't perform tests on patients themselves; rather, they help them deal emotionally and personally with the results of medical tests. It's still a relatively small field, but it's already booming, with more and more people going into the business.

If you're interested in genetics and have a background in science or medicine, genetics could be your calling.

Venture Coach

Don't be confused by the term "venture coach." A venture coach is not the same thing as a venture capitalist. Venture capitalists consult with companies in which they have invested money. But venture coaches are people who offer play-by-play mentoring in an office environment.

A venture coach works much like the coach of a sports team. He or she evaluates the performance of a company as a whole, and then works with individual employees to help them develop the skills they need to excel in the workplace. Often, venture coaches work with small start-up businesses that need help with organization and strategizing. They also help companies maximize their resources, which includes working one-on-one with staff members and helping them through transitions, promotions, and personal stumbling blocks.

Although it might seem like therapy, venture coaching isn't about listening to someone's woes and suggesting the root of the problem. It's more about innovating creative pathways for people and businesses to follow on their way to career success. The job is also more personal than traditional consulting. Venture coaches become close confidants and help their clients discover how anxiety and insecurity might be holding them back.

If you're interested in venture coaching, you should have a strong background in business. A little knowledge of psychology doesn't hurt either. You should also have good interpersonal skills and be willing to stay in constant communication with clients in person and via phone and e-mail.

Video Game Guru

Were you a video game geek as a child? Did you know all the secret codes for games, and all the ways to get past tricky levels to win? Does it feel more normal for you to hold a joystick or video game controller than a pen? Do you still find yourself spending hours in front of the TV or computer screen in a digital realty, racking up points and saving cyber-worlds? Did you know you could make a living from it?

Video games for computers and gaming systems are a $6-billion-a-year international industry and it shows no signs of slowing down. Put your years of adolescent game-playing to work as a video game guru. It can be a tough business, but every day is child's play—literally.

If you were always inclined to break the codes, solve the mazes, and envision ways to make games better, consider video game development. These are the people who develop the innovative ideas for new games. Artists are needed to design the graphics for the games. Computer-savvy individuals are needed to write the programs for the games. And then of course there is the all-important job of testing the games.

Smart Home Architect

It's a cold, blustery winter day. Outside your house, the wind is blowing and snow-drifts have buried your car. But it's not warm enough in your house. You wrap your arms around yourself and shiver. Your home heating system senses that you're cold and automatically raises the temperature to a snug 74 degrees. You're not living in a dream world—you're living in a Smart Home.

A Smart Home is one in which technology works alongside the home's residents to make life comfortable and efficient. Through a series of computers and sensors such as microphones and cameras, homes will be able to interpret speech, gestures, and expressions as commands to complete tasks like adjusting temperature levels, opening and closing doors, turning appliances on and off, and more. Technology has come a long way since The Clapper. Smart House technology isn't a thing of the distant future, either. It's already in place in millions of homes—burglar alarms, coffee pots with timers, remote-controlled light switches, and entertainment centers. And Smart Homes will be helpful to the elderly or disabled by performing daily tasks that are difficult for them, such as turning certain appliances on and off and transmitting a call for help if it's needed. The only place to go from an already wired home is more wired.

This creates a market for people to innovate and design increasingly advanced Smart Home technology, as well as for people to build, sell, install, and maintain such equipment. It won't always be easy for homeowners to master the use of these advanced systems, so tech support will be important, too.

> **The Water Cooler**
>
> Smart Homes are aimed, in part, to help out with the world's rapidly aging population. By 2050, the number of people age 60-and-over will comprise 33 percent of the population. "Smart" homes tend to produce technologies that make it easier for people to manage their houses.

Global Warming Consultant

Global warming means warmer, shorter winters, but that's not as good as it sounds. This phenomenon, caused by the waste products of human industry, is raising the earth's temperature, and that means big problems. Higher temperatures cause the ice caps to melt and ocean levels to rise, leading to shoreline erosion. The huge volume of pollutants in the air surrounding the earth increases health problems such as asthma, and also produces smog and acid rain. Forests and wildlife habitats are altered, endangering many species of plants and animals. It's a pretty grim picture.

But it's not one without a solution. The biggest factor causing global warming is the pollution released into the air through the burning of fossil fuels, like the gas we use to power our cars and the oil that heats our homes. Fossil fuels are also in limited supply—they won't last forever. The alternative? Natural energy, derived from wind, sun, and water, is cheap, plentiful, and pollution-free. Already many people are taking an interest in installing solar panels to power their homes and businesses. As more and more people start to "think green," natural energy-centered businesses will start to see green, with an increasing job market.

Scientists are needed to research and monitor global warming, and engineers are needed to innovate new and improved ways to harness and use natural and efficient energy, like hybrid cars and cars with lower emissions levels. Alternative energy companies will need project managers, analysts, and coordinators to manage operations. When natural energy becomes more widespread, employees will be needed to work at alternative energy provider companies, and laborers will be needed to build, operate, and maintain alternative energy sources, such as windmills and dams. And if no one knows about alternative energy, no one will use it, so there is a great need for marketing and publicity about these services. It's obvious that the greener companies get, the more greenbacks they'll see coming in as profits. If you've got an interest in the environment and have studied biological sciences, this might be the right job for you.

Failure Is Not an Option

Historians might say that what the real difference makers through the ages (people like Da Vinci, Franklin, Joan of Arc, and Edison) had in common was the elusive trait of genius. Maybe so. But I prefer to think they succeeded because of bull-dogged determination to prevail, damn the odds. I love the quote from the NASA mission commander played by actor Ed Harris in *Apollo 13*. Faced with a seemingly impossible task of bringing back the Apollo 13 astronauts safely from space, Harris coolly replied, "Failure is not an option."

When it comes to your career, failure should never be an option. Hopefully, in this book, you've seen a vocation or a job that ensures that you'll be happy with the choices you make in your career. Something that triggers a response deep inside of you that really resonates—that says, "Hey, I can do that!"

Or better yet: "Hey, I *want* to do that."

Getting paid for what you want to do is a big advantage in life. Just ask anyone lucky enough to love what they do for a living.

Hey, there's no reason that people shouldn't be asking you the same question someday.

The Least You Need to Know

- The dream job seeker should know what trends should gain strength as the new millennium progresses.

- Wireless technology isn't just for personal use. It's infiltrated the workplace, allowing more people than ever before to telecommute and conduct business from just about anywhere in the world.

- Genetics is a growing field of science, and it's affecting many areas of life, from the way we grow disease-resistant crops to the way we solve crimes.

- Video games for computers and gaming systems are a $6-billion-a-year international industry and it shows no signs of slowing down.

- Smart home technology creates a market for people to innovate and design increasingly advanced Smart Homes, as well as for people to sell, install, and maintain such equipment.

- Scientists are needed to research and monitor global warming, and engineers are needed to innovate new and improved ways to harness and use natural and efficient energy.

- When it comes to your career, failure should never be an option.

Appendix A

Great Job Websites

Landing your dream job takes some research and discipline. Chances are, if you're looking for a job as a rodeo clown or greeting card writer, you won't find those jobs advertised in your local paper's help wanted section.

In fact, your best bet is to log on to the Internet and begin researching the industry, joining (or at least contacting) key industry associations, and *developing relationships with people who actually do what you want to for a living.*

Even so, you should augment your industry research with access to some of the Internet's best websites. Why? A massive jobs database like the ones found on Monster.com or CareerBuilders.com can provide access to jobs in the industry you are targeting. The U.S. government, for example, actually does place job advertisements for agencies like the FBI, CIA, and the Peace Corps. And the film, media, and publishing industries do use such sites to find editors, scriptwriters, and even fashion models.

The best Internet job sites offer a huge list of jobs, broken down by trade or industry. They also include job search tips, interviewing techniques, and even salary comparisons and articles on career issues like finding a mentor, good business etiquette, or keys to getting along with co-workers and bosses.

The following career websites fit the bill:

AllJobSearch (www.alljobsearch.com)
This job search engine draws on all of the major job sites in the country, including Monster and CareerBuilder, to list the jobs you're interested in. In the dream job game, time is important. AllJobSearch enables you to save time by using all of the major Internet job search engines at once.

America's Job Bank (www.ajb.dni.us)
This is another free job search engine website that offers about one million jobs that can easily be broken down by category and/or industry. I'm not crazy about any site that wants your Social Security number to sign up, but the site does offer a privacy guarantee, along with nice perks like resumé and cover letter templates, and a "dream job" section that finds the jobs you want in the industry you want and e-mails them to you automatically.

CareerJournal.com (www.careerjournal.com)
Brought to you by *The Wall Street Journal* (full disclosure: I have written for *The Journal* as a freelance writer), CareerJournal.com provides a searchable database of interesting jobs by industry and region—even by commuting distance. The feature I like best is that you can search the jobs database by key word. So somebody looking for a Hollywood screenwriter gig or a job at a Washington lobbyist firm can dive down into CareerJournal's huge database and find exactly what they want, without wasting a lot of time.

EmploymentWizard.com (www.employmentwizard.com)
This useful site for dream job candidates enables you to really drill down and search by unique industry after unique industry. So if you want a job in cosmetics, care giving, or pet care, the site enables you to pick and choose from jobs in those sectors. A lot of sites say they can help you search by industry, but EmploymentWizard does that better than most.

FabJobs.com (www.fabjobs.com)
A nice little site that fits in well with dream job seekers whose career paths might be … well … off the beaten path. It's particularly useful in finding job opportunities and career information on sometimes hard-to-research careers like etiquette consultant or art curator.

JobHuntersBible.com (www.jobhuntersbible.com)
This site was created by Richard Bolles, author of the famous career tome *What Color is Your Parachute?* The site is wide-ranging, but if you know what you want, it's a big boost to your dream job search. As well as a comprehensive menu of great jobs, it offers unique add-ons such as an interactive test that can help you decide which career is best for you, an automatic resumé creator, and a section called "Find Out" that tells you about places, fields, companies, and salaries. The best feature? A section called "Contacts" that helps you find people in the field you are passionate about and talk to them about jobs in that industry.

Monster.com (www.monster.com)
This is perhaps the largest website for job seekers. It provides hundreds of thousands of available jobs, along with helpful tips and data on particular industries.

Dream Jobs Glossary

I'm not going to insult your intelligence with a traditional glossary that spells out what a resumé is or what a human resources executive does. What I want to do is provide some key terms that should resonate with dream job seekers. Each term has a quote or a story behind it that I hope will fill your heart with optimism and give you the notion that you, too, can find your dream job.

action   Hoping won't make something happen. An old Chinese proverb says, "Man who waits for roast duck to fly into mouth must wait very, very long time."

adversity   We grow from adversity. There is a great quote that says, "Life doesn't do anything to you, it only reveals your spirit."

ambition   Some people use ambition to get ahead. Judge to burglar: "You've committed six burglaries in one week!" Burglar to judge: "That's right—if everyone worked as hard as I do we'd be on the road to prosperity."

attitude   "Your attitude, not your aptitude, will determine your altitude."—Zig Ziglar

career   Former Ford Motor Co. CEO Donald Peterson tells this story about careers. "Three years of delivering over 400 copies of *The Portland Oregonian*, beginning at 3:30 A.M., seven days a week, rain or shine, was a powerful incentive to find a job that started later, paid better, and offered better working conditions. After wearing out several bicycles, maybe that's when I truly began my life's interest in cars."

challenge   We are our own biggest challenge. As Sir Edmund Hillary said, "It is not the mountain we conquer, but ourselves."

change   The biggest change we can make is on ourselves. "Progress is impossible without change, and those who cannot change their minds cannot change anything."—George Bernard Shaw

compensation   Salary—especially early on in your dream job—isn't nearly as important as the opportunity to demonstrate your talent and enthusiasm. Focus on the passion and the money will follow.

decisions   Don't be afraid to make a decision. Arm yourself with the facts, set your jaw, and go for it. As Harry Truman said, "Whenever I make a bum decision, I just go out and make another."

determination   Be like a postage stamp. Stick to your passion until you get there.

enthusiasm   It is the irresistible power of enthusiasm that …

◆ Enabled Noah Webster to spend 36 years on his dictionary.

◆ Kept George Stevenson working for 15 years on his locomotive.

◆ Saw Thomas Edison endure thousands of defeats before perfecting the incandescent lamp.

Remember, enthusiasm is as much a commodity as widgets or washing machines. It will find solutions where there appear to be none. And it will help you achieve success when success seems impossible.

excuses   "It takes less time to do a thing right than to explain why you did it wrong."—Henry Wadsworth Longfellow

failure   "My great concern is not whether you have failed, but whether you are content with your failure."—Abraham Lincoln

future   Plan for the future where you want to be—not where you are now. Hockey legend Wayne Gretzky said, "I skate to where the puck is going to be, not where it's been or where it is now."

goals   People who know where they are going know how to get there. When Apple co-founder Steve Jobs was 12 years old, he called Bill Hewlett, founder of Hewlett-Packard, and asked him for some spare computer parts. Hewlett, impressed with the young go-getter, made sure Jobs got the parts.

integrity   Integrity is not a 90 percent issue. It's not a 95 percent issue. Either you have it or you don't.

interviewing   Be prepared. "I'm turned off by people who have not done their homework."—Donald Kendall, former CEO, PepsiCo

job satisfaction   People rarely succeed at anything unless they enjoy it. "When people aren't having any fun, they seldom produce good work."—Advertising industry legend David Ogilvy

job security   "Too many people are thinking of security instead of opportunity." —James Byrnes

listening   Find an expert in the field you want to be in and listen to what he or she says. "A single conversation across the table with a wise man is better than 10 years studying books." —Henry Wadsworth Longfellow

marketing   Marketing is often simply positioning yourself properly in the dream job marketplace. A person's success in business today depends on his or her ability to convince people that he or she has something they want.

mistakes   Don't obsess over mistakes. After all, a mistake only proves that you stopped talking long enough to do something. And even the best make mistakes. Ford Motor founder Henry Ford forgot to put a reverse gear in his first Edsel. Babe Ruth was famous for his 714 homers, but he struck out 1,330 times.

motivation   "Keep away from people who try to belittle your ambitions. Small people always do that, but the really great make you feel that you, too, can become great."—Mark Twain

opportunity   When opportunity presents itself, don't dawdle. As Helen Keller said, "When one door of opportunity closes, another invariably opens. But often we look so long at the closed door that we do not see the one which has been opened for us."

optimism   Look on the bright side of things. As radio giant Paul Harvey says, "I've never seen a monument erected to a pessimist."

performance   Don't build a reputation on poor performance. A man once found an old shoe ticket at the bottom of a desk drawer. He noticed that the ticket was three years old. Out of curiosity, he stuck the ticket in his wallet and set out to visit the shoe repair store. Without saying a word, he handed the ticket to the old cobbler behind the counter. The old man studied the ticket for a moment, shuffled into the back room, and soon returned. "They'll be ready Wednesday," he said.

perseverance   The best recipe for success in finding your dream job? Not having the sense to quit until you find it.

planning   For everything you must have a plan. "If you don't know where you are going, you could wind up somewhere else."—Yogi Berra

preparation   Be ready. "If you don't do your homework, you won't make your free throws."—Larry Bird

results   Work hard to find your dream job, but have patience. Remember the old Chinese proverb, "A journey of a thousand miles begins with a single step."

risk   Go ahead. Take a shot. "Behold the turtle. He only makes progress when he sticks his neck out." —James B. Conant

success   Get out there and show people what you can do. As Woody Allen says, "Ninety percent of success is just showing up."

values   Values are important, but remember that values are also in the eyes of the beholder. A minister selected a 50-cent item at a convenience store, then discovered he didn't have any money with him. He told the clerk, "I could invite you to hear me preach in return, but I'm afraid I don't have any 50-cent sermons." Said the clerk, "Maybe I could come twice."

wealth   It's good to have wealth, but wealth can be defined in myriad ways. The best definition I've heard is that wealth is not only what you have, but what you are.

work   There are many formulas—but none of them work unless you do. "The common denominator for success is work."—John D. Rockefeller

Index